T0369624

Warriors' Wives

Warriors' Wives

*Ancient Greek Myth and
Modern Experience*

EMMA BRIDGES

OXFORD
UNIVERSITY PRESS

OXFORD
UNIVERSITY PRESS

Great Clarendon Street, Oxford, OX2 6DP,
United Kingdom

Oxford University Press is a department of the University of Oxford.
It furthers the University's objective of excellence in research, scholarship,
and education by publishing worldwide. Oxford is a registered trade mark of
Oxford University Press in the UK and in certain other countries

Published in the United States of America by Oxford University Press
198 Madison Avenue, New York, NY 10016, United States of America

British Library Cataloguing in Publication Data
Data available

Library of Congress Control Number: 2023938629

ISBN 978-0-19-884352-8

DOI: 10.1093/oso/9780198843528.001.0001

Printed and bound in the UK by
Clays Ltd, Elcograf S.p.A.

Links to third party websites are provided by Oxford in good faith and
for information only. Oxford disclaims any responsibility for the materials
contained in any third party website referenced in this work.

*For the women who held me together
when it seemed as though I might fall apart*

Acknowledgements

This book has been longer in the making that I had initially anticipated; it is probably around a decade since I first started contemplating some of the parallels between the ancient stories of warriors' wives and my own experiences as a military spouse. Once the women—fictional and real—of what has now become *Warriors' Wives* had taken up residence in my head, it became clear to me that I needed to share their stories with a wider audience. Early conversations with Edith Hall about the scope of such a project provided me with the initial impetus to explore the theme further; Edith's encouragement has been, as so often in the course of my career, a fundamental part of my academic journey.

A three-year stint (2017–20) as Public Engagement Fellow at the Institute of Classical Studies in London enabled me to conduct the majority of the research. I am especially grateful for Greg Woolf's insistence that I should prioritize writing the book while juggling various other professional endeavours during that time. The Institute, along with the extraordinary Combined Library of the ICS and the Hellenic and Roman Societies, provided the ideal setting for this work; this was due in no small part to the geniality of my colleagues there.

More recently, colleagues at the Open University, with their customary warmth, have provided friendship and encouragement at a time when I have been dealing with considerable personal challenges. The AHSENT Thursday/Friday writing group at the OU has been a particular source of collegiality and inspiration in the final stages of preparing the manuscript.

The input of friends and colleagues along the way has been crucial in shaping the final form of this book: Elton Barker, E-J Graham, Edith Hall, Jess Hughes, Helen King, and Jo Paul all read chapter drafts and provided thoughtful insights. Naoko Yamagata provided emergency advice in answer to my queries about ancient Greek. The audiences of papers I delivered on aspects of the research at the Durham Greek and Latin Summer School, the Institute of Classical Studies, the University of Liverpool, the Open University, and the University of St Andrews offered generous and perceptive feedback which helped to develop much of my thinking. OUP's anonymous reviewers also provided valuable perspectives on the work.

At OUP, Charlotte Loveridge's patience in the face of long delays to my submission of the final manuscript has been invaluable, as has her unwavering support of the project from proposal stage through to completion. My thanks also go to Henry Clarke and his colleagues for working their magic in transforming the manuscript into an actual book.

It has been a joy to work once more with Asa Taulbut, whose ability to create a beautiful image from my rather vague ideas about what the cover illustration might look like will never cease to astound me.

I look forward especially to being able to share the final volume with my family, David, Charlotte, and Joseph Bridges, and with my parents, Margaret and Terry Clough, all of whom have always been among my most ardent supporters.

Finally, one of the preoccupations of this book is the importance of recognizing the challenges faced by others, and of holding space for them in our minds and hearts even (or perhaps especially) when their experiences bear no resemblance to our own. In recent years, I and my family have experienced profound trauma which has fundamentally transformed our lives. Amid the horror and uncertainty, I have been fortunate to have alongside me an army of incredible women who have, each in their own way, held me together when it has sometimes seemed to me as though I might fall apart. It is to these women that this book is dedicated. Ruth Dare, Helen Dobson, E-J Graham, Ali Grimes, Jess Hughes, Laura Lonsdale, Helen Mallaby, Claire Millington, Helen Morgan, Jo Paul, Frédée Sardais, Karima Soutsane, Amy Stones, Sam Todd, Catherine Ward, and Helen West: I am grateful for all of you. Thank you.

Contents

Copyright acknowledgements

I would like to thank the copyright holders for their kind permission to quote the following material:

Excerpt from THE SILENCE OF THE GIRLS: A NOVEL by Pat Barker, copyright © 2018 by Pat Barker. Used by permission of Doubleday, an imprint of the Knopf Doubleday Publishing Group, a division of Penguin Random House LLC. All rights reserved.

Frances Cornford, 'Parting in Wartime', reproduced with permission of the Frances Crofts Cornford Will Trust.

Excerpt from Jehanne Dubrow, 'In Penelope's Bedroom', reproduced from Jehanne Dubrow (2010), *Poems: Stateside* with permission of Northwestern University Press.

Excerpt from Jehanne Dubrow, 'Ithaca', reproduced from Jehanne Dubrow (2010), *Poems: Stateside* with permission of Northwestern University Press.

Excerpt from Edna St Vincent Millay, 'An Ancient Gesture' from *Collected Poems*. Copyright 1954, © 1982 by Norma Millay Ellis. Reprinted with the permission of The Permissions Company, LLC on behalf of Holly Peppe, Literary Executor, The Millay Society, www.millay.org.

Dorothy Parker, 'Penelope', copyright 1928, renewed © 1956 by Dorothy Parker; from THE PORTABLE DOROTHY PARKER by Dorothy Parker, edited by Marion Meade. Used by permission of Viking Books, an imprint of Penguin Publishing Group, a division of Penguin Random House LLC. All rights reserved.

Excerpt from Ursula Vaughan Williams, 'Penelope', © Vaughan Williams Foundation, reproduced by kind permission of the Vaughan Williams Foundation.

Excerpt from Tino Villanueva, 'Twenty Years Waiting', reproduced by kind permission of the author and Grolier Poetry Press.

All reasonable effort has been made to contact the holders of copyright in materials reproduced in this book. Any omissions will be rectified in future printings if notice is given to the publisher.
   Translations of ancient texts are my own.

Introduction

When in the sixth book of the *Iliad* the Trojan warrior Hector tells his wife Andromache that 'the war shall be the men's concern' (πόλεμος δ' ἄνδρεσσι μελήσει, *Iliad* 6.492), the phrasing sums up a division of gender roles which not only pervades Homeric epic poetry but which is also still apparent where armed conflict is concerned today.[1] In ancient Greek epic poetry and drama, warfare is on the whole a male pursuit: warriors fight, kill, and die on the battlefield, while their wives, mothers, and sisters wait, worry, and mourn at home. In the modern world, the majority of armed forces are still overwhelmingly male-dominated.[2] Even in cases where strides have been taken towards admitting women to the military on equal terms with men, many of the conventional assumptions about gender roles, and the notion that warfare is a masculine pursuit, persist. When the focus of political discourse, media reporting, and the military itself rests primarily on combatants themselves, and when the majority of those combatants are still male, the sense that war is predominantly 'men's concern' can seem inescapable. Yet alongside the accounts focusing on those who do the fighting, there are other voices—like that of Hector's wife Andromache—which are heard less often. These are the voices of those whose lives are profoundly impacted by conflict although they themselves may never have set foot on a battlefield.

[1] I discuss this scene, and its relationship to wider gender stereotypes in military contexts, in greater detail in Chapter 1. On the significance of this particular line, and the way it is echoed elsewhere to reinforce the division of gender roles in Homeric poetry, see below, p. 30 n. 35.

[2] The 2020 Demographics Report by the Department of Defense (2020, p. 16) for the US military suggested that just over 81 per cent of active duty military personnel were male. The latest biannual diversity statistics available for the British armed forces at the time of writing suggest that in 2022, only 13.4 per cent of total UK personnel were female (Ministry of Defence, 2022). Statistics from NATO published in its most recently available Summary of the National Reports to the NATO Committee on Gender Perspectives of (NATO, 2019, p. 19) suggest that the average percentage of women in the armed forces of all member nations (discounting Iceland, which does not have regular armed forces) was 12 per cent in 2019.

Warriors' Wives: Ancient Greek Myth and Modern Experience. Emma Bridges, Oxford University Press.
© Emma Bridges 2023. DOI: 10.1093/oso/9780198843528.003.0001

This book unearths and examines the stories of one such group of non-combatants: the wives of warriors.[3]

Recently, there has emerged a strand of scholarship that compares ancient representations of armed conflict with the experiences of modern-day combatants. The first to explore this terrain in depth was Jonathan Shay, a clinical psychiatrist based in the US, whose work comparing the psychological traumas of Vietnam veterans with descriptions of the Homeric heroes' responses to war and homecoming in the *Iliad* and *Odyssey* was published in two volumes: *Achilles in Vietnam* (1994) and *Odysseus in America* (2002). Shay observed similarities between the experiences endured by his own patients and by the mythical heroes Achilles and Odysseus; he explored the ways in which the ancient Greek epics depict the lived experiences of soldiers and veterans. *Achilles in Vietnam* reads the *Iliad* as a study of how the stresses of warfare affect combatants. It focuses in particular on loss of faith in a commander who has betrayed what is right, as well as on the impact of the death in battle of a close comrade, examining how these experiences can lead—as in the case of Achilles—to a period of frenzied rage on the battlefield. Meanwhile, *Odysseus in America* employs the *Odyssey* as what Shay himself describes as '*an allegory for real problems of combat veterans* returning to civilian society'.[4] Shay's work was intended primarily to contribute to the understanding of the psychological experiences and treatment of present-day combatants and veterans, rather than as an analysis of the ancient texts. He perceived that the *Iliad* and *Odyssey*, as poems created for audiences who had first-hand experience of war, could be used to provoke reflections on war in present-day societies where the majority of citizens are unaccustomed to combat.

Since Shay's work was published, discussion about the relationship between ancient and modern experiences of conflict has developed in a range of directions. The work of Lawrence Tritle—a Vietnam veteran and historian—built on Shay's initial research and resulted in the publication, in 2000, of *From Melos to My Lai: War and Survival*. Here Tritle drew on a range of sources, including historiography and drama as well as epic poetry, from the ancient world. He discussed these alongside contemporary representations of combat in order to examine the impact of war on both soldiers

---

[3] As Fabre-Serris and Keith (2015, p. 3) point out, 'women are, in effect, the cause, stakes, and victims of war: indirectly, because they lose their male relatives in war (fathers, husbands, sons, and brothers); and directly, because they are sacrificed, raped, killed, and/or reduced to slaves'.

[4] Shay (2002, p. 2) (italics in original).

and civilians. More recently, a volume edited by Peter Meineck and David Konstan, *Combat Trauma and the Ancient Greeks* (2014), brought together a range of perspectives on the ways in which modern insights into the effects of combat can illuminate our understanding of ancient Greek representations of war. Peter Meineck and Bryan Doerries have opened up the conversation still further with their outward-facing work; both have developed (in US contexts) public projects which use ancient texts to explore issues relating to the impact of armed conflict. Meineck's *Ancient Greeks/Modern Lives* programme with Aquila Theatre has toured public venues with readings and discussions of Greek poetry and drama, and his *Warrior Chorus: Our Trojan War* initiative uses classical literature as a starting point for the discussion of issues affecting the veteran community.[5] Meanwhile Doerries' *Theater of War* stages readings of Greek tragedies in order to facilitate dialogue about social issues, including in particular the effects of combat on military personnel and those who are close to them.[6] Relatedly, Nancy Sherman—who is trained in both psychoanalysis and philosophy—has investigated some of the ways in which ancient philosophy might be applied in the modern world, especially in relation to the moral and ethical issues encountered by soldiers. In particular her 2007 work, *Stoic Warriors*, explored the interrelation between Stoic philosophy and military culture both ancient and modern, examining, for example, the impact of Stoic ideas on leadership, and on emotions such as fear, anger, and grief in military contexts.[7]

What unites this scholarship, however, is that its primary focus is on the (predominantly male) combatants themselves. Yet comparative analyses such as these, which centre the male experience of war, risk overlooking integral aspects of the social context and impacts of military action. One recent and welcome addition to the scholarly literature, which considers more broadly some of the ways in which the *Odyssey* can shed light on human emotions and experiences, is Joel Christensen's *The Many-Minded Man*, which suggests that the *Odyssey* has 'a therapeutic function for its ancient and modern audiences'.[8] Rather than focusing solely on the figure of Odysseus as returning warrior, Christensen examines the ways in which the

---

[5] See Meineck (2012).   [6] See Doerries (2015).
[7] Sherman (2007). See also Sherman (2010), which considers the moral and psychological impact of soldiering on individuals, and Sherman (2015), focusing on the experiences of combatants after their return from the wars in Iraq and Afghanistan and examining the 'moral injury' that many have sustained.
[8] Christensen (2020, p. 2).

epic can shed light on a whole range of aspects of human experience, including family life, politics, and work. On the whole, however, despite the prominence of warriors' wives—among them Penelope, Andromache, and Clytemnestra—in ancient epic poetry and tragedy, these figures have been given little attention in comparative studies. Yet exploring the ways in which these women are represented can shed light on the psychological, emotional, and social effects of being married to a soldier. At the same time, seeking out their stories can lead us to an enhanced understanding of the ancient texts, as well as of the experiences of modern-day warriors' wives.

The effects of war in both ancient and modern settings—although those settings differ considerably from one another, as I shall note later in this Introduction, and throughout this book—can be equally as profound for those left at home as for their serving partners. As will become clear, even when war was a far more pervasive aspect of life for whole populations than it is in the majority of modern states, the emotional and practical impacts of marriage to a soldier were considerable. To sideline the perspectives of soldiers' spouses is therefore to render invisible the women who bear a large proportion of the burden of war. This burden manifests in all sorts of ways for warriors' wives: the pain of separation; fear for the safety of their loved one and, in many cases, their co-parent; the need to assume additional responsibilities in a partner's absence; the risk to themselves of harm (whether physical or psychological); and the often considerable emotional labour which can be associated with the return of a serving soldier. If we fail to examine these aspects of the wartime experience as represented in the ancient texts, then the comparisons that we can draw with contemporary experiences will also be lacking. Too often, the military spouses of the modern world are also silenced or left unseen. My work here brings their voices to the fore, enabling them to be heard on an equal footing with those who serve on the front line.

While some of the scholarship I have referred to above touches in passing on the experiences of soldiers' families, there has not yet been a sustained attempt to place women who are married to the military, and the ways in which they are depicted, at the centre of a discussion comparing ancient and modern material. This is despite the fact that in recent decades a great deal of valuable scholarship has emerged which examines the ways in which women are represented in the ancient sources. The work of Helene Foley, Laura McClure, Nancy Rabinowitz, and Victoria Wohl on tragic drama, that of Beth Cohen, Nancy Felson, and Marylin Katz on epic poetry, and Froma Zeitlin's scholarship on both of these genres, has brought fresh feminist perspectives to bear on the female characters of ancient myth.[9] More specifically in relation to my own topic, the collection of papers in Jacqueline Fabre-Serris and Alison Keith's 2015 edited volume, *Women and War in Antiquity*, represents a wide range of possible approaches to women's experiences of war as found in the ancient source material.[10] Meanwhile Kathy Gaca draws on a variety of ancient sources from a broad chronological span to investigate one particular element of female wartime experience: the martial rape and capture of women and girls.[11] Women's experience of war in ancient myth has also been of interest to creative writers, several of whom have taken on the task of retelling the stories of Homeric epic and Athenian tragedy from the point of view of the female characters; these reworkings too offer alternative insights into the ancient material. For example, Margaret Atwood's 2005 novel *The Penelopiad* gave Penelope a voice to tell her version of the events of the *Odyssey*. More recently, Pat Barker's *The Silence of the Girls* (2018) and *The Women of Troy* (2021), and Natalie Haynes' *A Thousand Ships* (2019), revisit the stories of the Trojan War from the point of view of the women involved.[12] Although such feminist works—both creative and scholarly—all represent valuable contributions to discourse on the depiction and experiences of women in the ancient world, no analysis has yet set out to examine the representation of women specifically in their role as the wives of soldiers.

It is not my intention in this book to suggest that we can draw uncomplicated parallels between ancient and modern, or indeed between the mythical representations in epic poetry and tragic drama and the lived experience of today's military spouses. Instead I aim to show how both ancient

[9] Foley (2001) focuses on gender relations on Athenian tragedy, with particular attention to death ritual and lamentation, marriage, and ethical choices; McClure (1999) discusses the representation of women's speech in Athenian drama; Rabinowitz (1993) is an analysis of the ways in which the tragedies of Euripides represent women as the subjects of exchange (for example through marriage, or sacrifice) by or for the benefit of men; Wohl (1998) builds on the theme of the exchange of women in tragedy; Cohen (1995, ed.) is a collection of essays discussing the roles played by female characters in the *Odyssey*; Felson (1994) focuses on the agency of Penelope in the *Odyssey*; Katz (1991) considers the ways in which the representation of Penelope relates to the *Odyssey*'s overall narrative strategy; and Zeitlin (1996) collates the author's essays on gender relations in a wide range of ancient Greek poetry and drama.

[10] Papers in this edited volume range across a vast chronological and geographical scope, from Greece of the eighth century BCE to the Roman world of the fifth century CE. Authors also consider a range of different types of source material, including epic poetry, tragedy, historiography, and painted pottery.

[11] Gaca (2010), (2011), (2014), and (2015). Gaca's work also compares ancient wartime sexual violence with martial rape in other historical contexts.

[12] Cox and Theodorakopoulos (2019, eds.) show that these writers sit within a rich tradition of women's creative engagements with Homeric poetry.

representations and modern experiences can be illuminated by comparison with one another. Comparative work focusing on military personnel themselves has demonstrated that an awareness of modern experiences can enhance our appreciation of the representations of combatants in the descriptions of ancient warfare. In turn, it also shows that ancient texts can be used to facilitate discussion of contemporary issues surrounding military service. This is not as straightforward as suggesting, however, that it is possible to adopt a universalizing approach whereby ancient and modern experiences can be mapped on to one another precisely. In fact, the political, cultural, and social contexts in which soldiers operated in the ancient Greek world differed vastly in many ways from those of the present. The recent work of Jason Crowley, for example, challenging claims (in particular those advanced by Tritle) that post-traumatic stress disorder (PTSD) can be retrospectively diagnosed in some of the soldiers who are described by ancient authors illustrates the need for a sensitivity to specific contexts.[13] In relation to my own work, it would not be unreasonable to suggest that even the descriptor 'military spouse', or 'warrior's wife', or the notion of a distinct category of women who were married to soldiers, might seem meaningless to ancient Greek audiences. In ancient societies, where war was omnipresent, every adult male could expect to serve in the military at some point in his life. Therefore, the majority of women would have an understanding of the impact of military service on their intimate partner relationships. This means that the mythical narratives that I discuss draw on scenarios which would be widely familiar to the majority of their first audiences. By contrast, in the modern world, where in many societies the military is a career choice and the majority of the population has had no direct involvement in combat, marriage to someone who has spent time in a war zone can set apart the military spouse from other women in society; many of the experiences with which she is familiar are shared only by others whose partners are combatants.[14]

---

[13] Crowley (2012) and (2014). I discuss this issue further in Chapter 6. Rees (2019) provides a worked example of the problems that arise when an ancient example is removed from its historical context in order to apply the modern diagnostic model. Gardner (2019) uses modern research into trauma to re-examine the ways in which characters in the *Odyssey* are impacted by overwhelming events; she also argues against the notion of PTSD as a universal phenomenon.

[14] Taylor (2011, ed., p. 38) reports that in a study conducted among veterans who had served in the military post-9/11, eight in ten of them suggested that 'the public does not understand the problems faced by those in the military or their families'. Enloe (2000, pp. 157–8) articulates clearly some of the ways in which the experience of military wives compares with that of other married women.

There are other obvious ways in which the situation for military couples in modern society might differ from the marriages that are depicted in the ancient sources. The ancient representations of married couples in military contexts in the texts which I examine are exclusively heterosexual, each of them involving a male warrior and a female non-combatant. In many of the world's armed forces today, women and those in same-sex partnerships are eligible for military service, and in some cases both partners in a relationship may be service personnel. Other elements of the modern experience differ too, and are not mirrored by what we see in the ancient texts. For example, in twenty-first century societies with permanent military forces, frequent relocations are a typical feature of life for many military families. These impose particular additional pressures on spouses, in many cases exacerbating the sense of lives put on hold in service of the military. Meanwhile the existence of military communities, where families of service personnel live close together with one another—but separated to an extent from the wider world—on base, is a distinctive feature of modern military life. This can provide some advantages (for example, in the form of local support networks), but it also presents its own challenges, including enforced separation from a spouse's natal family or non-military friendship circles, and difficulties relating to continuity of employment or education.[15] This particular kind of camp following, whereby civilian families accompany military personnel as they move to new locations, is a phenomenon which is observable in other ancient contexts, but which is not apparent in the Greek material that I will be discussing. Despite these points of contrast, however, close attention to the ancient depictions of warriors' wives reveals that many of the emotional and practical aspects of being married to a soldier found there bear striking similarities to contemporary military spouses' experiences.

My own scholarship on this topic is deeply personal. I have lived experience as a military spouse; my husband David spent seventeen years as a military pilot in the Royal Air Force. I have therefore lived through some of the scenarios explored in this book, and my social network includes many women who have had similar personal experiences. As a result, I undoubtedly read the ancient sources in a way that differs from a reader without this background. This distinct perspective has been the driving force behind the writing of this book, and my familiarity with the terrain from a personal

---

[15] I discuss the kinds of sacrifices which spouses are expected to make in Chapter 2.

point of view has provided me with a valuable entry point to thinking about the issues I discuss.[16] Relatedly, one of my aims is that not only will this book offer those who are already familiar with the ancient texts new ways of thinking about the material, but that it also reaches readers who themselves share some of the experiences I describe, or who support or otherwise interact with military families in various contexts.[17]

Those unfamiliar with the realities of life as part of a military family might wonder to what extent the experience of the modern-day military spouse differs from that of other women who have experienced separation from, or the loss of, a partner (for example divorced spouses, or those who are widowed under circumstances other than war). I distinctly recall a conversation some years ago with a male acquaintance who—despite being aware of my own situation as a military spouse, and having no comparable experience of his own upon which to draw—was quite insistent that the experience of partners left behind when military personnel are deployed to war zones is no different from that of those whose partners travel away from home occasionally for other kinds of employment. On the contrary, there are several things which set apart the experience of the military spouse from other types of lone spouse. While other professions might demand high levels of commitment and sacrifice (manifesting in, for example, long working hours, stress, and time away from the family), there can be a vast gap between the lived experiences of a civilian spouse and their serving partner, especially when the latter is involved in situations which are far removed from those of ordinary civilian life. As Sherman notes, even in other demanding professions, 'There is no comparable arena divide or sacrifice of liberty and life characteristic of the military.'[18] In addition, military life imposes upon the partners of service personnel a sense of perpetual uncertainty. The repeated and often unpredictable cycle of deployments impacts

---

[16] A series of short essays collected in the online journal *Eidolon* under the heading 'Personal Classics' illustrates that there are many ways in which scholars' own identity and experience might influence the ways in which they interact with, write about, and teach, the ancient world. See https://eidolon.pub/personal-classics-46f41ee99788 (accessed 4 August 2022). Nancy Rabinowitz's 2001 piece (for a follow-up to Hallett and Van Nortwick's 1997 edited volume *Compromising Traditions: The Personal Voice in Classical Scholarship*) explores the relationship between (her own) 'personal voice scholarship' and feminism. Goldhill (2022) is a collection of essays reflecting on the author's own personal experiences and identity in connection with his classical scholarship.

[17] With my non-classicist readership in mind, I have aimed to make the sources I discuss as accessible as possible, by supplying translations and contextual information for the ancient texts which I cite.

[18] Sherman (2010, p. 18).

upon almost every aspect of the spouse's own life, from the possibilities of pursuing a career or further education to the disruption of day-to-day plans, family occasions, and life milestones. Most military spouses have stories of missed celebrations and important events, including even momentous occasions such as the birth of a child.[19] A further peculiarity of life for a military spouse is the ever-present knowledge that the departure of the serving partner to a war zone almost always carries with it the risk of death, serious physical injury, or psychological trauma. Every military spouse therefore bears the mental load associated with worry that each farewell could be their final moments together, or that a deployed partner may return home damaged in some way.

As will become clear in the course of this book, there exists in the modern world—just as in the ancient Greek material I discuss—an idealized 'myth' of the military wife. This is a figure who is passive, uncomplaining, supportive of her partner's career and his commitment to the military, and, like the wives whom we encounter in Homeric poetry, largely confined to the domestic sphere, except on occasions such as homecomings, repatriations, or other formal events where she is required to offer a public display of wifely support or of patriotism. She is a product of gendered ideas about feminine sacrifice as contrasted with military masculinity, which is usually conceived of as heroic, aggressive, and powerful.[20] She too, no less than the female characters of ancient myth, is the product of the particular rhetorical and ideological filters imposed by those who imagine her. As many of the modern-day examples cited in this book reveal, military institutions themselves can perpetuate traditional gender stereotypes, not least as they often rely on the unpaid domestic labour, and compliance with the military's demands, of a partner at home. Cynthia Enloe, whose pioneering work has been instrumental in shaping feminist discussions of militarism, has described this image of the model military spouse which is perpetuated by military institutions as one which is 'patriarchally feminized'. She sets out a lengthy list of the ideal characteristics of the 'Model Military Wife' as defined by modern standards.[21] This ideal spouse, to whom I shall refer

---

[19] I discuss in depth in Chapter 3 the sense of a life on hold as described by many military spouses.

[20] Elshtain (1995 [1987], pp. 3–13) describes the gender binary which has often asserted itself in times of war as the 'beautiful soul' (female) and the 'just warrior' (male). On these gendered oppositions, see also Cree (2018, pp. 23–39).

[21] Enloe (2000, p. 162). Enloe explores in detail the factors that shape the expectations placed upon military wives at pp. 153–97. She sets out her list of characteristics of the 'Model Military Wife' at pp. 162–4.

periodically throughout this book, is a woman who is content for all aspects of her life to be subordinated to her husband's military role; the stereotype created in service of patriarchal ideals emerges as being no less of a mythical construct than the women we encounter in ancient drama and epic poetry.

The modern evidence on which I draw in the course of my discussion is derived from a range of sources. As well as considering psychological and sociological research that pertains to military families, I have attempted where possible to seek out the stories of military spouses themselves. These can be hard to locate: they are often scattered and fragmented, published as anonymized quotations in academic papers, woven into articles and books written by investigative journalists, or shared informally as online blogposts or on social media. I also draw on autobiographical works and creative pieces produced by military spouses; in a few cases these types of sources draw their own direct comparisons between the writer's personal experience and those of figures from ancient myth. In addition, some of my sources are those written for and about military spouses. The former category includes, for example, 'handbooks' and self-help guides for military spouses, and the latter incorporates works written by serving members of the military as well as fictionalized or dramatized versions of military life. Like the ancient texts in my study, these types of sources often reveal as much (and in many cases more) about stereotypes and societal expectations as about the actual lived reality of being in a relationship with a member of the military. My contemporary sources relate primarily to conflicts in living memory, from the Vietnam War through to military action carried out since the 1990s by the US and their allies in Iraq and Afghanistan, although in places I touch also on sources relating to the First and Second World Wars. Geographically, the focus for much of my discussion of modern military spouses invariably centres on American and British contexts.[22] I recognize that there are therefore chronological and geographical limits to the scope of this study, but the scale of the work, and the limits of my own expertise—as a trained classicist with lived experience as a military spouse, but not a scholar of international politics, critical military studies, or psychology—simply have not allowed me to produce comparisons which look at wider contexts globally. I would be glad to see others taking inspiration from my work to develop this area of study further in order to draw

---

[22] The one exception here is Chapter 6, where, for reasons outlined in that chapter, I also consider sources relating to violence committed against women during the Rwandan conflict of the 1990s.

comparisons between the ancient material and other modern-day political settings.

Where the ancient Greek evidence is concerned, my primary focus is the extensive body of textual material that tells the stories of the mythical Trojan War.[23] There are two key genres of text here: the first of these are the earliest-surviving complete epic poems in the Greek language, the *Iliad* and the *Odyssey*, attributed to Homer and composed orally over several centuries. The *Iliad* tells the story of just a few days in a ten-year war waged by Greek forces at Troy (modern Hisarlik, in Turkey),[24] yet the poet's use of flashbacks and foreshadowing enables this epic to encompass the whole chronological span of the conflict, from the departure of the Greek fleet to the sack of Troy. The *Odyssey* tells the tale of the convoluted and fantastical return home (over the course of a further ten years) of Odysseus, another of the Greek heroes, to his wife Penelope, who has waited for him in their palace on the island of Ithaca during the course of their lengthy separation. Both poems sit within a much wider storytelling tradition, a mere fraction of which survives in fragmentary form, relating to the Trojan War. The characters whom we meet in the Homeric poems, and the stories of the wider epic cycle, continued to inspire creative responses in art and literature throughout antiquity, just as they have over the centuries to the present day. The second set of ancient texts on which my study focuses is a collection of tragic plays composed by dramatists working in Athens in the second half of the fifth century BCE. The writers of Athenian tragic drama produced a body of material which responded to the stories of the Trojan War in new ways, re-imagining the characters from epic in order to address some of moral, political, and social issues of their own time.[25] Plays written by Aeschylus, Sophocles, and Euripides, and performed as part of annual civic

---

[23] Ancient poetry and drama did not, of course, deal exclusively in myths of the Trojan War; other rich mythic traditions focused on the cycle of stories relating to civil war in the city of Thebes, for example, and tales involving other mythical heroes such as Heracles also deal with some of the themes I examine. My focus in this book, however, is solely on the Trojan War myths.

[24] The relationship between Homeric poetry and the nineteenth-century archaeological discoveries relating to civilizations which flourished in the second millennium BCE is complex. Much has been written about the extent to which the Homeric narratives of the Trojan War bear a relationship to actual historical events; this is not the place to enter into a discussion of the poems' historicity. For readers new to the topic, Barker and Christensen (2013) provide a series of useful insights. See also Graziosi (2016, pp. 15–42), and Sherratt and Bennet (2017, eds.).

[25] For a lucid overview of some of the ways in which Athenian tragedies reflect on contemporary issues relating to, for example, civic identity, gender, and social status in the fifth century BCE, see Hall (1997).

and religious festivals at Athens, offer their own contemporary takes on some of the wives of the warriors found in Homeric poetry. Of course, poetic and dramatic texts dealing with myth simply represent one possible way in to thinking about such issues, and several alternative approaches to the kind of comparative study on which I embark here are also possible. I hope that in future others will be inspired to consider different ways of tackling the themes of this book, whether by examining the ways in which soldiers' wives are depicted in other types of ancient source material— historiography, material culture, comic drama, or philosophy, for example—or by considering other periods and regions in antiquity.

A key point of context to note here is that the Homeric epics and Athenian tragic plays were produced by male authors and performed by men. The performers of epic poetry were rhapsodes—professional reciters who performed to the accompaniment of an instrument—and the actors on stage in Athens were all male. Similarly, ancient evidence suggests that Athenian theatre audiences were predominantly, if not exclusively, male.[26] All surviving tragedies were written by male authors, and all speaking parts were played by male actors. Therefore, although these texts depict a range of female experiences in wartime contexts, undeniably they represent male perspectives on women's behaviour and associated assumptions about gender roles.[27] As a result, it is impossible to assert that we can access authentic ancient female experiences and voices by reading these texts.[28] There are also some gaps in terms of the types of women who are represented most fully in these stories. The male warriors at the centre of epic and tragedy are invariably the foremost fighters, usually from aristocratic families, and most of them serve as military leaders. Their wives, therefore, are similarly from elite households. Even those women who are enslaved after being taken as war spoils have usually previously been part of families with high social status. Little attention is paid in the main plotlines of these texts to the soldiers who form the majority of the fighting force, the rank and file who fight and die in their droves as a result of the decisions made by their commanders. Careful inspection does reveal traces of these more ordinary figures and

---

[26] Goldhill (1994) summarizes the debate relating to the gender of Athenian theatre audiences in the fifth century BCE.

[27] See Fabre-Serris and Keith (2015, pp. 2–4).

[28] Shannon (2014, p. 83) notes, for example, that the female characters in tragedy are very different from actual Athenian women, suggesting that they 'served the necessary symbolic function of carrying themes of war-related anxiety and loss'. She explores the possibility that these women act as 'stand-ins' for male experiences.

their wives—in the catalogues of the dead in Homeric poetry, for example, or in the voices of some of the choruses of tragedy—but we must not assume that the women who occupy the most prominent roles represent typical households.

Why, then, use epic poetry and tragic drama as sources for comparison with the real-life experiences of women who are married to military personnel in the modern world? First, these renderings of the wives of mythical warriors are some of the most detailed depictions of soldiers' spouses which survive from the ancient Greek world. Even where they are given less attention than their husbands (this is particularly true of epic poetry, if less so in tragic drama), textual representations show these characters in situations which still today remain familiar to those in intimate relationships with members of the military. These are women who must variously deal with separation, readjust when warriors return home, or cope with bereavement and trauma. While the characters and the plotlines they inhabit are fictional, they nonetheless undergo experiences that would be familiar to ancient audiences too. Although it is rarely possible to disentangle entirely the cultural realities of women's lives from depictions of them as imagined in literature and art, representations of mythical figures can nonetheless offer an insight into the preoccupations of the societies from whose imagination they have sprung.[29] It is also often through the representation of female characters, and what they reveal about the human costs of war, that ancient poets and playwrights raise questions about the value, purpose, and effects of conflict. In addition, the lasting appeal of the stories of the Trojan War and its aftermath as subjects for poetry, drama, and art bears witness to the power of these myths as tools for exploring the phenomenon of war and its ethical, societal, and emotional implications. For ancient Greek audiences, myth was a ubiquitous part of their social and cultural milieu. Not only would they encounter live performances of the stories of the Trojan War as recitals of oral poetry or dramatic productions in the theatre, but these tales were also a key part of their visual culture. For example, the sculpture on and inside public temples, and the decorative images on painted pottery used in the home, often depicted episodes from these

---

[29] Murnaghan (2015) provides a helpful discussion of the way in which depictions of fictional women might be used to illuminate our understanding of lived realities, along with an overview of the history of scholarship in this vein. For sample case studies of some of the ways in which the ideological and rhetorical filters imposed by authors and artists can influence the representation of women's wartime roles, see Georgoudi (2015) and Cuchet (2015).

stories.[30] Mythical narratives tended to be set in a distant past, yet elements of the stories would usually bear at least some resemblance to the world inhabited by the audiences for whom they were reimagined. The critical distance afforded by settings that were remote in time meant that poets and playwrights could depict characters who were facing challenges and moral dilemmas which echoed some of their contemporaries' concerns. Without directly referring to potentially uncomfortable or controversial present-day issues, they could use myth to provoke reflection and to raise important questions surrounding some of those issues. As the public-facing work of Doerries and Meineck mentioned earlier has shown, ancient mythical narratives can even now be used to open up discussions about real-world topics which are often difficult to address, whether because those topics evoke painful emotions or because they are morally complex.

In what follows, I focus on a series of key experiences shared by women who are married to combatants in the ancient and modern worlds. Chapter 1 examines the moment of farewell, comparing the parting of Hector and Andromache in the *Iliad* with those of contemporary military personnel and their partners. In Chapter 2, which takes as its ancient starting point the literal sacrifice of his daughter Iphigenia by the military commander Agamemnon, and the effect of this on his wife Clytemnestra, I consider the different kinds of sacrifice that military organizations have always expected of the wives of soldiers. Chapter 3 examines the challenges brought by separation, focusing primarily on the figure of Penelope in the *Odyssey* in comparison with today's 'waiting wives'. Relatedly, Chapter 4, which retains a focus on Penelope but also compares her with Clytemnestra, the archetypal unfaithful wife of Greek mythology, considers the ways in which doubts about fidelity can pose challenges for couples separated by war. In Chapter 5 I turn to the process of reunion, and to Penelope's reactions to the return of Odysseus in comparison with the emotional responses to a soldier's homecoming as described by her modern counterparts. My final chapter discusses the traumatic aftermath of war as represented in tragic drama. Here I examine the experience of sexual violence and enslavement for women like Euripides' Andromache and Sophocles' Tecmessa whose homeland is ravaged by war, as well as considering how Tecmessa's relationship with Ajax—a deeply troubled warrior who dies by suicide—might relate to the experiences of women who live with traumatized veterans.

---

[30] Woodford (1993) provides an introduction to ancient visual depictions of episodes from the Trojan War.

This book presents a series of new perspectives both on the ancient stories and on the experiences of those who are married to military personnel today. If we observe that the wives of soldiers are silenced, idealized, or even at times demonized in the stories told by the ancient Greeks, does this prompt us to reflect on the ways in which contemporary discourse surrounding military wives feeds in to notions of the model military spouse and her opposite? In turn, does this inspire us to seek out, and listen more carefully to, contemporary voices which offer their own perspectives on life with a serving soldier? Do modern women's descriptions of the emotions associated with the processes of farewell or reunion offer new insight into the representations of Andromache or Penelope in Homeric poetry? If we listen to the voices of women in tragedy who have been raped and enslaved, or who articulate the challenges of living alongside a suicidal warrior, does this open our minds to the stories of women who have endured the reality of these situations? Can the ancient archetypes offer comfort for women dealing with their own challenges in a world where the role of the military spouse is often misunderstood? Conversely, can these often passive figures inspire resistance against the traditional models of femininity which military organizations often expect military spouses to exemplify? In asking these questions, and in bringing to light the stories of women who have been overlooked too frequently and for too long, I urge my readers to recognize that the often silent, unacknowledged, and unnamed sisters of Penelope, Clytemnestra, Andromache, and Tecmessa still walk among us.

1

Farewell: Andromache in the *Iliad*

> How long ago Hector took off his plume,
> Not wanting that his little son should cry,
> Then kissed his sad Andromache goodbye—
> And now we three in Euston waiting room.
>
> Frances Cornford, 'Parting in Wartime'[1]

Frances Cornford's poignant 1948 verse condenses into just three lines the final scene between Andromache, Hector, and their infant son Astyanax as told in the sixth book of the *Iliad*. In its final line, her poem makes a leap from the mythical setting of the ancient epic to an experience which was all too familiar to the generation of women for whom the wartime partings of the Second World War were a recent memory. The apparent ordinariness of the farewell scene in the waiting room at Euston station contrasts with the significance and emotional weight of the moment of goodbye for a couple parting for what might be the last time. For the reader who knows the *Iliad*, and the story of Hector's death which it tells, the verse carries a sense of the dread which spouses might feel as their loved ones leave them behind for a war zone. The poem was originally published alongside another four-line verse titled 'Parting in Peacetime', which presents a light-hearted tableau of a carefree couple kissing each other goodnight at the garden gate; the wartime image of the poem set at Euston station is made all the more affecting by this contrast. Earlier in the century Vera Brittain, in her memoir of the First World War, had also made the connection between the Homeric scene and a conflict of the recent past: she wrote that '...the lovely lines from the *Iliad* which describe Andromache holding out the child Astyanax to Hector and "smiling through her tears," will be for ever associated for me with those poignant early days of the War'.[2]

---

[1] Reprinted in Dowson (1996, ed., p. 35).
[2] Brittain (1978 [1933]). For a discussion of Brittain's engagement with Homeric models in relation to the First World War, see Murnaghan (2015, pp. 187–90). The scene between Hector and Andromache has inspired many literary and artistic retellings; see Graziosi and Haubold (2010, pp. 53–6) for a sample of these.

Warriors' Wives: Ancient Greek Myth and Modern Experience. Emma Bridges, Oxford University Press.
© Emma Bridges 2023. DOI: 10.1093/oso/9780198843528.003.0002

That these writers could find a connection between events in living memory and an ancient text's depiction of mythical characters might suggest that elements of the soldier's farewell to his family can have ongoing resonance. Regardless of historical, geographical, or cultural context, for every service member who is deployed on a military mission, there must first be a version of the goodbye scene. For some, final farewells might be exchanged with parents, siblings, or close friends, yet for many more these last moments at home will be spent with a partner and perhaps their children. This chapter will consider the ways in which the farewells of soldiers are represented in ancient texts and reports on contemporary military departures. Not only do such scenes highlight the emotions present at the moment of goodbye, but they often also work to reinforce conventional gender roles. I will begin with a brief discussion of representations of grand-scale military depart-ures, noting some of the ways in which these convey gendered expectations. The majority of my discussion will focus, however, on more intimate fare-well scenes between individual couples, primarily the parting of Hector and Andromache in the *Iliad*, and that of Penelope and Odysseus in the *Odyssey*. Some of the emotional aspects of these scenes, as well as the division of gen-der roles which they assume, can also be detected in modern-day represen-tations of the 'soldier's farewell'; I discuss several such contemporary examples alongside the ancient depictions. In some cases, like that of Andromache and Hector, the wartime farewell between a soldier and his partner is their final meeting before the soldier's death; I conclude the chap-ter with a brief discussion of the scene in the *Iliad* where Andromache learns that she has become a widow.

The spectacle of goodbye

When the six hundred uniformed soldiers gathered into a sea of digitized green, Kailani Rodriguez and the other Bravo Company wives drew together. They watched their soldiers stand at attention behind the red banner of unit colors, then march into the waiting buses. The women waved and finally let themselves cry, holding tight to the children who wanted to run after their fathers.[3]

---

[3] Fallon (2011, p. 103).

Siobhan Fallon's *You Know When the Men Are Gone* (2011) is a collection of fictional narratives derived from the author's own experience as an army wife. Her short story 'Inside the Break', quoted above, opens with the departure of a military unit as seen from the perspective of the wives left behind. The spectacle here is a public one, in which the massed troops merge into a single cohort as they head off to war. The uniformity of their dress and body language renders them unidentifiable as individuals as they perform the ritual of standing to attention before boarding buses for their departure point. Fallon's description reflects the heteronormativity that characterizes many contemporary representations; here gender roles are starkly divided. As indicated by the title of Fallon's volume too, it is the men who go off to fight and the women who remain at home, in many cases with children to care for in their husbands' absence. For the women left behind watching the departure, emotions are held in check until the moment the men are too far away to see them; only then do they feel able to surrender to the grief associated with separation. The wives' appearance, and their public display of emotions, also reflects traditional gender norms, as we see them,

> tears streaming, rivulets in the thick makeup on their cheeks, mascara pooling under their eyes, noses running. It was fine to look this horrible now that the men were too far away to see their faces, fine to finally grieve, messy and ugly. Crying in public offered a strangely satisfying relief. Most of them had been through this before, the good-bye, the long deployment, the jubilant return, and they cried now as much for themselves and the lonely year ahead as they did for the men heading off to the dangers of war.[4]

The scene of an army or navy assembled before departing for war would also be a familiar one for the ancient audiences of Homeric poetry and Athenian tragedy. For these audiences, such images were not only present in the myths which formed a key element of their cultural milieu, but they were also a part of their lived experience at a time when war was an ever-present aspect of life. The earliest and most elaborate surviving Greek textual depiction of a massed military force is the lengthy catalogue of ships of the *Iliad*'s second book (2.484–785). It describes the various contingents of the Greek force sent to Troy, and—although it comes in the poet's account

---

[4] Fallon (2011, p. 104).

of the events of the ninth year of the Trojan War—evokes the sense of spectacle associated with the gathering of a force at the start of a military mission.[5] The model would be appropriated and adapted by later authors in their own depictions of armed conflict. Aeschylus' 472 BCE tragic play *Persians*, for example, contains a roll call of the invading Persian forces and their commanders, which reads like a condensed version of an epic catalogue (*Persians* 21–58). Herodotus, in his historiographical account of the Greeks' conflict with Persia (written in the mid-fifth century BCE), also produced a detailed catalogue of the Persian forces who invaded Greece (Herodotus 7.61–99).[6] For audiences for whom the Persian conflict was within recent historical memory these works would provide powerfully resonant visual images of an army on the march. They would perhaps also evoke memories of moments of departure which their audiences had witnessed, or in which they had participated.

For the Athenian audience of Euripides' late-fifth-century-BCE tragedy *Iphigenia at Aulis*, for whom war was an ongoing preoccupation, this play's description of the Greek troops which had gathered on the eve of their mythical expedition to Troy would doubtless seem familiar too.[7] There, Euripides' chorus, a group of women from Chalcis, near to the location where the troops are gathered, report that they have heard from their husbands of the army's encampment (*Iphigenia at Aulis* 176–7), and they have come to witness the spectacle.[8] After identifying the famous Greek heroes whom they have observed (192–230), they sing of how they counted the ships, listing by region of origin the various components of the fleet (231–95). For these female spectators, the sight of the army and fleet about to head off for war is a thrilling display of military prowess; as Zeitlin notes, 'these women have no reason for being there other than the simple fact that they live in the vicinity and are driven by curiosity to take in the impressive sight'.[9]

---

[5] For a detailed discussion of the Homeric catalogue of ships, see Sammons (2010, pp. 135–96).

[6] See Bridges (2015c, pp. 114–17) for a discussion of the Homeric and Aeschylean catalogues of Persian forces.

[7] I discuss this play and its historical context at length below, at pp. 62–72.

[8] On the representation of the Euripidean chorus' interest in the army, and its relationship to Homeric epic, see Michelini (1999–2000, pp. 45–6).

[9] Zeitlin (2004, p. 157). The trope of women viewing the spectacle of military action is at its most prominent in the *teichoskopia* ('viewing from the walls') scenes of epic poetry. On this, see Fuhrer (2015, p. 53), arguing that 'female focalization is used in the context of epic narrative or dramatic action not only to describe a battle and its heroes and make emotional associations with them, but also to comment on the dark side and negative consequences of the phenomenon of war'.

The sense of pageantry connected with the departure of a military force as they set out with one common purpose can still be detected in farewell scenes such as the one described by Siobhan Fallon, and in the official farewell ceremonies which, particularly in the US, take place as a battalion readies itself for departure. News reports on these large-scale farewells typically focus on the sense of unity, purpose, and order of the massed troops, as contrasted with the emotion and individuality of the families left behind. One such report describes a departure ceremony for troops about to leave the base at Fort Hood for Iraq in 2004:

> A brisk wind blew across the parade grounds outside the 1st Cavalry's headquarters, where a farewell ceremony for its first deployment of soldiers to Iraq was under way...On this winter day, 3,000 soldiers in desert fatigues stood at attention, silently, for as far as the eye could see. In the stands, wives clutched camcorders and toddlers, who tried to wrestle out of their arms; a large American flag billowed above them. There were speeches and an inspection of the troops by the major general and an old-fashioned cavalry charge, after which a bugler played with great flourish. 'We say farewell and Godspeed,' the announcer told the troops. The children grew restless, chasing one another around the bleachers, while a few women wiped away tears. Some looked on stoically, lips pinched together. Others slid on sunglasses even though they sat in the shade. The troops marched by, their young faces flushed from the cold. Their expressions were solemn, their chins held high. They would have two weeks of leave. Then they would go off to war.[10]

In observing such a scene, a viewer without an emotional connection to any of the individuals involved might, like the chorus of women observing the army in Euripides' *Iphigenia at Aulis*, become caught up by the sense of occasion. The combination of solemnity and anticipation for what is to come, along with the exhilarating spectacle of disciplined uniformity 'as far as the eye could see' is constructed in such a way as to mark the momentousness of the departure for the viewer, or for the reader of such a news report. Yet the grandeur and scale of such occasions, played out in a public space, is a world away from the intimacy and domesticity of the personal goodbyes which take place between individual soldiers and their spouses. In the rest of this chapter, I focus on these intimate goodbyes, exploring

[10] Colloff (2004).

such scenes both for their insights into the emotions connected with departure and for their representation of gender roles in military partnerships.

'The war shall be the men's concern':
Andromache and Hector

The familiarity of the 'soldier's goodbye' in ancient Greek life is attested by
the fact that images of departing soldiers were a common type-scene on
painted pottery. By the classical Athenian period, such departure scenes
seem to have been particularly popular as subjects for pottery painters.[11]
These visual depictions suggest that the departure of a soldier was a culturally recognized event, a key moment in the life of the family as well as of the
city that the soldier served. Sometimes in these images, an inscribed name
identifies the departing soldier as a figure from myth, although in other
examples it seems that a contemporary scene is being depicted. In many
cases, the departing warrior is portrayed arming himself, or being assisted
with arming, accompanied by a woman who is explicitly identified as his
mother. Such tableaus are perhaps inspired by the Homeric story of Thetis'
presentation of new armour to her son Achilles, which features on some
early examples.[12] Often the woman in these images is performing a libation
as an offering to a god, and in some cases there is also present an elderly
man, usually presumed to be the warrior's father. Some scholars have also
suggested that on occasion the female figure shown alongside a departing
soldier may be identified as his wife, although this is difficult to say with
certainty.[13] Nonetheless, such scenes allude strongly to the division of wartime activity along gendered lines. The images usually have a domestic setting, with the male combatants—wearing the armour which marks them
out as such—heading out to war while the women, like the Andromache of
the *Iliad* and the Penelope of the *Odyssey*, remain behind at home.[14] The
presence of the warrior's armour acts as a reminder of the striking contrast
between the household and the battlefield, as the male figure transitions

[11] Matheson (2005, p. 24).

[12] The story of Thetis' arming of Achilles is told in the *Iliad* at 18.368–19.39. Von Bothmer
(1949) discusses several examples of the scene as depicted on painted pottery. On the motif of
women arming men more generally in art and literature, see Lissarrague (2015).

[13] Ducrey (2015, p. 188) and Matheson (2005, p. 30) suggest the possibility that a wife may
be present in some of these scenes.

[14] On the predominantly domestic setting of these images on painted pottery, see Matheson
(2005, pp. 31–2).

from home to the theatre of war. Meanwhile the women in such scenes are about to begin their period of waiting for their loved ones' return. Images like these might also evoke in the viewer the complex range of emotions felt by those who have experienced first-hand such a farewell scene.

Warriors' personal farewells, despite their ubiquity in ancient Greek life, and their popularity in visual culture, feature only rarely in surviving literary texts. The most detailed ancient textual depiction of the moment of farewell is the departure scene between Andromache and Hector which takes place in the sixth book of the *Iliad* (6.390–493). It is a scene which expresses profoundly the experience of the warrior's wife as her husband goes to battle. For this mythical couple the war is not being fought in some faraway land, with a lengthy journey from home to the front; instead, Hector will fight on his own native soil against the army threatening his city, his home, and his family. The farewell scene with his wife Andromache and their child Astyanax (or Scamandrius, as we are told Hector calls his son, after the river that flows near Troy, 6.402) therefore takes place in close proximity to the battle, at the very gates of the city which Hector is defending. This is the liminal point between home and the war. The location, as well as the emotional exchange between Hector and Andromache, emphasizes the marked contrast between the safety and comforts of domestic life, and the horrors and danger of the fighting.

The scene takes place as follows: Hector, having been unable to find Andromache at home, learns from one of the women of his household that she rushed out of the house and headed for the city walls when she heard the Trojan troops faring badly in the latest development in the battle. He meets his wife, along with their baby Astyanax and the child's nurse, close to the Scaean gate, which is the entrance to Troy and the place from which he will exit the city as he heads back to the fray. Andromache makes a lengthy plea, begging her husband to take pity on her, and on their son, and to rethink his battle strategy. In response, Hector insists that despite the risk to himself and his family, he cannot hang back from the fighting, as he must fulfil his duty to his fellow Trojan warriors. Having removed the plumed helmet from which the child initially shrank in fear, he takes hold of his infant son, then expresses his wishes that Astyanax will grow to inherit his father's heroic qualities, before engaging in a final embrace with his wife and child. After instructing Andromache not to grieve excessively for him, but to return to the house and carry out her domestic tasks at the loom, he rejoins the battle.

Much has been written about the couple's farewell scene, its pathos in illustrating the impact of war, and its representation of the characters of Hector and Andromache.[15] In what follows I focus on the ways in which the scene represents the emotions associated with wartime farewells, as well as its portrayal of the conventional gender roles which often become particularly conspicuous in times of war. The scene between husband and wife comes at the culmination of a series of encounters between Hector and the women inside the walls of Troy in the course of *Iliad* 6; these encounters focus our attention on the repercussions of war for the members of a soldier's family. The women all attempt in some way to delay his departure (at 6.251–62 his mother Hecuba, for example, offers him wine to pour a libation to Zeus; and at 6.342–68 Helen, partner of his brother Paris, invites him to sit and rest). In a detail with which the poet anticipates Hector's final encounter with his own wife, as soon as the hero enters the city walls he is waylaid by the female relatives of the Trojan warriors. The women clamour for information about their own sons, brothers, and husbands (6.237–41); the poet's comment that 'many had grief (already) tied to them' (πολλῇσι δὲ κήδε’ ἐφῆπτο, 241) suggests that several had already received news of their loved ones' deaths.[16] The subsequent scene between Hector and Andromache (and, later in the poem, her response to his death) is therefore framed as having already played out countless times over for all of the other women whose family members are enmeshed in the war. While epic poetry focuses overwhelmingly on the experiences of elite men and their families, such details hint at the way in which the challenges brought by war touch those of all ranks. Despite being the focus of our attention as the foremost Trojan fighter, Hector too is aware that his experience is one among many; he instructs Hecuba to arrange a sacrifice to Athena, in hope that 'she will pity the city and the wives of the Trojans and their infant children' (6.276).

The fear of death or injury overshadows every wartime departure scene, and the audience knows that this may be the final time that Hector sees his wife and child; before he meets his family, Hector tells Helen that he does not know if he will live to return to them (6.365–8). Andromache's own opening words to her husband, spoken through her tears (δάκρυ χέουσα,

---

[15] For a detailed commentary on the scene, see Graziosi and Haubold (2010, pp. 188–223). Katz (1981, pp. 26–36) discusses the exchange between Hector and Andromache in the context of the representation of gender roles and the contrast between domesticity and war in the sixth book of the *Iliad*. Tsagalis (2004, pp. 118–29) analyses in detail Andromache's lament.

[16] On the interpretation of the Greek here, see Graziosi and Haubold (2010), commenting on line 241.

6.405) as she takes hold of his hand (6.406), convey a blend of fear, grief and resentment. She admonishes Hector, addressing him as δαιμόνιε (6.407), a Greek term which is difficult to translate precisely (it implies that the addressee has been manipulated by a god) but which has negative connotations and is often used as a reproach.[17] She goes on to accuse him of being reckless and uncaring, suggesting, 'Your bravery will destroy you! You have no pity for your infant child, nor for me, the wretched woman who will soon be your widow' (6.407–9). This is the first time we, as the poem's audience, have encountered Andromache; there is a palpable sense here of her feeling that Hector is choosing to put his military duty, and with it certain death at the hands of the Greeks (6.409–10), before his family. In reality for this warrior, however, there is no choice but to fight if he is to live up to his reputation and defend his city, as we shall learn from Hector's later response to his wife (6.441–6), which I shall examine shortly.[18] The combination of anguish and anger seen here has been identified too in the responses of modern-day military spouses to a partner's imminent deployment. Black, in a discussion of family separations, summarizes the stages of the 'pre-deployment' process for spouses of US military personnel: 'Separated wives tend to go through set stages of a grief reaction. Some experience shock or denial at the impending loss about two weeks before the separation. As the departure date draws closer, many feel anger about the prospect of being left alone. Some may then feel guilty because they were angry.'[19] In our encounter with Andromache, this range of emotions is compressed into just one brief scene. In her case, as we shall see, there is perhaps a sense of denial in her later attempt to dissuade Hector from the tactical strategy that he plans to pursue.

Andromache's distress stems not only from concern for Hector's life, but also from fear about the dangers that will await her and her child after Hector dies in battle. Her reflections on this future are a reminder of the patriarchal structure of the world depicted in the *Iliad*; this is a world where women are subordinate to their fathers and husbands. She points out that the lives of her parents and her seven brothers have already been claimed in

---

[17]   Graziosi and Haubold (2010) note on line 326 that 'the word refers to somebody who is familiar to the speaker and yet behaves in an extraordinary and objectionable way'.

[18]   The conflict between the competing sets of obligations—to the family and the military— is a recurring feature of the lives of those who serve. I discuss this at length in Chapter 2.

[19]   Black (1993, p. 277). See also Wilson and Murray (2016, pp. 109–10), summarizing recent research on the array of emotions experienced by military spouses at the point of deployment. For a discussion of the story of one spouse whose response to her husband's military service abroad exemplifies the combination of anger and anxiety hinted at in Andromache's opening words to Hector, see below, p. 70.

the course of the war, with her male relatives having been killed by the Greek warrior Achilles (6.413–24), and her mother—who was captured as war booty, but later set free for a ransom—also now dead (6.425–8). As a consequence of this loss of her natal family, she is wholly dependent on Hector, and recognizes that her own identity and security are connected entirely to those of her husband: 'Hector, you are my father and my revered mother, my brother and my strong husband' (6.429–30). Hector too knows what lies in store for Andromache when Troy is taken. Widowed and captive, she will be taken away as a slave by the victorious army: one of the city's Greek conquerors will 'lead [Andromache] away weeping, taking away the day of freedom (ἐλεύθερον ἦμαρ ἀπούρας)' (6.455). Enslaved, she will be expected to perform domestic tasks in another household far from home, weaving at the loom or carrying water 'very much against [her] will' (πόλλ' ἀεκαζομένη, 6.458). In death, Hector will no longer be able to protect her from this 'day of slavery' (δούλιον ἦμαρ, 6.463); he imagines her being violently dragged away (6.465) once he is no longer there to save her. The presence of their infant son adds pathos here, anticipating the fate that awaits the child too. When Andromache later learns of Hector's death, she imagines the cruel future of grief and poverty, and the taunts of his peers, which await the orphan child of the dead hero (22.484–505). Elsewhere in the poem, she also alludes to an alternative and more horrific version of Astyanax's fate, in which he is not allowed to live but is thrown from the battlements of Troy by one of the victorious Greeks (24.734–5).[20]

These hints at Andromache's future in the *Iliad* say little about the full horrors that will await her as the wife of a dead warrior on the losing side; it is in tragic drama where we find the fullest exploration of the violation of the women of a sacked city.[21] Yet epic poetry makes it clear that the capture, rape, and enslavement of female survivors is the norm in Homeric society. As documented by Kathy Gaca, references to captive women sharing the

---

[20] I discuss further below (p. 38) Andromache's response to Hector's death in the *Iliad*. The death of Astyanax at the hands of a Greek warrior features in other versions of the Trojan War myth: the *Ilias Mikras* ('Little Iliad') has Achilles' son Neoptolemus throw Astyanax from the battlements of Troy, and an ancient summary of the *Iliou Persis* ('Sack of Troy') suggests that in this poem Odysseus was responsible for the child's murder. In the fifth century BCE, Euripides' tragic retellings of Andromache's story would draw out this detail; in her opening speech in his *Andromache*, she recalls, 'I witnessed my husband Hector killed by Achilles, and Astyanax—the child I bore to my husband—thrown from the lofty walls when the Greeks captured Troy' (*Andromache* 8–11). Euripides' *Trojan Women* incorporates a lament for the dead child by Hecuba, grandmother of Astyanax, after he has been murdered by the Greeks in the course of the play (*Trojan Women* 1156–1206).

[21] In Chapter 6 I consider in detail the fate of Andromache after Hector's death, and the ways in which her story after the fall of Troy is represented in Athenian tragedy.

beds of the Homeric warriors are often made in passing, and in ways which gloss over the violence of their capture.²² The aged Nestor in the *Iliad* exhorts the Greeks, 'Let none of you rush to sail home until each of you has slept with (κατακοιμηθῆναι) the wife of a Trojan' (*Iliad* 2.354–5); the euphemistic phrasing conceals the horror that lies behind such an act of sexual violence.²³ Meanwhile in the *Iliad* the captive women Chryseis and Briseis are repeatedly referred to using the term γέρας, meaning 'gift of honour', including one awarded as a prize for conduct in war.²⁴ As the possessions of men—Agamemnon and Achilles—these women are expected to serve their captors sexually as well as to carry out domestic tasks. Agamemnon, for example, envisages Chryseis back at home with him in Argos, working at the loom and sharing his bed (1.31) and later reflects that she is more attractive to him than his own wife (1.113–15). Achilles describes Briseis as 'won with my spear' (δουρὶ δ' ἐμῷ κτεάτισσα) after he sacked her city (16.57, cf. 2.689–94).²⁵ The phrasing here refers to the violence with which war captives were treated; women ravaged by the victorious army are often referred to as 'spear-won', although the *Iliad* offers little elaboration as to what this might mean in practice. It is by way of a simile in the *Odyssey* that we gain a fuller sense of how events might play out for a widowed survivor of war, and of the brutality that she will most likely suffer when captured by those who killed her husband. There (*Odyssey* 8.523–30), Odysseus is described as weeping,

> as a woman weeps, embracing her dear husband, who has fallen in battle before his city and people while warding off the pitiless day from the town and its children. She sees him dying and gasping for breath, and, throwing herself upon him, she shrilly screams. But [enemy soldiers] at her back strike her torso and shoulders with their spears and drag her off to slavery, to endure toil and misery.   (εἴρερον εἰσανάγουσι, πόνον τ' ἐχέμεν καὶ ὀϊζύν)

---

²² Gaca (2015, pp. 285–8). Abducted women in the Homeric epic are sometimes also referred to euphemistically as 'wives' (ἄλοχοι, as at, for example, *Iliad* 2.355), even though they are often unmarried adolescent girls, see below, pp. 177–80, for a fuller discussion of this point. On rape in Trojan War narratives, see also Deacy and McHardy (2015).

²³ A chilling twentieth-century echo of this promise of sex with the wives of the defeated enemy came during the conflict in Vietnam, when in some cases, as an incentive to volunteer, US Marines were told that they would be authorized to rape local women. See Bourke (2007, pp. 367–8).

²⁴ See, for example, *Iliad* 1.118, 1.120 and 1.123.

²⁵ At *Iliad* 19.291–6 Briseis recalls that Achilles slaughtered her husband and three brothers, and sacked her city.

Modern scholars of conflict-related violence now refer to such large-scale brutalization of female survivors as 'mass martial rape'.[26] These are, therefore, the risks to which Andromache will be exposed upon the death of Hector. For this warrior's wife, who exists in a society where women's fates are inextricably tied to those of their male relatives, the stakes could not be higher.

The portrayal of Andromache's farewell to her husband, while framing her as Hector's vulnerable dependant and foreshadowing what her fate will be after his death, also works in other ways to assert conventional gender roles. Having pleaded with Hector on the grounds that she has already lost so many of her family members, and having repeated her entreaty that he shows her pity so as not to 'make your son an orphan and your wife a widow' (6.431–2), Andromache then attempts to step beyond the domain to which, as a woman and the wife of a warrior, she is confined by social convention. She tries to influence her husband's military tactics, adopting what Graziosi and Haubold refer to as the 'technical language of siege warfare'.[27] Rather than suggesting that he refrain from rejoining the fighting, she tries instead to persuade Hector to adopt a more defensive strategy by positioning troops at a place by the wall where the city is most vulnerable to attack; she reminds him that on three occasions the Greeks have tried to scale the wall there (6.433–9).[28] There is perhaps a remnant here of a pre-Homeric version of her character, whose name in Greek means 'fighter of men' and who is associated elsewhere with the mythical Amazons, warrior women who defied gendered norms.[29] Here, however, her suggestion is dismissed by Hector. He acknowledges that he shares her concerns (6.441), but tells her that he would be ashamed (αἰδέομαι, 6.442) if he were to shrink from the fighting 'like a coward' (κακὸς ὥς, 6.443). Instead he seeks glory for both his father and for himself (ἀρνύμενος πατρός τε μέγα κλέος ἠδ' ἐμὸν αὐτοῦ, 6.446: the Greek concept of kleos, variously translated as 'glory', 'fame', or 'honour', is what all Homeric heroes strive to achieve). As a warrior, and as a carrier of the reputation of his family's male line, he has been conditioned to fight and to strive for honour, and for the immortality that this will bring

[26] For the application of the term 'mass martial rape' in modern contexts, see Card (1996). In Chapter 6, I discuss martial rape in other ancient and modern contexts.
[27] Graziosi and Haubold (2010), commenting on line 434.
[28] Nappi (2015, p. 40) notes that this suggested strategy is later echoed by the Trojan seer Polydamas (18.273–9), and that Achilles says that it has been used by Hector himself in the past (9.352–4). See also Payen (2015, pp. 219–20).
[29] Tsagalis (2004, p. 128, with n. 347).

through the stories that will be told about him by subsequent generations. He, like his fellow warriors, will follow through with these actions in spite of the fact that—as he goes on to acknowledge at 6.447–65—this will end in defeat for the Trojans, as well as his own death. Meanwhile the women of Troy can only watch and grieve.

Hector's assertion of these conventional gender roles is present through-out the scene, as he goes on to express his wish that his son will inherit his own reputation as a heroic warrior. His hope is that Astyanax will one day outstrip Hector's own achievements, killing his enemy and returning home with spoils so as to please his mother (6.476–81). There is added poignancy here for the audience, who know that with the inevitable fall of Troy these desires will be thwarted. The emphasis placed on the presence of Astyanax in the scene also serves to remind the audience of the domestic, child-bearing, nurturing role of the wife left behind, as contrasted with the outward-facing role of the warrior whose responsibility it is to act as protector for the women and children who are unable to defend themselves. The tableau of wife, husband, and child as it is visualized here enacts vividly the division of traditional masculine and feminine roles which are made even more pro-nounced when a soldier husband departs for battle. Hector is fully armed and ready for combat: Astyanax's fear at the sight of the plumed helmet and Hector's removal of the alarming headgear (6.466–73) highlight his role as warrior.[30] The poet also alludes to this defining element of his identity, with the use of the formulaic epithet κορυθαιόλος, 'of the glittering helmet', to describe Hector at line 440. By comparison, Andromache is to return to her domestic role as mother of the child whom Hector hopes will continue the male line; this is re-emphasized by Hector's action as he places the child in Andromache's arms towards the end of their exchange (6.482–3).

Wartime images of couples saying farewell as a soldier heads out into the field in more recent contexts often replicate versions of this gendered tab-leau, with servicemen in the uniform which marks them out as military personnel and their partners in civilian dress. If there are children present the spouse left behind (still most often, although not always, female), in whose care they will remain in the soldier's absence, often carries them in her arms or holds them by the hand. The image is summed up neatly by

---

[30] Griffin (1980, p. 7) notes that 'The function of armour is to terrify…but not to terrify one's own children', and suggests that the scene emphasizes the way in which 'the Hector who carries out a man's task of defending his wife and child must, in doing so, become alien and terrifying to his own son, as all things are changed from what they were "beforetime, in peace, before the sons of the Achaeans came"'.

Donna Moreau, in her *Waiting Wives*, a fictionalized memoir which explores the lives of the women waiting at Schilling Manor, the US military base set aside for the wives and children of soldiers deployed to Vietnam.[31] Describing the last time one of her characters, Bonnie, saw her husband in 1964, before he was killed in the war, Moreau writes,

> At the airport Bruce hugged his two boys and then Bonnie, who held her arms tight around Colleen Joy, a sprightly, blond toddler with a contagious smile...
>
> ...the little ones would keep her busy.
>
> Bruce let go of his family. The children waved good-bye. They blew air kisses. He never turned back to glance at his high school sweetheart and their three beautiful babies. Bonnie watched her tall, athletic husband—dressed in his crispest khakis and wearing a new pair of black-framed, Army-issue glasses—and wondered why he did not turn around for a last wave good-bye. Then, he was gone.[32]

The similarities between this scene and the mythical parting of Hector and Andromache are striking. Moreau emphasizes Bonnie's role as mother to Bruce's children, while her husband is marked out as a military man by the army kit he wears. In not turning back to look at his waiting family, Bruce maintains a focus on the mission that lies ahead of him. The sense of separation, between home/family and military service, is repeated elsewhere too in Moreau's account of wives' goodbyes to their soldier husbands during the Vietnam conflict:

> Lorrayne and the boys walked with Bob to the chain-link fence that divided those leaving from those staying. Farewells were brief. Lorrayne had said good-bye to her husband five or six times during their marriage. Still, tears welled, spilling down her cheeks. She kissed her husband one last time before he went through the gate, alone. Terry and Robbie noticed their mother's tears. They had never seen her cry.

---

[31] Moreau (2005). The book, which the author describes (p. xv) as 'part memoir, part history, and part portrait of three women' (including the author's own mother), is based on the personal memories of the women whose stories it tells, along with anecdotes from others who lived at Schilling Manor during the Vietnam War.

[32] Moreau (2005, p. 25).

Bob climbed the portable stairway, turned to his family, and waved good-bye. He entered the aircraft.

Gone.[33]

In the scene described by Moreau, it is a chain-link fence which serves the same symbolic purpose as the walls of Troy in the Homeric goodbye scene. For Lorrayne, as for Andromache, this boundary marks the division between her husband Bob's two worlds; the world of the war for which he is about to set out is contrasted with that of the home and family he leaves behind as he walks through the gate to perform his military duty. On the 'home' side of the fence are wives, children who need to be cared for, and the outward displays of emotion—in Lorrayne's case, as in Andromache's, tears—associated with farewell. The other side of the fence is out of bounds for Lorrayne and her children and accessible only to the men whose domain is the war. That domain, with all its horrors, is one that these soldiers' wives will never experience directly themselves, yet the repercussions of the war will impact their lives at home for many years to come.

In the *Iliad*, it is in Hector's final words to his wife that the contrast between the warrior's wife and her husband is stated most clearly. As Andromache smiles through her tears (δακρυόεν γελάσασα, 6.484), there is a moment of physical connection and tenderness between the couple; moved to pity her, Hector strokes his wife's hand (πόσις δ' ἐλέησε νοήσας, / χειρί τέ μιν κατέρεξεν, 6.484–5). He goes on, however, to instruct her not to grieve excessively for him (6.486), reminding her that there is an allotted time for all men to die (6.487–9).[34] For her this is little consolation. His final words to her are, 'Go back to the house and see to your own tasks, the loom and the distaff, and order your female attendants to go about their work. The war shall be the men's concern (πόλεμος δ' ἄνδρεσσι μελήσει)—all those who were born in Troy, but me in particular' (4.490–4).[35] With these words,

[33] Moreau (2005, pp. 54–5).

[34] The term with which Hector addresses Andromache here, δαιμονίη, is not one of affection but of reproach. It echoes Andromache's own reproachful use of the term to address Hector at line 407, when she criticizes him for his lack of pity. See above, n. 33. On the use of the term in the *Odyssey*, see below, p. 147 and p. 154.

[35] Rousseau (2015) shows how these words—in which a woman is put in her place and told to attend to her domestic duties—fulfil a similar function to two scenes in the *Odyssey* (1.356–9 and 21.350–3), where Penelope is told by Telemachus to return to her loom and not interfere with men's business. See below, pp. 78–9 and p. 95. The words 'The war shall be the men's concern' (πόλεμος δ' ἄνδρεσσι μελήσει) would later be repeated by the eponymous heroine of Aristophanes' 411 BCE comic play *Lysistrata* (*Lys.* 520), in which Lysistrata reports that her

Hector picks up his crested helmet, the symbol of his role in the fighting, as his wife turns homewards (4.494–5). Andromache is described as 'turning back again and again, and shedding swollen tears' (ἐντροπαλιζομένη, θαλερὸν κατὰ δάκρυ χέουσα, 6.496). The *Iliad*'s description of her final moments with her husband is all the more affecting because the audience knows that Troy will fall and that Hector will not return home alive.[36] Andromache's reluctance to take her eyes off her husband for the last time reflects her foreboding that he will not return to her. Unsurprisingly, this fear that a warrior may not come home is a feature typical of many military goodbyes; as one US Air Force wife, Danette Long, told journalist Karen Houppert, 'The minute they're walking away down the airport terminal you say, "Is this the last time I'm going to see him?" You memorize his gait, his smile, and everything. Just in case.'[37]

Not only, then, does this goodbye scene convey a sense of the range of emotions—fear, grief, and anger—experienced by a spouse as they bid farewell to a soldier who is setting out for combat, it also foregrounds the gender binary, which, on the eve of war, appears all the starker. The scene makes clear that this warrior's wife has no place interfering with military strategy or even being outdoors near to the battlefield. Hector's parting words quite literally put Andromache in her place, at home, performing the tasks of cloth production which take place indoors and which are conventionally associated with women in Homeric poetry.[38] As represented by Andromache, the home, domestic tasks, and the care of children are configured here, as elsewhere in Homeric poetry, as female. Meanwhile Hector—with his battle-ready appearance, his words to his wife and child, and his departure for the fray—is firmly associated with the male domains of politics and war, which take place outside the home.[39]

As an image of wifely dependence, Andromache might serve as an ancient mythical archetype for the vulnerability and femininity which are still today envisaged by some (in UK and US contexts, at least) as defining

---

husband has dismissed her concern for military matters since these are beyond the remit of a woman. See also Payen (2015, pp. 216–17).

[36] Andromache's words in the scene prefigure her later laments for Hector in Books 22 and 24 of the *Iliad*. See Tsagalis (2004, pp. 129–36).

[37] Houppert (2005, pp. 74–5).

[38] The weaver *par excellence* of Homeric poetry is Penelope in the *Odyssey*. I discuss the significance of Penelope's loom below, at pp. 97–101.

[39] Rousseau (2015, p. 19) notes that the very fact that Andromache is outside at this point, rather than inside the house where she—as a respectable woman—ought to be, is 'an indication of the state of crisis and disorder that had befallen Troy'. On the correlation between woman/man and indoors/outdoors in Greek thought, see Payen (2015, pp. 216–17).

characteristics of the model military spouse. These gender divisions are reinforced by military structures which still often rely on the—at least partial—dependence of the partners of serving personnel.[40] The idealized, and still heavily gendered, image of a soldier's spouse has proved to be astonishingly persistent. This is despite progression towards greater gender equality in the twentieth and twenty-first centuries as well as developments which have seen women occupying ever more active—and traditionally 'male'—roles in response to the necessities brought about by conflict.[41] Elshtain conceived of the gender binary which has periodically asserted itself in wartime in the modern day as a contrast between the 'beautiful soul' (female, vulnerable, in need of protection, centred on the household and producing children) and the 'just warrior' (male, concerned with war and politics, honourable, protector of the 'beautiful souls' and all that they represent).[42] Of course this image of the military spouse today, and any assumption that one single definition will suffice to categorize all military spouses, is no less a myth than the character of Andromache. In the course of this book, it will become clear, however, that the idealized 'feminine' stereotype frequently reasserts itself in relation to those who are married to service personnel.

Practical preparations: Penelope and Odysseus

Like the *Iliad*, the *Odyssey* also shares an insight into the farewell of a warrior and his wife. In this case, however, the audience knows that the departing warrior, Odysseus, will return to his wife Penelope alive, albeit after an extended absence.[43] This poem, which focuses primarily on Odysseus' protracted homecoming, has no single description of the couple's goodbye scene. Instead we are given a series of glimpses of the behaviour of Penelope and Odysseus in the days before his departure. In contrast with the parting of Hector and Andromache, the focus in the *Odyssey* is less on the emotional aspects of the farewell, and more on some of the practical

---

[40] I discuss at greater length in Chapter 2 some of the ways in which military organizations obstruct the independence of the spouses of service personnel.

[41] For a survey of the ways in which women's lives have changed, specifically in the UK, as a result of the wars of the twentieth century, see German (2013).

[42] Elshtain (1995 [1987], pp. 3–13 and *passim*).

[43] I discuss Odysseus' homecoming in depth below, in Chapter 5.

preparations which the couple made before they parted.[44] As depicted on the painted pottery discussed earlier in this chapter, the moment of a soldier's departure marks the start of his transition from the domestic space of home to the theatre of war. In the case of Andromache and Hector, this transition happens almost immediately, as the war is on their doorstep in Troy; for Odysseus and Penelope it marks the start of the warrior's lengthy journey to war in a faraway land. There is also at this point a transition for the waiting wife as well as for the departing soldier. She moves from a state of anticipation of the inevitable departure, and the uncertainty associated with the predeployment period, to the early stages of awaiting either his return, or the news of his death.[45] At this moment, Penelope also becomes the guardian of the household in Odysseus' absence. There is an expectation that—as for many military spouses even today—she will temporarily assume a role that would ordinarily belong to her husband, and the usual gendered division of responsibilities is put on hold while the warrior is gone.[46] This is a state which cannot last forever, however, since if Odysseus does not return, his wife must choose a new man to be the head of the household.

In contrast with the detail provided in the *Iliad*, the *Odyssey* gives only the merest hint of a departure scene featuring wife, young child, and warrior. When in the course of his adventures in this poem Odysseus journeys to the underworld, he meets the shade of the dead Greek leader Agamemnon, who recalls that Penelope 'was just a young bride when we left her as we set out to war; and her son was still an infant at the breast' (*Odyssey* 11.447–8). Elsewhere too, the female spouse is associated with domesticity and childrearing; earlier in the poem Menelaus had recalled that Odysseus left behind, along with his father Laertes, 'prudent Penelope, and Telemachus, whom he left a newborn in the house' (4.111–12). On only two other occasions in the text, once in Book 18 and once in Book 19, does the poet elaborate further on what passed between Penelope and Odysseus

[44] Fragments of the epic cycle preserved elsewhere make no mention of the farewell of Penelope and Odysseus, although later summaries refer to a version in which Odysseus feigns madness in order to avoid joining the Trojan expedition, and a play by Sophocles with the title *Odysseus Mainomenos* ('Odysseus gone mad') is attested. See Gantz (1993, p. 580).

[45] On the phases of deployment as experienced by a military spouse—from the 'anticipation phase' (characterized by emotions including fear, resentment and denial, and by practical actions related to preparing for the time apart) through separation to reunion—see Norwood et al. (1996, pp. 170–3).

[46] For discussions of the reversal of gender roles in the absence of the serving partner, see below, pp. 90–2 and pp. 121–31.

before he departed. The first of these insights comes when Penelope addresses the suitors, at the point in the epic where it is becoming apparent that she can no longer delay the decision as to whom she will marry. Unknown to them all, however, Odysseus is already in the house in disguise. Penelope recalls that as he left, he grasped her by the right wrist (18.257–8). Such a gesture may seem aggressive to a modern audience, but as Steiner notes, in the Homeric poems it is often a sign of affection associated with saying goodbye.[47] Here Penelope relates the words which Odysseus said to her before he left: initially, she says, he speculated as to how the war at Troy might pan out, reflecting on the Trojans' reputation as great fighters, and musing that he could not be certain whether he would return home alive (18.259–66). He then gave his wife a series of instructions. In light of his uncertain fate he directed Penelope to 'take care of everything here (σοὶ δ' ἐνθάδε πάντα μελόντων); keep in your mind my father and my mother in these halls, as you do now, but still more when I am far away' (18.266–8). The exhortation to take care of the household hints at the reversal of conventional gender roles which often takes place when a soldier husband is away at war, when the spouse left behind must undertake tasks which would not ordinarily be her responsibility.

It is made clear, however, that in the world which Penelope and Odysseus inhabit, the lack of a male head of the household can only ever be a temporary state. The final piece of advice which Odysseus gives to Penelope is that she must choose someone new to marry should he have failed to return home by the time their son Telemachus has grown a beard (18.269–70).[48] The immediate plot of the *Odyssey* hinges upon this instruction, since it is becoming more urgent that Penelope should choose which of her suitors to marry. Odysseus' words before his departure function in a similar manner to the 'just in case' letters still written today by combatants to their families as they set out for war. Such letters, to be delivered to next of kin should their loved one not return home alive, may contain final words of comfort and expressions of affection as well as practical instructions about, for example, the distribution of an individual's belongings, or details about how

---

[47] Steiner (2010, ed.), commenting on line 258.

[48] In antiquity, the model of a soldier issuing instructions to his wife seems to have filtered beyond the *Odyssey*. Sophocles' mid-fifth-century-BCE tragic play *Trachiniae* has Deianeira, wife of Heracles, recall the guidance given to her by her husband before he set out on his latest expedition: he instructed her as to how his inheritance should be divided between his children, and related a prophecy that he should either die one year and three months after his departure, or otherwise from then on live his life free from pain and grief (*Trachiniae* 161–8).

they wish to be remembered.[49] Penelope's report of Odysseus' words offers little insight into the emotional connection she might have with him; her immediate concern at the point in the poem where she recalls his parting advice is that imminently she faces a 'hateful marriage' (στυγερὸς γάμος, 18.272) to one of the suitors. Nor do we gain any sense of Penelope's own part in the interaction with her husband or her feelings at the point of his departure. Her silence on this, and the attribution of several lines of direct speech to Odysseus, fits with the way in which he takes centre stage throughout the poem. It anticipates too some of the ways in which the experiences of the serving partner have so often been foregrounded in accounts of conflicts ever since.[50]

The only other glimpse of the couple's preparation for Odysseus' departure comes in Book 19, when Odysseus, in disguise, pretends to be a stranger who 'met' Odysseus while the wanderer was on his travels. Penelope, having been tricked before by visitors to Ithaca telling false tales of her husband, is keen to test the 'stranger' to ascertain whether he might be telling the truth. She asks for a full description of what Odysseus was wearing, what kind of man he was, and who was with him. In the detailed description given at 19.225–35 of Odysseus' clothing—a purple *chlaina* (warm woollen travelling-cloak), a gold pin decorated with an image of a hound pinning down a fawn it had caught, and a fine *chitōn* (tunic)—she recognizes the garments which she prepared for him before he left. She recalls, 'I myself gave him those clothes of which you speak; I folded them in my chamber, and attached the shining pin to be an adornment for him' (19.255–7). The memory shows her undertaking a task that illustrates her concern for her husband's well-being, as she carefully gathers practical items for his journey. At the same time, however, the decorative gold brooch that she gives to Odysseus is a keepsake by which he might remember her while they are apart.[51] As things turn out, the brooch becomes for her one of the tokens by

[49] Price (2011) is a compilation of these 'just in case' letters written by soldiers across a chronological span from the Napoleonic Wars to recent conflicts in Iraq and Afghanistan.
[50] For discussions of some of the ways in which military spouses are silenced, see below, pp. 47–9, pp. 78–80, pp. 94–5, p. 170, pp. 189–90, and p. 201.
[51] Felson-Rubin (1996, p. 175 n. 28) notes the significance of the scene depicted on the brooch, pointing out that 'As a departure gift from wife to husband, it binds Odysseus, reminding him of Penelope's claims', and suggesting that the image of the dog capturing a fawn might hint at an erotic chase, either that of Odysseus' first 'capture' of Penelope in their youth, or the way in which Penelope later ensnares her husband using the trick of the marriage bed. See also Rutherford (1992, ed.), on lines 226–31, suggesting that the hunter/hunted motif could also allude metaphorically to Odysseus and the suitors.

which she recognizes Odysseus on his return.[52] Once again, however, the poignant expression of emotion which is apparent in the farewell scene between Hector and Andromache in the *Iliad* is absent from the *Odyssey*'s descriptions of Penelope and Odysseus' parting. In the latter, of course, the sense of immediacy is lacking, since Penelope is recalling events that took place almost twenty years ago. Here the reminders of Odysseus' departure act as plot hinges, with his instructions to Penelope a reminder of the urgency of action if Penelope's marriage to a suitor is to be averted. Meanwhile the memory of Penelope packing his clothes—distinctive items which he still possesses—is the start of a recognition process by which she comes to learn that he is still alive, and indeed already in the house.

Penelope's silence in the *Odyssey* as to her own emotional processes has left the way open for later authors to imagine her thoughts and feelings at the point of her husband's departure. In one poetic version of Penelope's story, Ursula Vaughan Williams, who was herself widowed during the Second World War, reflects on the pain of farewell. Published in 1948, at a time when wartime partings were a recent memory, Vaughan Williams' 'Penelope' opens with the following lines:

> Certain parting does not wait its hour
> for separation; too soon the shadow lies
> upon the heart and chokes the voice, its power
> drives on the minutes, it implies
> tomorrow while today's still here.[53]

Already, then, in the moments spent waiting to say goodbye to her husband, Vaughan Williams' Penelope anticipates the pain of separation and the challenges which time apart will bring. The poem's final stanza imagines Penelope trying to recall her husband's appearance while he is absent, and even before his departure she is already, in its last line, imagining 'the future days of solitude and fear' which she will endure while he is gone. This twentieth-century reimagining of Penelope encapsulates what it is which makes the anticipation of farewell so painful. As one contemporary military spouse shares on her personal blog, for many the anticipation of departure can be

---

[52] The recognition token *par excellence* for Penelope and Odysseus is, however, the olive-tree bed at the centre of their home. See below, p. 150, for a full discussion of the role of the bed in the process of recognition and reunion described in the *Odyssey*.

[53] Extract from Reilly (1984, ed., p. 125).

more difficult than the separation itself: she writes that 'the days leading up to saying goodbye are sometime [*sic*] more painful than him finally being gone. You want to savor every moment, but also just want the weight of waiting to be over.'[54]

This sense of the awfulness of the countdown to departure is captured too in a short story written by Mollie Panter-Downes, and published during the Second World War. 'Goodbye, My Love' tells the story of Ruth and her husband Adrian, in the days leading up to Adrian's departure for the front line. After he leaves, Ruth moves from a dazed and aimless state to acceptance that Adrian has gone and determination to keep herself busy during his absence. This new state is shattered, however, when Adrian calls to say that he will be returning home temporarily as his departure has been delayed by ten days. The story closes with Ruth's realization that she will have to endure the anguished anticipation of goodbye once more: 'The clock on the table beside her sounded deafening again, beginning to mark off the ten days at the end of which terror was the red light at the end of the tunnel. Then her face became drawn and, putting her hands over it, she burst into tears.'[55] Panter-Downes recognizes that the emotions associated with saying farewell can be even more powerful than those that surface for a spouse during a soldier's absence. This is due in part to the anticipation of the loneliness and stress of separation.[56] It also reflects the fact that parting moments such as those explored in this chapter are infused with the sense that this may be the final time when a couple will be together. Panter-Downes' description of the goodbye of her characters Ruth and Adrian reflects the impossibility of knowing whether the separation will be permanent: 'Language was inadequate, after all. One used the same words for a parting which might be for years, which might end in death, as one did for an overnight business trip. She put her arms tightly round him and said, "Goodbye, my love."'[57] The concluding section of my chapter considers briefly the impact when, as for Andromache in the *Iliad*, the moment of parting does turn out to have been a couple's last goodbye.

---

[54] Huffman (2018). See also Provost (2019) for a similar personal reflection from a military spouse on the pain of the time before deployment.

[55] Panter-Downes in Boston (1988, ed., p. 33).

[56] I discuss the emotional impact of the period of separation on the waiting spouse in Chapter 3.

[57] Panter-Downes in Boston (1988, ed., p. 31).

When the farewell is final

The awareness that war turns wives into widows is present throughout Homeric poetry; as discussed earlier in this chapter, the farewell of Hector and Andromache is given added pathos as the audience knows that this is the last time the couple will see one another alive. Every death of a soldier brings pain for loved ones left behind: the poet acknowledges this in allusions to warriors' wives and families as he recounts deaths on the battlefield. Of those killed by Agamemnon in Book 11, for example, we learn that Iphidamas was married to Theano, daughter of Cisses, but left for Troy soon after his marriage (11.224–9); later, when Alcathous falls at the hands of Idomeneus, the poet sings of his wife Hippodameia (13.427–33). While Andromache's grief as the widow of Hector is the most fully drawn in the poem, even these brief obituaries remind the audience that hers is merely one among many such agonizing bereavements.

The moment of realization for a waiting wife that a warrior has been killed in the line of duty, anticipated in Hector and Andromache's final exchange with one another, is played out poignantly in the *Iliad* when Andromache learns of Hector's death. That moment comes towards the close of the poem, in its twenty-second book. As in the earlier farewell scene, events which take place on the (male-dominated) battlefield once again intrude upon the female-centred domestic setting within which Andromache operates. This is especially noticeable in Troy, where the front line is only just outside the city walls and therefore very close to home for Andromache and Hector. At the moment when Hector is killed, we find Andromache weaving, having instructed her attendants to prepare a bath for her husband (22.440–4).[58] Her train of thought is interrupted by the sounds of Hecuba's lamentation from the city wall: limbs shaking, she drops her shuttle (22.448). This abrupt cessation of an everyday household task marks the moment of impact of the news from the front line. In what follows, the poet captures the physical and emotional effects as Andromache receives the worst possible news. Her words describe the physical symptoms of shock: 'the heart in my breast leapt up to my mouth, and my knees beneath me were numbed' (στήθεσι πάλλεται ἦτορ ἀνὰ στόμα, νέρθε δὲ γοῦνα / πήγνυται, 22.452–3). She articulates too the fear (αἰνῶς / δείδω, 'I am terribly afraid', 22.454–5) as she speculates that Hector's heroism and

---

[58] I discuss further the significance of the preparation of a bath for Hector in relation to homecoming rituals below at p. 159.

willingness to fight at the forefront must have led to his death at the hands of Achilles. The poet then follows Andromache as she rushes through the palace, 'heart pounding' (παλλομένη κραδίην, 22.461). As she sees Hector's corpse being defiled by his killer, a vivid metaphor describes the physical impact, as she faints in shock: 'Black night descended and covered her eyes as she slipped backwards and gasped for breath' (τὴν δὲ κατ' ὀφθαλμῶν ἐρεβεννὴ νὺξ ἐκάλυψεν, / ἤριπε δ' ἐξοπίσω, ἀπὸ δὲ ψυχὴν ἐκάπυσσε, 22.466-7).[59] On regaining consciousness, Andromache sobs as she laments Hector in a longer speech (22.477-514) in which she imagines the infant Astyanax's future, bereft of his father and cruelly treated by his peers. Here she also visualizes Hector's decaying corpse, no longer dressed in his fine clothes, which lie unworn in the palace. Andromache appears only once more in the *Iliad*, at Hector's funeral, where she mourns her widowhood and future enslavement, anticipating too the death of Astyanax at the hands of the victorious Greeks (24.725-45).[60] Her lament closes with a heart-breaking reflection on her final memories of Hector, with an implied con-trast between a good death in peacetime—in bed, at home, and close to his loved ones—and the violence which he suffered in war: 'I especially am left with terrible grief (ἐμοὶ δὲ μάλιστα λελείψεται ἄλγεα λυγρά); for you weren't reaching your arms out to me from bed as you died, nor did you say a tender word to me which I could always remember as I weep night and day' (24.742-4).

Individual stories of bereavement in wartime differ from one to the next; as one twenty-first-century war widow, Beate Medina, sharing a detailed reflection on her own story of loss observes, 'Every journey is different.'[61] The Homeric Andromache's reactions, like those of every war widow since, are deeply personal; yet she shares with many other bereaved women the sense that she was denied a final goodbye at the moment of her husband's death.[62] Andromache's lamentation is a reflection of the very real responses to grief experienced by women in similar situations. Murnaghan points out the similarities between Vera Brittain's description of her feelings after her fiancé, Roland Leighton, was killed during the First World War, and the

[59] Griffin (1980, p. 2) notes also the detail here that the headdress which Andromache was given on her wedding day falls off her head, describing this as 'a vivid symbol of her loss'.

[60] I discuss the enslavement of surviving women and children, including Andromache and Astyanax, after war in further detail in Chapter 6 below.

[61] Medina (2013, p. 323).

[62] See, for example, Bedell (2009), sharing the stories of three women whose husbands were killed while on military service.

Homeric portrayal of Andromache's grief, suggesting that Brittain's account 'provides the closest thing to authentication of Homer's text that we can hope to have', and interpreting this as 'an indication that real women's voices have been effectively integrated into the *Iliad* through episodes of lamentation'.[63]

In modern times, the death of a soldier is often represented as the 'ultimate sacrifice' made by military personnel in pursuit of the cause for which they fight; yet a warrior's wife too bears the cost of her husband's service. In the US today the widows of fallen soldiers are known as 'Gold Star Wives' in recognition of their partners' service, and the loved ones of those deceased in war are issued with lapel pins featuring a gold star; the practice of adding a gold star to the service flag to designate a member of the family killed in war dates back to the First World War.[64] Gestures such as this might seem to some an inadequate reflection of their suffering: for Josie, one of the widows imagined by Siobhan Fallon in her short story collection, the gold star carries patronizing 'imagery of schoolchildren receiving A's and stickers for a job well done',[65] masking the true horror of what she has endured. In a similar vein one of the women in Moreau's *Waiting Wives*, on being given the news that her dead husband will be awarded a posthumous medal, asks through her excruciating emotional pain, 'What good is a medal if my husband never comes home?'[66]

The farewells on which this chapter has focused—whether the precursors to temporary or permanent separation—are integral to the lives of those whose partners serve in the armed forces. A we have seen too, each parting is overshadowed by the ever-present fear for the waiting spouse of losing their loved on in a war zone. For the majority of military couples their lives are punctuated by many such moments of goodbye, which disrupt, sometimes irrevocably, the course of their relationships. The farewell scene often marks the suspension of normal family life for the waiting spouse, in some cases bringing with it the expectation that she will assume roles more normally carried out by her husband. In Chapter 3 I examine more closely this aspect of separation itself. Tableaus such as the scene between Andromache and Hector (and, in some cases, their modern counterparts) can reflect traditional ideas about gender roles, whereby men go out into the world

---

[63] Murnaghan (2015, pp. 189–90).

[64] The Gold Star Wives of America organization was created in 1945. See further Hedayat (2019).

[65] Fallon (2011, p. 210).   [66] Moreau (2005, p. 230).

to fight while their wives wait and tend to matters at home, including childrearing. Emotions expressed at the point of departure can encompass sadness at parting and fear for what the future holds, as well as anger and denial. Time spent apart from a partner, with its associated emotional and practical challenges, is just one of many demands that the military imposes on the spouse of a serving soldier. In my next chapter I consider some of the ways in which military spouses ancient and modern are affected by the 'sacrifices'—including wartime separation—which they are expected to make.

2

Sacrifice: Clytemnestra in Aeschylus' *Agamemnon* and Euripides' *Iphigenia at Aulis*

'The sacrifice of life begins at home.'[1] The words of the Greek military commander Agamemnon to his wife Clytemnestra in director Robert Icke's 2015 adaptation of Aeschylus' *Oresteia* might ring true for many military spouses. Icke's version of this myth traces events from before the departure of the Greek fleet for the war against Troy through to the aftermath of Clytemnestra's murder of her husband upon his return.[2] The myth on which Icke's play draws has at its heart a sacrifice in its quite literal sense: this is the sacrifice at Aulis of a human child, Clytemnestra and Agamemnon's youngest daughter Iphigenia. In the ancient tradition dramatized by the tragic playwrights Aeschylus and Euripides, this sacrifice was an appeasement to the goddess Artemis for Agamemnon's killing of one of her sacred stags; the goddess demanded the sacrifice in return for a fair wind to carry the Greek fleet to Troy.

Icke's reworking of the story casts Agamemnon as a recognizably modern military leader who is torn between obligations to his family and to the army he commands. On learning that Agamemnon plans to take Iphigenia's life, Icke's Clytemnestra pleads with him to reconsider, berating him for the choice he has made: 'Your eyes are open—and you choose your war. Your men.'[3] As in the ancient versions of the myth on which I will focus throughout this chapter, Agamemnon's decision to put the military first has grave and enduring consequences for his whole family, and in particular for his wife. From the outset, Icke frames Clytemnestra's eventual murder of her husband

---

[1] Icke (2015, p. 54). Note that Icke uses the spelling 'Klytemnestra' in his version of the story. For the sake of consistency I use 'Clytemnestra' throughout my discussion.

[2] Icke's play adopted a four-part structure (as compared with Aeschylus' *Oresteia* trilogy), in order to incorporate a version of events at Aulis, and the sacrifice of Iphigenia, to make the overarching narrative more comprehensible to a modern audience. See Bridges (2015b) for Icke's own insight into his work, and McConnell (2016) for a review of the production.

[3] Icke (2015, p. 52).

Warriors' Wives: Ancient Greek Myth and Modern Experience. Emma Bridges, Oxford University Press.
© Emma Bridges 2023. DOI: 10.1093/oso/9780198843528.003.0003

as motivated strongly by her desire to avenge the killing of their child. The actions that he takes are beyond her control, yet she too will bear the devastating consequences; the sacrifice he chooses becomes her sacrifice too.

The conflict between familial and military obligations which lies at the heart of Agamemnon's story, and the impact which this has upon his wife and children, is an extreme version of the 'sacrifices' which military families have always had to make in support of serving members' commitment to their roles in the armed forces. For ancient audiences, the notion of 'sacrifice', which usually related to the practice of making an offering to a god, often involving the slaughter of an animal, carried complex religious and ritual associations.[4] In comparison, the modern use of the term, while retaining religious echoes in some contexts, has to a large extent become detached from any such ritual connotations, yet it still recurs frequently as a concept in discourse surrounding military service and the families of military personnel. In this chapter, I consider the notion of the military and the family as 'greedy institutions' which each make competing demands on service members. I explore the impact of this tension on military spouses, considering some of the ways in which, still today, they are expected to make 'sacrifices' in service of their partners' role. I also present a reading of the myth of Iphigenia's sacrifice, as represented in the fifth-century-BCE tragic dramas of Aeschylus and Euripides, which sees it as an ancient worked example of the impact of the 'greedy' military upon Clytemnestra as warrior's wife.

'Greedy institutions': the competing obligations of family life and the military

'If the Marines wanted me to have a wife, they would have issued me one!'[5]

This quip, as recalled by the wife of the US Marine who would habitually parrot the phrase when she asked to spend more time with him, sums up a

---

[4] There is a rich Greek vocabulary relating to sacrificial rites, although no term specific to the sacrifice of humans: see Naiden (2015, pp. 453–4). The term 'sacrifice' as I use it in this chapter in discussion of the death of Iphigenia in ancient texts is usually translated from the Greek noun θυσία and forms of its related verb θυσιάζω. There is no evidence that human sacrifice was actually practised; as Bremmer (2010, p. 143) points out, it features only in mythical narratives, where it is presented as a transgressive act, 'meant to suggest a monstrous offering, not a pleasing gift'.
[5] Sherman (2010, p. 17).

key aspect of the lives of modern-day military spouses. The apparently light-hearted tone of the comment glosses over the complex nature of the challenges posed for a couple when one or both partners serve in the military. The competing pressures placed on service personnel by, on the one hand, their families and, on the other, their duty to the military can have a profound effect on the lives of their partners. Modern-day autobiographical accounts and fictional narratives focusing on soldiers' spouses often reflect an awareness, and sometimes a resentment, of these conflicting loyalties. In some cases, military spouses liken the experience of being married to a serving soldier or a veteran to being married to someone who is having an affair.[6] For the wives of some Vietnam veterans, for example, Vietnam itself would become the metaphorical 'other woman', occupying traumatized veterans' every thought and denying them the possibility of a return to normality. Matsakis, in her detailed study of the impact of the Vietnam War on the soldiers' wives, draws this analogy clearly:

> Although still living with Ed, Jessica feels alone and abandoned. Her husband, it seems, is involved with another woman. The other wives have the same complaint: their husbands are involved with another woman, too—the same other woman.
>
> Her name is Vietnam. She is ugly and battle-scarred, but her power is great. Somehow this other woman still controls the men who knew her.[7]

Similar sentiments have been expressed too in relation to more recent conflicts, as seen in the stories told by journalist Tanya Biank of the army wives whom she encountered on the US Army base at Fort Bragg in 2002; typical of this view is 'Rita', who, Biank reports, 'sometimes thought [her husband] cared more about the Army than their marriage. She felt the Army was another woman; heck, sometimes she felt as if *she* were the mistress.'[8]

Studies carried out by sociological and psychological researchers have sought to explore the impact of these conflicting loyalties on military families. In an influential article first published in 1986 which is often still cited in research into modern military families, sociologist Mady Wechsler Segal proposed that because of the demands which both the family and the

---

[6] I discuss the literal sexual infidelity of service personnel below, at pp. 110–14.

[7] Matsakis (1996, pp. 19–20). I discuss the impact of combat on veterans' mental states and the lives of their partners in further detail below at pp. 197–99.

[8] Biank (2006, p. 149).

military make on the loyalty, time, and energy of individuals, these two institutions share many of the characteristics of what Lewis Coser first defined in his own sociological work as 'greedy institutions'.[9] Both the family and the military require a level of commitment which limits the extent to which a person who belongs to these institutions can devote attention to other aspects of their life. If an individual is both a member of the military and has a family of their own (a partner and perhaps children), suggested Segal, this means that they will have dual loyalties which are frequently in competition with one another. In addition, the military makes demands not just on the serving member but also, by extension, on their spouse and family.

In her original piece, which was published towards the end of the Cold War, Segal observed that she was writing at a time of social change in America, when both the shape of the military and family patterns there were changing. For example, there had been an increase in the proportion of active-duty women and a greater number of single-parent families, along with a growing trend towards women being more likely to undertake employment outside of the home than had previously been the case. In 2015 Segal, now with a co-author, Karin De Angelis, revisited the original 1986 article to reflect on the extent to which the 'greedy institutions thesis' in relation to the family and the military still remained relevant. In this new piece of scholarship, the authors concluded that 'the greediness of the military lifestyle for modern families in the United States and its allied nations has at least remained constant, if not grown, since Segal originally applied this concept'.[10] Recent conflicts in Iraq and Afghanistan had imposed new demands on personnel and their families; De Angelis observed that these political developments, along with demographic shifts, changes in family structures, and changing gender roles led, in the US at least, to 'formal policy changes that recognize the sacrifices experienced by military families'. However, they noted, 'These policies and programs are aimed at helping service members and their families to adapt to the military's greedy demands, not at reducing those demands'.[11] In modern times, the recogni-

---

[9] Coser (1974). Segal's article first appeared in the journal *Armed Forces and Society* in 1986 but was reprinted as Segal (1988); it is the 1988 version to which I refer here.

[10] De Angelis and Segal (2015, p. 22).

[11] De Angelis and Segal (2015, pp. 24–5). On the family as a support system for the military, and ways in which US government policies relating to military families act to promote the interests of the state, see Horn (2010). Booth and Lederer (2012) discuss the ways in which, in what they describe as an 'era of persistent conflict', policy makers have responded to the needs of families.

tion that the family can exert a pull on a service member's time and loyalty, and one which competes with military obligations, has historically exercised policy makers to the extent that in some contexts service members have been actively discouraged from marrying.[12] The rhetoric of military institutions also still very often promotes the notion that the armed forces themselves are a 'family'; this fosters an individual's sense of allegiance to their unit and the wider military, often at the expense of time spent with, and emotional energy invested in, their natal or marital family.[13]

One aspect of the 'greediness' that Segal identified in the military is the expectation that serving members must make 'sacrifices' in the course of their service. The language of sacrifice has long been a part of the rhetoric surrounding war and those who fight, and it has, over time, become a key element of the concept of heroism in military contexts.[14] Contemporary discourse often favoured by politicians and the media in relation to recent wars continues to use the language of sacrifice to convey a sense that those who serve must often, in 'doing their duty', give up things which they hold dear.[15] Some are said to make the 'ultimate sacrifice' by losing their life or sustaining life-changing injuries, but there is also an expectation that they will make sacrifices in other ways: by putting the military before their personal relationships, by spending long periods of time away from their family, or by relinquishing the ability to make choices about other aspects of their life. Military personnel may, for example, have little choice about where to live or when to relocate, and the lack of predictability of military life can mean that making even short-term future plans is impossible.

This language of sacrifice and duty now also extends beyond referring only to combatants themselves. It has become part of the vocabulary surrounding the representation of military spouses in popular culture and the media, by the military itself, and by policy makers. In the UK, in recent years this came to the fore most forcefully with the media's construction and promotion of a group of 'Military Wives' Choirs' orchestrated by celebrity choirmaster Gareth Malone, initially for a 2011 BBC programme *The Choir:*

---

[12]   Enloe (2000, pp. 154–60).

[13]   Enloe (2000, p. 161) and Houppert (2005, p. 85). For an extreme example of the way in which one US military academy, the Virginia Military Institute, uses a warped 'family' structure as part of its initiation/indoctrination program, see Adams (1997).

[14]   Elshtain (1991) gives a wide-ranging historical overview of the concept of 'sacrifice' in relation to military service. For a discussion of the use of language and symbolism relating to sacrifice on war memorials, see Turner (2015).

[15]   Ware (2010).

Military Wives.[16] These groups of women, whose husbands were combatants, would become emblematic of the supposed stoicism of the idealized 'military spouse'. The way in which they were represented would also serve to reinforce the traditional gendered ideals perpetuated by the military; images of wholesome domesticity and displays of emotion in the television series call to mind the division between home/family and military service, which I explored in the farewell scenes I discussed in Chapter 1. Alice Cree suggests that the women of the military wives' choirs have been presented as modern-day 'Penelope'-figures, because of the 'feminine stoicism and sacrifice' which they embody.[17] She argues too that this gendered image has been manipulated by the media in service of a patriotic cause: 'In the frailty and grief of the military wife we can see a metaphor for wider civil society in need of protection, and at the same time can see what is sacrificed "at home".'[18]

The sacrifices which contemporary military spouses make—often relinquishing careers of their own, enduring repeated and prolonged separations from their partner, and allowing their own identity to become subsumed into their spouse's military role—may seem less dramatic than those made by service personnel themselves, yet the sense that they do this in service of their spouses' careers is often striking. One US Marine's account of the 'sacrifices' made by his wife offers a powerful insight into the way in which the narrative of 'willing sacrifice' can operate in a contemporary context:

> Marine Corps Col. Christopher Conlin assumed a command position in August 2003 and left for Iraq five months later. His wife assumed the role of key volunteer advisor, becoming point person for the families of 900 infantrymen. He applauds her. "[M]y wife Ava selflessly resigned her commission in the U.S. Navy Medical Corps to be a stay-at-home mom for our two daughters," the colonel wrote. "This was no small sacrifice, as she was a Lieutenant Commander with 8 years of service as a board-certified preventive medicine physician. She did this without complaint because she felt it was her duty as a spouse, mother, and American."[19]

---

[16] Baker (2018) outlines the history of these choirs and examines the way in which they relate to gendered constructions of military heroism in the UK. The movie *Military Wives*, which was based on the story of the choirs, premiered (in Canada) in 2019. Kermode (2020) captures a sense of the way in which the film represents the women's roles.

[17] Cree (2019, p. 1).

[18] Cree (2019, p. 7). On gendered narratives of heroism and sacrifice in relation to contemporary military personnel and their spouses, see also Cree (2018, pp. 23–39).

[19] Houppert (2005, p. 168).

A striking element of this individual account is the way in which, rather than presenting Ava's own perspective, the situation is perceived entirely through the eyes of her husband, who projects his own ideas of duty and patriotism onto his wife. Ava's own voice remains unheard; we cannot know the extent to which her husband's interpretation truly reflects Ava's own motivations for giving up her own career in service of his, or whether for her this felt like an active choice rather than a necessity driven by the demands of his job.[20] Here Ava's own identity is erased, and she fulfils gendered expectations to become the image of the idealized military spouse. She does so by performing childcare and emotional support roles traditionally perceived as feminine, retreating from her own military and medical career into the domestic sphere as wife and mother, and assisting others in similar situations. In her husband's account, Ava's service to the country is configured only in relation to his own role. The fact that Ava is said by her spouse to have done this 'selflessly' and 'without complaint' reinforces the idealized image of the loyal but largely silent (and silenced) partner; there is an echo here of the Penelope-figure of ancient myth, whom I shall discuss in depth later in this book.

The erasure of the identity and experience of the military spouse hinted at in the reflections of Ava's husband is a common feature of accounts of military life. Donna Moreau's fictionalized memoir *Waiting Wives* (2005) gives a satirical insight into how this can play out when the military community has a tendency to define women in relation to the role occupied by their serving partners.[21] Woven between chapters focusing on individual named women are sections which recount the exploits of a committee of wives formed to organize social events. In these 'Committee' chapters, the women are never referred to by name, but only by their husbands' ranks: they are 'the captain's wife', 'the sergeant major's wife', 'the warrant officer's wife', and so on. Meanwhile, the institutional culture of the military, reinforced by media representations like *The Choir: Military Wives*, cultivates admiration for those who stoically bear the challenges of being married to a service member: as Enloe sets out wryly, the 'Model Military Wife' is, among a long list of other things, one who supports her husband unreservedly in the performance of his job.[22] One woman cited by Enloe

---

[20] The notion of the modern western military as a 'two-person career', in which only one partner is paid as an employee, but the other also contributes their labour to the organization, has been much discussed. See, for example, Weinstein and Mederer (1997).

[21] On Moreau's book, see further pp. 28–30 above.

[22] Enloe (2000, pp. 162–3).

described a relationship of total interdependence between the military and the family, pointing out that often even the promotional prospects of the serving partner depend on the behaviour of his wife: 'If your husband is in the military, everyone [in the family] is in the military; it is the only way to survive and advance in the military...social activities can help in the advancement of your husband, because the more visual [sic] you are, the more people know who you are, the more you get...'[23]

This notion that, particularly for higher-ranking personnel, the character and actions of a military spouse reflect positively or negatively on the reputation of her husband has proved surprisingly persistent.[24] Some twenty-first-century 'handbooks' for military spouses, for example, still make the assumption that a wife's behaviour (and her relationship with other men's spouses) should relate closely to her husband's rank; as one such guide phrased this, 'spouses need to understand what the pecking order is, generally speaking, and what the appropriate protocol is'.[25] Behaviour deemed by the military as inappropriate for the wife of an officer, for example, might affect the serving partner's prospects for future promotion, and there is still a sense in some military circles that the rank structure among service personnel also applies to their wives. Marriage to a higher-ranking officer often carries with it particular expectations for a woman too, as one US military spouse revealed to journalist Karen Houppert. 'Heidi', married to a commander, reported that she felt coerced into carrying out labour which was ostensibly 'voluntary' (charity events, family support activities, and so on) in service of the military cause: '[My husband] wanted me to do this because if I didn't people would say I wasn't supportive of the military. That really upset me. We had quite a struggle with that.'[26]

Just as in the account given by Ava's husband, the construction of the idealized (and often faceless) image of the military spouse described by Enloe, satirized by Moreau, and investigated by Houppert often contributes to the silencing of individual women's voices. As one writer and campaigner, drawing on her own lived experience as a military spouse, commented in a piece written about the military wives' choirs, these women are mostly 'conveniently silent', representing 'an ideal of womanhood, the wife who waits and hopes, like Homer's famously faithful Penelope, who is loyal to husband and country and doesn't make a fuss'.[27] The silencing of their voices is yet one more sacrifice that spouses are expected to make by the 'greedy

---

[23] Quoted in Enloe (2000, p. 158).   [24] Harrell (2001).
[25] Leyva (2003, p. 44).   [26] Houppert (2005, p. 199).   [27] Shotbolt (2011).

institution' that is the military; many feel unable to share their stories as they fear that speaking out about problems may damage their partners' military careers.[28] Those who publicly express their discomfort, whether about the demands and disruptions imposed on family life by the military, or about the morality of the wars to which governments have committed their loved ones, are in the minority.[29] When women like Ava are not given a voice of their own, they have little opportunity to correct erroneous assumptions that their own sacrifices are made willingly in support of their husbands' careers and the causes for which they fight.

As discussed in the introduction to this volume the conditions under which contemporary military families live, work, and form relationships do not replicate those of the soldiers and their families whom we find in the ancient stories of the Trojan War. The 'sacrifices' made by modern-day military spouses are, therefore, the products of social and historical contexts which differ considerably from those which produced ancient mythical narratives. Nonetheless, I suggest, the story of Agamemnon's literal sacrifice of Iphigenia is a scenario in which the demands made by the 'greedy institution' of the military are at odds with those of the soldier's family. The fifth-century-BCE tragic versions of this myth, as told by Aeschylus and Euripides, highlight the far-reaching consequences of this sacrifice for the warrior's family; they do so largely through the figure of Agamemnon's wife Clytemnestra. It is this ancient story which will be the focus of my discussion in the rest of this chapter.

Resentment and revenge: Aeschylus' Clytemnestra

The story of the relationship of Clytemnestra and her husband, the Greek military commander Agamemnon, is used in Athenian tragedy of the fifth century BCE to think through several of the challenges which a warrior's military obligations impose upon a couple, and indeed on a whole family.

---

[28] See Jervis (2011, pp. 247–54). Heiselberg (2017, pp. 69–71) opens with a good example of such silencing, in the form of a letter written to the Danish Minister of Defence—but never sent—by 'Trine', wife of a senior sergeant in the Danish Defence Forces. In the letter Trine writes of the many things which she and her son have given up for the military; she chose not to post the letter out of fear of the consequences which it might have for her husband's career. On the ways in which military spouses are silenced, and the need for their 'unsilencing', see Davis, Ward, and Storm (2011).

[29] Houppert (2005, pp. 195–221) discusses some of the challenges faced by women who have openly criticized the military.

A key characteristic of Athenian tragic drama is its tendency to explore how humans might behave when placed in extreme situations. Playwrights manipulate mythical narratives in order to ask questions surrounding moral responsibility, the cause and effect of individuals' actions, and humans' relationships with their family, their community, and wider society. In particular, stories relating to the House of Atreus (from whom Agamemnon and his children were descended) presented ample opportunities for playwrights to impose a 'pressure test' on characters from the myths. Mythical narratives relating to the ongoing impact of an ancestral curse on the descendants of Atreus, and in particular on the household of Agamemnon, often take centre stage in these retellings. The curse is said to have originated with a quarrel between the brothers Atreus (father of Agamemnon) and Thyestes (father of Aegisthus, who in the mythic tradition would become Clytemnestra's lover when Agamemnon left for Troy). In revenge for Thyestes' adultery with his wife Aerope, Atreus had banished his brother, but later murdered two of Thyestes' sons and invited him home, where he served him a ghastly feast from the flesh of his own children; this brought down a curse upon Atreus and his descendants. It is within this framework of ancestral guilt that Agamemnon's sacrifice of his daughter Iphigenia before setting out for Troy, and his murder at the hands of Clytemnestra upon his return, take place; for example, in Aeschylus' *Agamemnon*, the curse is alluded to several times as a reason for the disasters which befall the family.[30]

Tragic playwrights were not the first to tell the story of Agamemnon and his family. Centuries earlier, the *Odyssey*—which almost certainly drew on pre-existing traditions relating to the homecomings of the Greek heroes— referred to his murder at the hands of Aegisthus, assisted by Clytemnestra (*Odyssey* 1.35–41, 1.298–300, 3.248–312, 4.512–37, 11.405–34).[31] There are also allusions to Agamemnon's return from Troy in fragmentary texts from the sixth century BCE, including the *Nostoi* ('Homecomings'), the Hesiodic *Catalogue of Women*, and an *Oresteia* by the lyric poet Stesichorus.[32] Pindar's eleventh Pythian ode (probably performed in 474 BCE) also

[30] See *Agamemnon* 1095–7, 1217–25, and 1583–1603. On the notion of inherited guilt, see Gantz (1982).
[31] Wolfe (2009) traces chronologically the changing representation of Clytemnestra. The tragedians generally give Clytemnestra greater individual responsibility for plotting Agamemnon's death than she is given in the epic tradition. I discuss Clytemnestra's murder of Agamemnon in tragedy in more detail in Chapter 5, at pp. 160–63.
[32] Garvie (1986, pp. x–xiii) considers the relationship of the *Odyssey* with other versions of the story of Agamemnon's homecoming.

mentions Agamemnon's homecoming; this poet raises the possibility that Iphigenia's sacrifice provided a pretext for the murder of Agamemnon, but then suggests that Clytemnestra's lust for Aegisthus was her true motive (*Pythian* 11.22-7).[33] It is in the hands of the tragic playwrights, however, that the relationship of Clytemnestra and Agamemnon becomes an extreme example of an irreconcilable conflict between the 'greedy institutions' of the family and the military. For this couple and their children, the consequences of Agamemnon's divided loyalties are devastating, and, as Nancy Rabinowitz has suggested, 'the Atreus myth as presented in tragedy reveals that war takes its toll on the family structure it was supposedly waged to protect'.[34] Assigning Clytemnestra responsibility for Agamemnon's death (rather than showing her merely as assisting Aegisthus) also enables the tragedians to explore the relationship between his sacrifice of Iphigenia and Clytemnestra's plan to murder him. Aeschylus and Euripides in particular portray a Clytemnestra who is driven by a desire for revenge for her daughter's death.

The various retellings of Clytemnestra's story share key plot points: that she and her lover Aegisthus contrived to murder Agamemnon on his return from Troy, and that Orestes, son of Clytemnestra and Agamemnon, later returned from exile to avenge his father by killing his mother and Aegisthus. Each version differs, however, in its treatment of the character and role of Clytemnestra; for example, in different texts she is given a range of motives for killing Agamemnon, and her degree of personal culpability varies, as does the extent to which the playwrights paint her as a sympathetic character.[35] One thing which the fifth-century-BCE tragic versions of Clytemnestra and Agamemnon's story have in common, however, is the fact that they all deal in some way with the impact which war can have on a marital relationship. In later chapters, I examine how the character of Clytemnestra is used in Athenian drama to examine the challenges of separation, the need for a soldier's partner to take on new roles when he is absent, concerns about potential infidelity, and anxieties surrounding the homecoming of a returning warrior.[36] For now, however, I am concerned primarily with tragic

---

[33] On Pindar's eleventh Pythian, see Finglass (2007, pp. 5-19). On the suggestion in this ode that Clytemnestra was motivated by adultery, see below, p. 118.

[34] Rabinowitz (2014, p. 191).

[35] Sommerstein (2012, pp. 137-45) details the ways in which versions of the story differ in the textual sources. Wolfe (2009, pp. 698-713) explores the extent to which the audiences of tragic plays (Aeschylus' *Agamemnon*, Sophocles' *Electra*, and Euripides' *Electra* and *Iphigenia at Aulis*) are encouraged (or not) to sympathize with Clytemnestra.

[36] See pp. 119-35 on infidelity in relation to Clytemnestra and Agamemnon's relationship, as well as on gendered role reversal in Agamemnon's absence, and pp. 159-63 on Clytemnestra's 'welcome' of Agamemnon as a distorted version of an ideal homecoming.

representations of Clytemnestra's response to Agamemnon's sacrifice of Iphigenia; this is the act which epitomizes his decision to place his obligations to the military before his wife and family. In particular, I examine in this chapter two tragic plays which represent the sacrifice of Iphigenia as a primary motive for Clytemnestra's murder of Agamemnon on his return from Troy.[37] The first of these is the *Agamemnon*, which deals with Agamemnon's return home and his death at Clytemnestra's hand. This was the opening play in Aeschylus' *Oresteia* trilogy, which was first performed at Athens in 458 BCE along with his *Choephoroi*, or *Libation Bearers*, and *Eumenides*.[38] The second play which I discuss is Euripides' *Iphigenia at Aulis*, which was left unfinished at the playwright's death in 407/6 BCE, and which deals with the circumstances surrounding Agamemnon's sacrifice of his daughter before the Greeks set sail for Troy.[39]

The Athenian theatre audiences who first watched tragic drama being performed at civic festivals in the fifth century BCE were accustomed to dealing with the real impact of conflict on their families; the plays were produced during an era of almost constant military action. Conflict with Persia had begun towards the end of the sixth century BCE, and, even after the defeat of Persian forces at the battle of Marathon (490 BCE) and later Salamis (480 BCE) and Plataea (479 BCE), the threat of a fresh Persian invasion remained present.[40] Tension between Athens and other Greek states (in particular Sparta), already apparent as a result of Athenian expansionism in the years following the Persian Wars, later escalated, and the middle decades of the fifth century were characterized by intermittent military engagements. Later in the century came the Peloponnesian War, a drawn-out conflict between Athens and Sparta with their respective allies, from 431 until 404 BCE.[41] Dramatists who staged episodes from the Trojan War on the Athenian stage could therefore expect spectators to view these stories

---

[37] I discuss at pp. 119–35 representations of Clytemnestra which focus on her adultery with Aegisthus as a motivation for her actions.

[38] The *Choephoroi* and *Eumenides* focus on the vengeance taken by Agamemnon's children, Orestes and Electra, on their father's murderers. The actions of Electra and Orestes in the years following their father's death are also the focus of Sophocles' *Electra* (possibly first performed between 420 and 410 BCE), and of two plays by Euripides, his *Electra* (dating from between 422 and 413 BCE) and *Orestes* (408 BCE).

[39] The story of Iphigenia's sacrifice at Aulis predates the tragedies of the fifth century BCE; it is not mentioned by Homer but appears in fragments of early poems from the so-called 'epic cycle' dealing with the wider narratives of the Trojan War, as well as in an *Oresteia* by the sixth-century-BCE lyric poet Stesichorus. See Gantz (1993, pp. 582–8), for a summary of the sources and their variant versions.

[40] On the impact of the Persian Wars in classical Greece, see Rhodes (2007).

[41] For an overview of the Peloponnesian War and its aftermath, see Welwei (2006).

of the mythical past through the lens of their own experiences of war.[42] That said, caution is in order: the representations of the warriors' wives found in the tragedians' work were not originally conceived as a means by which women might see elements of their own experience reflected back to them.[43] Instead, they were performed by and for men who brought with them their own experiences of participation in combat and its impact on their families. Given this context, the presence on the Athenian tragic stage of a significant number of women (mothers and daughters of soldiers, as well as soldiers' wives) who have endured war and its aftermath is perhaps all the more striking. This proliferation of female characters seems in part to derive from tragedians' concern to explore the consequences of war not just for those directly involved in the fighting but also for wider families and communities.

Aeschylus' plays engage with contemporary politics in a variety of ways: unusually for surviving Athenian tragedy, his *Persians* (produced in 472 BCE) had focused on recent history, envisaging the response at the Persian court to the defeat of the Persian king Xerxes at Salamis in 480 BCE.[44] The *Oresteia* trilogy shows that mythical narratives too could address contemporary issues: for example, the *Eumenides* provides an aetiological narrative for the foundation of the Areopagus as a homicide court, after recent reforms to that Athenian court by Ephialtes. The trilogy, in which both *Agamemnon* and *Choephoroi* are set in Argos, may also allude to the recent alliance between Athens and Argos, enemy of Sparta, which came about after a breakdown in Athenian-Spartan relations.[45] The *Agamemnon*, which focuses on the homecoming of a warrior from war, would have been likely to resonate strongly with its audience of 458 BCE, the majority of whom would be combat veterans. In the years preceding the play's production Athens had been involved in multiple military campaigns, and, at a time when all Athenian citizen males participated in military service, a large proportion of the audience would have experienced combat at first hand.[46]

---

[42] Aeschylus himself had fought against the Persians at Marathon in 490 BCE, and according to the historian Herodotus (6.114), the playwright's brother had died in that battle.

[43] I discuss this issue further in Chapter 6, at p. 171.   [44] See Rosenbloom (1995).

[45] See Macleod (1982, pp. 126–9) on the relationship between the *Oresteia* and Athenian politics.

[46] Raeburn and Thomas (2011, p. xxi) suggest that references in the *Agamemnon* to deaths in the Trojan War and the hardships of campaign were influenced by the Athenians' experience of recent military campaigns. Most would not have served as military leaders (trierarchs in command of naval vessels or *strategoi*, senior military commanders) but as hoplite soldiers, cavalry force, lightly armed peltasts, or—in a city which relied heavily for its military power on its fleet—rowers in the Athenian navy. For an overview of the components of the Athenian

The ancient audience of *Agamemnon* would therefore also be familiar with the 'enduring grief' (πένθεια τλησικάρδιος, 429–30) felt by the families of fallen warriors of whom the play's chorus sing; they too had known what it was like when, in place of the men who left for war, only urns containing their ashes returned home (433–44).

It is also possible to read *Agamemnon* as a comment on the futility of the loss of life in war, and on the morality of commanders who pursue their own agenda at the expense of the lives of the masses. The chorus, for example, allude to the resentment that can arise among the populace at the actions of military leaders: 'in secret they snarl, [they died] "For another man's wife"', and, mixed with grief, resentment creeps [φθονερὸν δ᾽ ὑπ᾽ ἄλγος ἕρπει] against the sons of Atreus, the leading advocates [of war]' (448–51). The reference here to the war as having been fought for the sake of another man's wife refers to Menelaus' pursuit of the Trojan Paris after his abduction of Helen, spouse of Menelaus. The commanders of the various Greek contingents were themselves Helen's rejected suitors and included Menelaus' brother Agamemnon. At the time of Menelaus' marriage to Helen, these men had sworn a binding oath to support Menelaus in time of need; it was this which obliged them to accompany Menelaus to Troy on his quest to retrieve his wife.[47] The resentment to which the chorus allude in a sense foreshadows some of the responses towards political decision-makers of generations robbed of their family members by war ever since.[48] Indeed, some recent reinterpretations of the Trojan War myth have seen the retrieval of Helen as merely an excuse for the Greek leaders to pursue their own expansionist or glory-seeking ambitions, linking this to the ways in which more recent wars have been fought on the basis of spurious pretexts. Playwright Marianne McDonald, for example, who has adapted many Greek plays for the contemporary stage, has suggested that 'Helen is a perfect metaphor for the Iraqi [*sic*] War', and that she is the ancient equivalent of governmental claims in 2003 that Iraq held weapons of mass

army, see Rawlings (2013, pp. 18–21); on the structure and operation of the navy, see de Souza (2013).

[47] The oath is also alluded to at *Agamemnon* 448–51. The extent to which Helen herself is cast as responsible for the Trojan War varies considerably in ancient versions of the story. Maguire (2009) examines a range of versions of Helen's story from antiquity to the present day, and at pp. 109–14 considers the ways in which some of these retellings treat the question of her responsibility for the war. See also Blondell (2013, pp. 123–41) on Helen in the *Oresteia* and the issue of blame for the war.

[48] A twenty-first-century example of criticism levelled at politicians by the families of fallen soldiers is the public response to UK Prime Minister Tony Blair after the Chilcot inquiry into the 2003 invasion of Iraq. See, for example, Brown (2011).

destruction.[49] These claims, which have since been revealed as misleading, were used as a justification for the US-led invasion of Iraq.

It is, however, in its depiction of Agamemnon's own family that Aeschylus' *Agamemnon* brings into the sharpest focus the price paid by the families of those who fight. By focusing on just one household, Aeschylus' trilogy draws attention to the psychological and emotional impacts of war on those who are closest to the combatant. In this play, Aeschylus uses the story of Agamemnon and Clytemnestra, and in particular the recurring memory of the sacrifice of Iphigenia, to foreground the sense of competing obligations between family and war which even now remains at the heart of the experience of many soldiers and their partners. The story of the sacrifice made by Agamemnon before the Greeks left for Troy is present almost from the very start of Aeschylus' play, as the parodos (the chorus' opening song) relates the course of events at Aulis. Here the chorus recall the delay of the fleet at Aulis, and the storm that was destroying the Greek naval force before they had even set off (184–98). They go on to relate the advice of the prophet Calchas as to how the delay could be resolved by way of an offering to Artemis (198–204), and Agamemnon's response to the demand to sacrifice his daughter (205–27). The recollection of Agamemnon's arrival at the decision to comply and thus offer his daughter in sacrifice here conveys something of the sense of his being caught in an impossible choice. The chorus relate his words articulating this dilemma (206–17) as he considers that, by not sacrificing his daughter, he would desert the fleet and renege on his obligations to his allies. Ultimately, however, the chorus report that Agamemnon donned the 'yoke of necessity' (218) by accepting the sacrifice of his daughter, so that he might pursue the 'woman-avenging war' (226).[50] There follows a brief but harrowing account of the sacrifice itself, including Iphigenia's pleading and being gagged so as to prevent her from uttering a curse (the chorus add the poignant detail that the voice which often used to sing in her father's house was now silenced), so that she could plead with her sacrificers using only her eyes (228–47).[51]

[49] McDonald is cited in the transcript of an interview conducted by Peggy Shannon (Shannon (2014), p. 279). Playwright Simon Armitage (2014) drew a similar parallel in relation to his play *The Last Days of Troy*: 'Helen is an Iraqi supergun or the 45-minute claim. She is, ostensibly, the reason why the Greeks go to war—but she is not the reason' (Gardner (2014)).

[50] The allusion here is to the retrieval of Helen as the reason for the Trojan War. See above, n. 47.

[51] The story of Iphigenia's sacrifice highlighted here is part of this opening ode's much longer narrative of events before the Greeks' expedition to Troy. For a detailed analysis of the Aulis narrative in the ode, see Egan (2007). Several scholars have pointed out the allusions here

Much has been written about the impossibility of Agamemnon's choice, and the morality of his decision to sacrifice Iphigenia, but my concern in this chapter is to consider further the impact of his actions on Clytemnestra as both wife and mother.[52] When Agamemnon prioritizes the military campaign over his family, putting the army's needs before the very life of his child, the long-term emotional impact is greatest for Clytemnestra. Where other tragic versions of her story would foreground her adultery and lust for Aegisthus, her hunger for power, or her sexual jealousy of Cassandra as the driving force behind her crime against Agamemnon, Aeschylus' Clytemnestra is a warrior's wife who cannot forgive her husband's actions in putting his loyalty to the army and his political obligations before the life of their daughter. This motive is present from the start of the play, even before we meet Clytemnestra. In the opening ode in which they describe the sacrifice, the chorus of *Agamemnon* foreshadow the terrible events which will unfold. They sing that in Agamemnon's house, 'there waits a fearsome, irrepressible, devious housekeeper, a still-remembering, child-avenging Wrath' (μίμνει γὰρ φοβερὰ παλίνορτος / οἰκονόμος δολία, μνάμων Μῆνις τεκνόποινος, 154–5) It is this 'child-avenging Wrath' (Μῆνις τεκνόποινος), personified in the chorus' description and nurtured by Clytemnestra during the ten years of Agamemnon's absence, which in the course of the play drives her to murder her husband. There are also other more oblique allusions to Clytemnestra's vengeful anguish in the chorus' words; for example, their comparison of the battle-cry of the sons of Atreus in their quest to retrieve the lost Helen to the screams of eagles who have lost their chicks (48–54) might hint at Clytemnestra's maternal grief.

---

to the story that Iphigenia was brought to Aulis on the pretext of marriage, and that the sacrifice is conceived of in the text as taking the place of the marriage ritual (see, for example, Zeitlin (1965, p. 466) and Mitchell-Boyask (2006)). Euripides' *Iphigenia at Aulis* explores this element of Iphigenia's story in greater detail (at *Iphigenia at Aulis* 1110–14, for example, Agamemnon uses the language of sacrifice ambiguously in relation to both her marriage and her death). See Foley (1982) and Foley (1985, pp. 68–91).

[52] On the ethics of Agamemnon's decision to proceed with the sacrifice, see in particular Nussbaum (2001, pp. 32–8). Meineck (2012, p. 13) contends that an ancient audience with experience of combat might respond to Agamemnon's decision in a very different way to a modern, civilian audience. He suggests that 'Aeschylus' portrayal of Agamemnon is not an account of a king who heartlessly kills his daughter to gain a blessing for a war he is resolved to see through until complete victory; rather, it is a terrifying picture of any soldier who has had to wrestle with his/her competing obligations between home and family and the responsibilities between duty and command'. Meineck also relates a 'thought experiment' presenting an audience of military veterans with a contemporary scenario echoing Agamemnon's choice between the lives of his troops and that of his daughter. He reports (p. 15) that most audience members 'reluctantly agreed' that a general in Agamemnon's position would choose to save his army over his child.

In this play, Clytemnestra rarely describes her own emotional state explicitly, yet after her killing of Agamemnon and Cassandra she articulates clearly the motive for her actions. Her murder of Agamemnon resulted, she says, from a long-held resentment: 'This struggle, which I have thought about for a long time, stemming from an ancient grievance, has come at last' (ἐμοὶ δ' ἀγὼν ὅδ' οὐκ ἀφρόντιστος πάλαι / νείκης παλαιᾶς ἦλθε, σὺν χρόνῳ γε μήν, 1377–8). The repetition in the Greek text of πάλαι... παλαιᾶς (which I translate here as 'for a long time' and 'ancient'), along with σὺν χρόνῳ ('at last'), emphasizes just how long she has been plotting to take her revenge. Clytemnestra also repeatedly frames Agamemnon's death as payment for his sacrifice of their daughter, and her own actions as the meting out of justice (δίκη in the Greek) for Iphigenia's death; she describes even the hand which she used to stab Agamemnon as a 'worker of justice' (δικαίας τέκτονος, 1406).[53] When the chorus suggest that she should be punished with exile, she reflects in response that they did not challenge Agamemnon, 'this man who, caring no more than if it had been the death of an animal, one of many sheep from his fleecy flocks, sacrificed his own child, dearest offspring of my own labour [ἔθυσεν αὐτοῦ παῖδα, φιλτάτην ἐμοὶ /ὠδῖν'], to charm the Thracian winds' (1415–18). It is Agamemnon, she asserts, who should have been exiled for this act (1419–20). Shortly afterwards, Clytemnestra swears an oath 'by Justice [Dikē], fulfilled for my child, by Ruin [Atē], and by the Fury [Erinys], through whose agency I killed this man' (μὰ τὴν τέλειον τῆς ἐμῆς παιδὸς Δίκην / Ἄτην Ἐρινύν θ', αἷσι τόνδ' ἔσφαξ' ἐγώ, 1432–3). Clytemnestra casts herself in the role of avenger, envisaging the personifications of Justice, Ruin and the avenging Fury to whom she refers here as joining her in seeking retribution from Agamemnon for Iphigenia's sacrifice. She later asserts too that Agamemnon's murder was an appropriate punishment: as the chorus mourn for the dead leader, she asks them, 'Did he too not bring ruin [atē] on this household through deception?' (οὐδὲ γὰρ οὗτος δολίαν ἄτην / οἴκοισιν ἔθηκ'; 1523–4) and refers to 'the offspring whom I conceived by him, the much-lamented Iphigenia' (ἀλλ' ἐμὸν ἐκ τοῦδ' ἔρνος ἀερθέν / τὴν πολυκλαύτην / Ἰφιγένειαν, 1525–7).

---

[53] This emphasis on justice is foreshadowed ironically too in Clytemnestra's welcome speech to Agamemnon, where she suggests that he will be led by δίκη into the house (911), and that events will transpire δικαίως ('in accordance with justice', 913). Justice is also a theme of the play as a whole (in relation to both the sack of Troy as justice for Paris' theft of Helen, and in connection with the ancestral curse of the House of Atreus), and recurs repeatedly in the choral odes as well as in Clytemnestra's speeches. See Raeburn and Thomas (2011, pp. xxx–xxxv).

Although there are some gaps in the original Greek text here which make it difficult to reconstruct precisely what is said about Iphigenia's sacrifice, Clytemnestra appears to say that Agamemnon 'has suffered what he deserves' (ἄξια πάσχων, 1527), and that he has 'paid with death, slain by the sword, for what he began' (ξιφοδηλήτῳ / θανάτῳ τείσας ἅπερ ἦρξεν, 1528-9).

In Aeschylus' version of events, the murder of Agamemnon's forced concubine,[54] the Trojan war captive Cassandra, is presented as an unplanned additional bonus for Clytemnestra (1446-7), and Clytemnestra's own adulterous relationship with Aegisthus offers her a source of security (1435-7). However, neither jealousy of Cassandra nor Clytemnestra's adultery feature in her own reflections on her motives for the murder of her husband; she casts the resentment which she has nursed over Iphigenia's death as the driving force for her actions. Similarly, the Clytemnestra of Sophocles' late-fifth-century-BCE Electra, in the face of accusations from her surviving daughter Electra that she was driven by her lust for Aegisthus, asserts too that she was motivated instead by revenge for the sacrifice of Iphigenia (Electra 525-51). Sophocles' Clytemnestra reminds Electra that Iphigenia was sacrificed for the sake of Menelaus, suggesting that Menelaus' children should have died instead and asking, 'Did your accursed father care for Menelaus' children, but not for mine?' (544-5). Like the Clytemnestra of Aeschylus' Agamemnon, Sophocles' Clytemnestra also presents herself as an agent of justice (δίκη, Electra 528) in avenging the death of her child.[55]

Agamemnon's sacrifice of his daughter takes the notion of the military as a 'greedy institution' to its furthest extent; the repercussions of his actions are catastrophic, and the murder which Clytemnestra carries out in response is the most extreme reaction possible. I suggest that we might see Aeschylus' Clytemnestra, her actions driven by years of resentment at her husband's decision to prioritize his military obligations over his family, as standing metaphorically for the generations of military spouses whose husbands have been caught between the pull of two 'greedy institutions'. Time and again, the pressures exerted by the military mean that there are times at which it insists on taking precedence over the family. Granted, for today's military spouses the literal sacrifice of a child seen in the tales of ancient

[54] On my choice to use the term 'forced concubine' to describe women who have been captured in war and then expected to submit sexually to their captors, see below, p. 184 n. 59.
[55] By comparison, Euripides' Clytemnestra in his Electra (1011-50) says that she felt wronged by Agamemnon's sacrifice of Iphigenia for the sake of the campaign to retrieve Helen, but that she would not have been driven to murder had he not returned with Cassandra as his concubine.

myth is a world away from their own experiences, which may seem prosaic in comparison to the sagas of the House of Atreus, yet the sacrifice imposed upon Clytemnestra might nonetheless stand in for what they too have given up. As I noted earlier, the media, policy makers, and the military itself often use the language of sacrifice to discuss service personnel and the impact of their actions on their families. While in the modern world, members of the armed forces have usually made an active choice to sign up and therefore to yield to the demands of their role, this decision has a ripple effect for civilian partners and children who did not themselves volunteer for military service. As the authors of one report into the experiences of contemporary military spouses write, 'In many ways, military wives not only espouse their husbands but also the military and the mission. The three make up the marriage.'[56] By default, then, spouses become co-opted into the military organization, and as a result they are expected to relinquish control over significant parts of their lives.

These contemporary soldiers' spouses are women like those encountered by Alexandra Hyde, whose sociological research involved spending six months living on a British military base in Germany. There she met women dealing with the personal impact of their husbands' allegiance to the military: 'Carol', who shared her experiences of leaving behind her home town, her natal family, and her career because of the frequent relocations demanded by her husband's job, and of being left alone with a four-week-old baby when her husband deployed to the Gulf for the first time;[57] 'Annie', who spoke of the incorporation of her own identity into that of her husband— 'my identity is Henry's wife, John and Hannah's mum'—and her lack of fulfilment, doing voluntary work on camp to plug the gaps left by the suspension of her career;[58] and 'Joanne', whose children, like those of many military parents, were in boarding school because of the educational stability it provides when moving home is a frequent occurrence, and who confessed, 'I'm not particularly happy about the fact that half their childhood I've not

[56] Aducci et al. (2011, p. 241).   [57] Hyde (2015, pp. 54–5).

[58] Hyde (2015, p. 56). In contemporary accounts of military spouses, the relinquishing of a promising career is a recurring theme; it is often brought about by frequent relocations and the need for flexibility around childcare resulting from the unpredictability of a serving partner's schedule. See also, for example, the stories of 'Toni', one of the 'invisible women' in Margaret Harrell's book which gives a voice to some of the wives of junior enlisted US Army personnel (Harrell (2000), pp. 53–98), and of Crystal, who wrestles with the impossibility of pursuing her own education and a career, as told by Houppert (2005, pp. 89–92).

seen them.'[59] The lack of rootedness, loss of identity, and absence of control over her own destiny for a military spouse are also themes picked up in several of Abby E. Murray's poems in her volume *How to Be Married After Iraq*, which draws on her own experience of marriage to an active duty soldier. In 'A Portable Wife' the poet gives voice to a woman who is 'portable as a jug of water…easy to lift, easy to set down', and whose friendships are as transient as her husband's postings.[60] Meanwhile, Murray's 'Army Ball' features a colonel's wife whose career has been put on hold and who 'talks to me / about her family law practice, / eight years untouched now / on account of her boys and the traveling.'[61]

While some military spouses meet these challenges with resigned acceptance or by way of displacement activity (throwing themselves into voluntary work on base, like 'Annie'), others feel anger, resentment, or grief. In Jervis' study of the impact of relocation among British military spouses, 'Claire', who was married to a Royal Air Force serviceman, referred to herself as 'grieving for the life…you had previously and the relationships you had previously'. Her reflections focus particularly on the sense of loss which she felt when her identity became subordinated to that of her husband: 'I was working…in a responsible job, in a career…so I lost that part of me, I lost my friends and I lost the world I knew I suppose…all the little bits that you build up around yourself to make your life how you lead it, I lost those.'[62] One recurring element of these reflections on life as a military spouse is the extent to which these women are at the mercy of the demands placed by the military on their husbands, and the lack of control which they themselves have over what happens to their own life and family. In this respect, there can often be a stark contrast between the experiences of the military spouse and those of other women within wider society; still today the patriarchal ideals of military institutions impact on gender roles within military families.[63] Ancient Greek warriors' wives, by comparison, existed within a society that was entirely patriarchal. The expectations placed upon them therefore aligned more closely with wider societal conventions relating to female subordination and lack of agency; this is a recurring feature of

---

[59] Hyde (2015), p. 57. On the effects of military life on child development (including stress factors relating to parental deployments and relocation, as well as lack of educational continuity), see Centre for Social Justice (2016, pp. 55–62).

[60] Murray (2018, p. 13).   [61] Murray (2018, p. 11).

[62] Jervis (2007, pp. 112–13). Jervis (2011, pp. 241–77) provides several other detailed examples of military spouses who have experienced loss of various kinds, primarily as a result of the need to relocate with their husbands.

[63] See Enloe (2000, pp. 153–97).

the ways in which mythical soldiers' wives are represented in tragic drama.[64] This becomes particularly apparent in Euripides' dramatic portrayal of Clytemnestra's response to the sacrifice made by Agamemnon, in his *Iphigenia at Aulis*. It is this play which will be my focus for the remainder of this chapter.

When the women pay the price for war: Euripides' *Iphigenia at Aulis*

Where Aeschylus dramatized Clytemnestra's long-planned revenge for the sacrifice of Iphigenia on Agamemnon's return from Troy, Euripides' *Iphigenia at Aulis* examined in detail the events immediately prior to the Greeks' departure for war, with a focus on the sacrifice itself. This was the second of Euripides' Iphigenia plays; his earlier *Iphigenia in Tauris* (414/413 BCE) envisaged an alternative version of Iphigenia's story in which she was living as a priestess of Artemis among the Taurians, on the Black Sea, having been rescued by the goddess and replaced with a deer at the moment of her sacrifice. *Iphigenia at Aulis* was left unfinished at the playwright's death, and was first produced posthumously by Euripides' son or nephew in around 405 BCE.[65] By the last decade of the fifth century BCE, the Athenians had been at war with Sparta almost continuously for more than twenty years, and the questions which this play considers relating to the responsibility of military leaders in times of conflict would doubtless be as timely for Euripides' audience as those which had been raised by Aeschylus' earlier representation of Agamemnon. *Iphigenia at Aulis* has been read as engaging with late-fifth-century politics in a variety of ways, whether as a discussion of the issues relating to the proper exercise of democracy versus tyranny in the wake of the oligarchic coup at Athens of 411 BCE, or as a comment on the politics of 'panhellenism' which, towards the end of the Peloponnesian War, advocated for the warring Greek states to unite against a common external enemy rather than fighting among themselves as they had done since the outbreak of war between Athens and Sparta earlier in the

---

[64] Aeschylus' Clytemnestra is portrayed as transgressive precisely because she defies gendered expectations. I discuss this element of her character in Chapter 4, at pp. 121–25.

[65] At least the play's final scene (from line 1510 on, where a messenger reports on the replacement of Iphigenia with a stag by Artemis) is thought to be a later addition to the original text. See Collard and Morwood (2017, pp. 55–9) for a summary of issues surrounding the authenticity of the text.

century.[66] At the same time, Euripides' play highlights the challenges faced by families and communities in times of conflict, and reflects on the psychological, social, and emotional pressures under which individuals and groups are placed by war. The sacrifice of Iphigenia once again epitomizes the intractable conflict between family loyalty and military duty; Euripides' treatment of Clytemnestra and Iphigenia provides food for thought about the ways in which women in particular are impacted by the decisions made by (or imposed upon) a serving soldier.

Iphigenia at Aulis opens with the Greeks unable to sail to Troy because of a lack of wind to propel the fleet.[67] The events of the play take place as follows: Agamemnon has agreed to sacrifice Iphigenia in order to appease Artemis, and has sent for his daughter on the pretext that she will be married to the great warrior Achilles, who is as yet unaware that he is being used as bait. At the opening of the play Agamemnon has, however, had second thoughts, and attempts to send a second message revoking the first, only for the messenger to be intercepted by Agamemnon's brother Menelaus. After the ensuing debate between the two men, Menelaus becomes convinced that it would be wrong to sacrifice Iphigenia and that instead the expedition should be disbanded. Agamemnon, meanwhile, has had a change of heart in the opposite direction and has resolved that his daughter's death is necessary, on the basis that the army will revolt and slaughter him, along with his family, should he decide not to proceed.[68] In the meantime, Iphigenia and Clytemnestra have arrived from Argos; in what follows, both Clytemnestra and Achilles discover the real purpose of Agamemnon's invitation to bring Iphigenia to Aulis. The audience then witnesses Clytemnestra's unfolding response to her husband's decision to prioritize the army over their child. Euripides explores here the motivations that

---

[66] Michelakis (2006, pp. 73–81) and Collard and Morwood (2017, pp. 12–18) provide helpful overviews of some of the scholarly discussions about the play's relationship with current political issues. On the representation of 'panhellenism' in the play—particularly in relation to Iphigenia's motivation for agreeing eventually to sacrifice herself—see also Michelini (1999–2000, pp. 54–7) and Bacalexi (2016, pp. 65–9).

[67] Note that there is a contrast with the Aeschylean version of events, in which Agamemnon's force is beset by stormy winds. Luschnig (1988, pp. 2–4) outlines the main points of contrast between Aeschylus' and Euripides' treatment of the story.

[68] Siegel (1981) considers some of the reasons suggested by scholars as to why Euripides' Agamemnon changes his mind here, whether as a result of compulsion—from pressure put on him either by the army or by Artemis—or ambition. See also Luschnig (1988, pp. 6–20), on Agamemnon's indecision and his interactions with Menelaus in the first part of the play. Gibert (1995, pp. 206–22) provides a detailed analysis of the ways in which both Agamemnon's and Menelaus' vacillations play out.

would lead to the future actions (outside the chronological scope of this play) for which Clytemnestra's character had become notorious.

Euripides' play transplants Clytemnestra and the whole of her family to the army's encampment—the liminal space between the soldiers' homes and war—as they await their departure for Troy. The setting itself is unusual for Athenian tragic drama, where the action normally take place within a household.[69] Clytemnestra and her children (Iphigenia and the infant Orestes), along with the chorus of local women from Euboean Chalchis, intrude on the military camp, which is ordinarily a male space. In their opening ode, the all-female chorus draw attention to this division of space along gendered lines, commenting on their own blushes and suggesting a bashfulness at being so close to the camp (*Iphigenia at Aulis* 185–8). Much of this ode is devoted to describing the hyper-masculinized scene before them, as they list by name the male warriors whom they have seen engaged in athletic pursuits, as well as the commanders of the contingents of the fleet. Clytemnestra—described by Achilles as 'a woman among armoured men with shields' (γυνὴ πρὸς ἄνδρας ἀσπίσιν πεφραγμένους, 826)—appears in this male-dominated location uninvited by Agamemnon. He had sent for Iphigenia alone so as to proceed with the sacrifice without his wife's knowledge (456–7; cf. 538–41, where Agamemnon instructs Menelaus to ensure that Clytemnestra does not learn of the plan until it is done, 'so that I may pass through my troubles with the fewest tears'). The setting therefore focuses our attention upon the way in which Agamemnon's familial and military obligations compete for his loyalty; home and the front line are no longer clearly separated, and the physical presence of his wife makes it all the harder for the commander to ignore his responsibility towards his family.[70] In this play, the two 'greedy institutions' which compete with one another for Agamemnon's loyalty—the family, as represented by Clytemnestra and Iphigenia, and the military, as represented by the proximity of the army, and by Menelaus—are both present throughout. Just as the Homeric scene with Andromache and Hector discussed in Chapter 1 casts into sharp focus the contrast between domestic life and warfare, the

---

[69] The liminal setting of this play might be compared with that of Euripides' *Trojan Women*—discussed below at pp. 172–82—which is set after the Trojan War and in the Greek camp at Troy.
[70] Michelini (1999–2000, p. 46): 'The alien setting of the camp enhances the focus on relations within the nuclear family of Agamemnon. No longer embedded in a normal community whose ties and traditions could otherwise form a counterweight to their interactions, the family is thrown into a particularly close dependency.'

proximity of Agamemnon's wife and child to the army under his command on the eve of its expedition to Troy presents a striking image of the warrior caught between a military mission and his family.

Where Aeschylus' *Agamemnon* reported in brief, as part of a choral ode, Agamemnon's eventual decision to sacrifice Iphigenia, Euripides chose instead to play out the military commander's deliberations on stage. In *Iphigenia at Aulis*, we see Agamemnon's apparent changes of heart and the factors which influence his eventual actions. He outlines the reasons for making war on Troy (49–84): the marriage of Helen to Menelaus; Paris' taking of Helen; the Greeks' agreement to fight to retrieve her in accordance with the oath they had sworn to her father Tyndareus; and their choice of Agamemnon as general. By his own account, Agamemnon's military actions are driven by several motivations: obligation to the wider Greek force; familial duty to his brother Menelaus; the need to adhere to the oath he swore; and the responsibility he has as commander-in-chief. He relates that when the prophet Calchas announced that Iphigenia must be sacrificed, he initially refused and was ready to dismiss the army, 'for I could never bear to kill my daughter' (ὡς οὔποτ᾽ ἂν τλὰς θυγατέρα κτανεῖν ἐμήν, 96), but was persuaded by Menelaus to yield (97–8). Menelaus later asserts that Agamemnon has long been motivated by personal ambition to command the army (337–49), and that as a result he panicked when the lack of wind meant that he could no longer lead the planned expedition (350–7). He suggests to Agamemnon that, when a solution was presented in the form of the sacrifice, 'your heart rejoiced; you promised gladly to sacrifice your child' (ἠσθεὶς φρένας / ἄσμενος θύσειν ὑπέστης παῖδα, 359–60), and that he sent for her 'willingly, not under force' (ἑκών, / οὐ βίᾳ, 360–1). Later Agamemnon claims that his eventual decision to proceed with the sacrifice (after an earlier change of heart) is a 'fated necessity' (ἀναγκαίας τύχας, 511).[71] He tells Menelaus that 'the whole gathered army of the Achaeans' (514) compels him to do so, despite the fact that they do not yet know of Calchas' prophecy. His fear is that once the army discover what has happened, Odysseus will lead the troops to kill him and his family, and perhaps even to destroy Argos, Agamemnon's homeland (528–37; cf. 1267–8, where he repeats a similar argument to Clytemnestra and Iphigenia when they plead with him

[71] The Greek phrase here, ἀναγκαίας τύχας, might remind us of the 'yoke of necessity', ἀνάγκας...λέπαδνον, in the Aeschylean chorus' account of his decision at *Agamemnon* 218. See above, p. 56.

not to go ahead with the sacrifice).[72] The case for sacrificing his own child rests largely, therefore, on Agamemnon's military obligations, although the suggestion that, if he refuses to comply, his family may die at the hands of his own army allows him to claim that he has no choice; by this reasoning, the demands of the military will always prevail. Yet the picture that Menelaus paints of his brother as an ambitious leader adds a new dimension to the idea of a conflict between family and military. It suggests the possibility that Agamemnon's actions might be driven, at least in part, by his own desire to maintain his position of power, and to lead the army into battle regardless of what the personal cost will be to him and his family. For this Agamemnon, the 'greediness' of the military—whether as a result of his personal ambition, his sense of obligation, or his fear of reprisal from his troops—outweighs any claims to his loyalty which his family might make.

The entrance of Clytemnestra, with Iphigenia and the infant Orestes, highlights dramatically the commander's competing obligations. The chorus hail the arrival of Agamemnon's family at line 590, and Clytemnestra's first words in the play (from line 607 onwards) reveal that she has been tricked into believing that her own familial priorities are compatible with Agamemnon's military and political concerns. A marital bond with Achilles, himself a pre-eminent warrior of high birth (101) would be of benefit to Iphigenia's family (625–6).[73] Initially Clytemnestra is preoccupied with this fictitious marriage, and is keen to participate in the wedding rituals (609–10, 691–741). Meanwhile Iphigenia's obvious adoration for Agamemnon underscores the pathos of her impending death. She rushes to embrace her father (631–2, 640), and Clytemnestra comments that Iphigenia is the child who loves him the most (639). Agamemnon, in turn, is moved to tears (650) and there ensues an exchange in which he speaks cryptically of Iphigenia's impending fate (651–80). Clytemnestra eventually learns from Achilles that the marriage is a ploy (841–2), and when an elderly enslaved member of the household subsequently reveals the plan to sacrifice Iphigenia (873),

---

[72] Synodinou (2013) discusses in detail Agamemnon's possible motivations here, suggesting that his claim to have decided against sacrificing Iphigenia may be disingenuous.

[73] Note that in the ancient context marriage to Achilles, even if it were a genuine proposition, is not about Iphigenia's own desires, but about furthering the allegiances of the men for whom the transfer of a woman from her father's household to that of her husband is a transactional relationship. See Rabinowitz (1993, pp. 38–54) on Euripides's Iphigenia as a woman in an 'exchange economy'.

it becomes clear that her own concern for her child is at odds with Agamemnon's true devotion to his military obligations.

Clytemnestra's emotional response at these revelations turns from initial disbelief (she suggests at line 874 that the old man who exposed the plot is not of sound mind, then at line 876 that Agamemnon has gone mad) to self-pity. She repeatedly describes herself as τάλαινα, 'wretched' (876, 880, 888), reflecting at line 888, 'I'm wretched, lost; I can no longer hold back streams of tears' (οἴχομαι τάλαινα· δακρύων νάματ' οὐκέτι στέγω). She then pleads with Achilles to protect Iphigenia (900-16), after which the chorus comment on the power of the maternal bond (917-18). Having secured Achilles' assurance (motivated by the insult to his honour that was Agamemnon's deceitful use of him as a lure for Iphigenia) that he will assist if Agamemnon does not yield to her supplication, she speaks directly of her own suffering once again. Again the emphasis is on self-pity: she reflects, 'I'm ashamed to bring up my piteous tale, my private sickness' (αἰσχύνομαι δὲ παραφέρουσ' οἰκτροὺς λόγους, / ἰδίᾳ νοσοῦσα, 981-2), and asks Achilles to 'Show us pity, for we have suffered pitiably' (οἴκτιρε δ' ἡμᾶς· οἰκτρὰ γὰρ πεπόνθαμεν, 985). Clytemnestra touches only briefly on Iphigenia's suffering—she describes Iphigenia too as τάλαινα, 'wretched', at lines 880 and 1100, and comments on Iphigenia's lamenting in response to the news at 1100-2. Her primary focus throughout is on the impact of Agamemnon's actions on her as his wife; before confronting Agamemnon directly, she reflects on what she describes as 'my own troubles' (τῶν ἐμῶν... κακῶν, 1124). Spurred on to challenge Agamemnon, she repeatedly demands that he speak the truth (1131, 1132-3, 1135). Her assertion that 'I know everything and have learned what you are about to do *to me*' (πάντ' οἶδα καὶ πεπύσμεθ' ἃ σὺ μέλλεις με δρᾶν, 1141) focuses our attention on Clytemnestra's own experience. The sacrifice which Agamemnon makes, leading to the loss of her child, is one over which Clytemnestra has no control. It is something which will be done to her, and by extension it becomes her sacrifice too.

If the military is greedy for the literal sacrifice which Agamemnon will make, Clytemnestra shows that she too, as his wife, expects to be able to make demands of him; again the army and the family exert competing pressures on the warrior. In a lengthy speech (1146-1208), Clytemnestra sets out in detail her perspective and stakes her own claim to her husband's loyalty. We learn here that she has had a previous life wrested from her in the most violent way imaginable. Euripides shares an element of Clytemnestra's backstory which is rarely treated in other surviving ancient versions of the myth, and one which means that she emerges in this play as an altogether more sympathetic character than the Clytemnestra of Aeschylus' *Agamemnon*. She sets out how her current marriage originated in death and violence; Agamemnon killed Tantalus, her first husband, and their baby, before taking her by force and marrying her against her will (1148–56). Despite this violent start, Clytemnestra says that she became a model wife and an asset to his house, remaining sexually faithful (1158–61).[74] In addition she bore him four children, 'one of whom you are cruelly stealing from me' (ὧν μιᾶς σὺ τλημόνως μ᾽ ἀποστερεῖς, 1165). The comparison between herself as good wife and her sister Helen as bad wife is made explicit as she points out that Iphigenia is to be the price paid for Menelaus' retrieval of Helen (1168–70); again the point is made that Agamemnon's wife and children are of secondary importance to his military commitments.

In what follows, Clytemnestra attempts to dissuade Agamemnon from his planned course of action, turning to her imagined future response to his killing of Iphigenia. Alongside her sorrow, we begin to see hints of the resentment whose culmination Aeschylus had dramatized (1171–8):

> Come! If you go to fight, leaving me behind at home and staying there in a long absence from me, what do you suppose will be my feelings at home whenever I see all of her chairs empty, and her rooms vacant, while I sit alone weeping, always singing my lament for her: 'The father who conceived you has destroyed you, child!'

Here Clytemnestra anticipates already her time as 'waiting wife'; the absence she will feel most keenly is not that of her husband while he is at war, but that of the child he will have taken from her, in pursuit of his military ambition. She then alludes to the 'welcome' which Agamemnon can expect upon his eventual return from Troy: 'For it needs only a slight pretext, and I and the girls who were left behind will receive you with the reception you ought

---

[74] Michelini (1999–2000, p. 50) notes that 'Clytemnestra's past transforms the moral significance of the current conflict'. See also Gibert (2005), discussing the ways in which the story of Agamemnon and Clytemnestra's marriage connects with the broader themes of the play (including its function in justifying further Clytemnestra's later anger over the sacrifice of Iphigenia, having already transferred her allegiance from her first husband to Agamemnon and the children she bore him). Gibert is careful to stress that, for an ancient Athenian audience, it would be accepted that a woman would have no choice in her marriage, but that the violence which Agamemnon has committed reveals him as a hypocrite in his pursuit of the punishment of Paris.

to receive [δεξόμεθα δέξιν ἥν σε δέξασθαι χρεών]' (1180–2; note also her reference to his 'sorry return'—νόστον πονηρόν—at line 1187). Although Clytemnestra's imagining that his children will share her gnawing resentment towards Agamemnon, and will join her in executing revenge, runs counter to the myths of Orestes and Electra as they are retold elsewhere in the tragic corpus (where they seek to avenge their father's death), the hints at the gruesome homecoming which she will prepare for Agamemnon are clear. Yet in this play, Clytemnestra does not directly name her own negative emotions which lead to this resentment; as we have seen, she focuses primarily on self-pity. Instead it is Iphigenia who will later identify explicitly her mother's feelings of anger and hatred towards Agamemnon: at lines 1369-70 she says to Clytemnestra, 'I can see that you are angry with your husband, but in vain' (μάτην γάρ <σ'> εἰσορῶ θυμουμένην / σῷ πόσει·), and later she exhorts her mother, 'Do not hate my father, your husband' (πατέρα τὸν ἀμὸν μὴ στύγει, πόσιν γε σόν, 1454). These are the emotions that the audience knows will breed the bitterness which in turn will lead to Clytemnestra's eventual murder of Agamemnon.

The point at which Clytemnestra articulates most concisely the conflicting loyalties between which Agamemnon is torn—and his decision to value his political and military obligations more highly than those towards his wife and children—comes towards the end of this speech. Having set out her two key arguments—that Agamemnon should feel obligated towards her, as his loyal wife, and that he should fear the reception he will receive at home after Troy if he proceeds with the sacrifice—Clytemnestra asks, 'Have you already considered these things, or do you care only about carrying your sceptre and leading your army?' (ταῦτ' ἦλθες ἤδη διὰ λόγων, ἢ σκῆπτρά σοι / μόνον διαφέρειν καὶ στρατηλατεῖν μέλει; 1194-5). Her question recognizes that Agamemnon's ambitions as commander operate in direct opposition to his wife and family's desire for his loyalty. The phrasing here, in which this is not merely about the lure of military service per se, but about his ambitions for the power conferred by a position of command, echoes Menelaus' earlier suggestions that Agamemnon's actions are driven by his desire for leadership over the army. A similar sense that, for some soldiers, the military might always come before their family—whether because of career ambition, loyalty to their comrades, or simply because active service provides an escape from the responsibilities of family life—remains today a source of anxiety for some military spouses. As US Air Force wife Danette Long confessed when interviewed by a journalist, 'I worry sometimes that he likes it too much.'[75] Danette's concern that her husband might prefer being on operations in Korea, where he had only his own schedule to worry about rather than the demanding domestic life of a family with teenagers, reflects in simple terms the family/military conflict. Her description of this ongoing worry pinpoints an issue that rings true for many military spouses, who often have good reason to doubt whether they, and their children, will ever be their partners' first priority.

Clytemnestra concludes her speech to Agamemnon with a reflection on the unfairness that she should have to suffer by losing her child; the Greeks, she suggests, should have drawn lots or, given that the mission to Troy is for Menelaus' sake, his and Helen's child should be sacrificed (1196–1202). Instead, she reflects (1202–5), 'As things are I, who am faithful to your bed, will be robbed of my child, and she [Helen] who did wrong will take care of her own girl in Sparta, and will become happy.' As Agamemnon's wife, she has done all that was expected of her, and yet still he has chosen the needs of the army over her needs and the life of their own child. The sense of betrayal which Clytemnestra feels is palpable here; it is echoed too in the words of Iphigenia which follow. When it becomes apparent that, despite Iphigenia's lengthy plea (1211–52), Agamemnon intends to proceed with the sacrifice, she asserts that she too has been betrayed by her father. After Agamemnon departs, having made clear that he will indeed prioritize the military mission over his family ('I must sacrifice you for Greece, whether I wish to or not', ἀλλ' Ἑλλάς, ᾗ δεῖ, κἂν θέλω κἂν μὴ θέλω, / θῦσαί σε, 1271–2), Iphigenia reflects on her own situation. The vocabulary which she uses in her lament here indicates clearly that she also perceives Agamemnon's decision as a betrayal. The words she uses in Greek, οἴχεται προδοὺς ἔρημον (1314), can be translated in various ways, as perhaps 'he has gone, betraying me to abandonment', or 'he has gone, giving me up to abandonment', but προδούς (from the verb προδίδωμι) can carry the sense of both 'betrayal' and 'forsaking' or 'giving up'.

The impact of Agamemnon's choice on his family is profound, and Clytemnestra ultimately has no influence over his decision; the pull of his obligations to the army, and to his male relative Menelaus, is far stronger than any ties to his wife and child. The feelings of betrayal and resentment which surface in Euripides' play (and in Aeschylus' earlier version of

---

[75] Houppert (2005, p. 76).

Clytemnestra's story) recur too in contemporary accounts of military spouses who feel let down by their husbands' loyalty to the military, and aggrieved by the impact which this has on them and their children. One striking example of these emotional responses is the story of 'Pernille', the wife of a member of the Danish Defence Forces who had been deployed to Iraq.[76] For Pernille, her husband's military role put at risk both the well-being and the safety of her family. She repeatedly told the researcher interviewing her that she could not understand how her husband Erik could leave her and the children to serve in Iraq, reflecting frankly, 'I have been let down.' This resentment at what Pernille framed as Erik's own choice to leave (although presumably he was under operational orders) gave way during the course of his absence to overwhelming anxiety when the safety of his family at home became compromised. When his name was printed by a newspaper while he was still in the field, Erik was advised to conceal his identity (and his relationship with his wife) on social media. Pernille subsequently became convinced that there was a threat to her and their children back home. When she shared her fears with her husband, he offered to return home to the family; at this point, she reported, 'that made me feel like, we actually are the most important thing for him ... I don't feel angry at him any more.' Pernille's story crystallizes elements of the effect which membership of a 'greedy' military might have on a family today, and the way in which, for some, anger and bitterness can build when the military's demands take precedence.[77] In this case, the sacrifice made by the service member also had the potential to put his immediate family in jeopardy. In order to forgive Erik for what she perceived as his betrayal, Pernille needed some form of proof that her husband's first priority was not his military duty but instead his family at home.

For Clytemnestra, of course, such reassurance never comes; Agamemnon will make the sacrifice regardless of its impact on his family. Yet towards the end of Euripides' play, there is a twist by which ultimately Iphigenia decides to go willingly to be sacrificed (1374–6). After Achilles' thwarted attempt to save her, Iphigenia has a change of heart, suggesting that she will die 'as liberator of Greece' ('Ελλάδ' ὡς ἠλευθέρωσα, 1384). She goes to her death having instructed Clytemnestra not to mourn her (1442), and not to hate

---

[76] Pernille's story is told by Heiselberg (2017, pp. 80–1).
[77] Wilson and Murray (2016, pp. 109–10) summarize recent research relating to anger directed at a deployed partner or the military institution.

Agamemnon (1454), asserting that 'unwillingly he has destroyed me for the sake of Greece' (ἄκων μ' ὑπὲρ γῆς Ἑλλάδος διώλεσεν, 1456).[78] While Iphigenia's words appear once again to underline the way in which Agamemnon's obligations to his family are at odds with those towards his country and his army, this change of heart on her part takes away any suggestion that Agamemnon has betrayed his family. It also effectively absolves him of responsibility for the final decision to send Iphigenia to her death. Any notion that Iphigenia has made an active choice is an illusion. Instead, her apparent willingness to die for the sake of the war waged by her father and the men who are his comrades is a product of the patriarchal structure of the society into which she has been born.[79] She is ultimately a commodity whose value lies for Agamemnon and the army in the fact that she can be offered up in service of the military mission.[80]

Euripides' decision to represent Iphigenia as a voluntary—and necessary—casualty of the conflict effectively reframes her not as a female victim of war but as a stand-in for the experience of soldiers (such as those who would have originally watched this play in late-fifth-century-BCE Athens) who fight and die in service of the state. Although in this case it is the soldier's daughter, and not his wife, who chooses to sacrifice herself, the reconfiguration of the death of this female character as voluntary self-sacrifice might put us in mind of the 'sacrifices' made by the wives of service personnel whom we met earlier in this chapter. Just as Ava Conlin's husband claimed that she had given up so much of her former life and identity 'without complaint because she felt it was her duty as a spouse, mother, and American' (see above, pp. 47–8), the male playwright who tells Iphigenia's story imagines her voice too as one of assent to the ideals espoused by the military. By this reckoning, the female members of a soldier's family—in both the ancient and modern worlds—become merely material assets to the military. If the men who serve create the illusion that the values of their families and their military mission align, they will be able to persuade

[78] Gibert (1995, pp. 222–39), considers the possible motivations for Iphigenia's change of heart, and provides a discussion of critical and scholarly responses to this (beginning with Aristotle's criticism of Euripides' characterization of Iphigenia as inconsistent). See also Michelini (1999–2000, pp. 50–4).

[79] Rabinowitz (1993, pp. 31–54) explores the illusion of the willing sacrifice in *Iphigenia at Aulis*, suggesting (p. 51) that 'Iphigenia chooses "death with her father" because her society predisposes her to condemn the women she has around her and consequently to condemn herself'.

[80] On sacrificial virgins as commodities in tragedy, see Scodel (1996). Wohl (1998, pp. 67–82), within a wide-reaching study of women as objects of exchange in Greek tragedy, explores in detail the transactional aspect of Iphigenia's sacrifice.

themselves and those around them that there is in fact no conflict between the 'greedy institutions' of the family and the military. At the same time, asserting that their sacrifices are made voluntarily also effectively erases the experiences of the women on whom the impact of their husbands' service is profound and often damaging. We are left wondering whether, as in the case of Clytemnestra and Iphigenia, the military will always win out, no matter the cost to a soldier's family.

3

Separation: Penelope in the *Odyssey*

The archetypal 'waiting wife' of ancient literature is Penelope in the *Odyssey*, immortalized as the spouse of Odysseus, the returning soldier and adventurer who takes centre stage in this epic poem. With her customary pithiness the American poet and critic Dorothy Parker, writing in 1928, when the First World War was still a recent memory, drew attention in her own memorialization of Penelope to the unglorified courage of the wife left behind:

> In the pathway of the sun,
> In the footsteps of the breeze,
> Where the world and sky are one,
> He shall ride the silver seas,
> He shall cut the glittering wave.
> I shall sit at home, and rock;
> Rise, to heed a neighbor's knock;
> Brew my tea, and snip my thread;
> Bleach the linen for my bed.
> They will call him brave.
>
> Dorothy Parker, 'Penelope'[1]

Penelope's situation was one with which Parker herself could empathize: she had been a wartime bride, married in 1917 to a husband who would soon leave her behind to enlist in the armed forces.[2] The details of the lives of Penelopes ancient and modern may be less exhilarating and more mundane by comparison with those of their husbands, yet nonetheless, Parker suggests, they too deserve recognition. For evermore, however, Parker's Penelope

---

[1] Parker (1928, p. 34).
[2] On Parker's first marriage, to Edwin Pond Parker II, the couple's subsequent wartime separation, and their later divorce, see Meade (1989, pp. 38–50 and pp. 191–2).

Warriors' Wives: Ancient Greek Myth and Modern Experience. Emma Bridges, Oxford University Press.
© Emma Bridges 2023. DOI: 10.1093/oso/9780198843528.003.0004

suspects that it is her husband—'him'—and not her who will be remembered by others as brave.[3]

Parker's poem alludes not only to the gulf between the experiences of the serving soldier and those of the partner left behind but also to the fact that Penelope as waiting wife has traditionally been given far less attention than her husband. Nowhere is this more apparent in the *Odyssey* than after the couple's eventual reunion when the two exchange accounts of their time apart. Here, despite the fact that the majority of the poem is given over to descriptions of Odysseus' exploits, the poet summarizes Penelope's story in only four lines (23.302–5) as compared with the thirty-two lines that are devoted to recalling Odysseus' adventures (23.310–41). As I shall discuss in the course of this chapter, Penelope's experience is erased or overlooked in other ways too in the *Odyssey*. The representation of her as the model wife at times allows little space for an insight into her own responses to her situation, and on occasion when she does attempt to express her emotions she is overtly silenced by her son Telemachus. As the idealized loyal, but largely silent, partner she has much in common with the modern-day military spouses whom we met in Chapter 2, women who are expected to make sacrifices in support of their husband's military service selflessly and without complaint.

In what follows, I reflect on what, despite this repeated silencing, we might learn about the experiences of waiting wives (contemporary as well as ancient) when we examine the relatively brief moments in the poem which do reflect on Penelope's emotions and actions during Odysseus' absence. I begin with an analysis of our first encounter with Penelope in the *Odyssey*; here I discuss how the poet frames her from the outset as a model wife, before examining what we might learn about her emotions in Odysseus' absence, as well as about the ways in which her experience might be disregarded or dismissed by observers. I then consider the way in which the concept of 'ambiguous loss', used in this context to describe the psychological impact on those left behind when a person is physically absent but without the certainty or closure which death usually brings, might be applied to Penelope's situation as well as to those of some modern military spouses. This includes the ways in which waiting spouses may be desperate for information about their loved ones whilst simultaneously living in fear of receiving bad news. Penelope, in common with the partners of military

---

[3] For an analysis of Parker's representation of the figure of Penelope here, see Clayton (2004, pp. 106–7).

personnel today, also faces particular challenges as lone spouse; she is expected to assume new responsibilities in Odysseus' absence, including those which are traditionally perceived as 'male' roles. Having explored some of these responsibilities I examine Penelope's primary coping strategy—the 'shroud trick' by which she holds off the unruly suitors as they vie for her hand in marriage—and reflect on how this might relate to some of the coping techniques used by her modern counterparts.

Penelope: a first encounter

> She carried her worry night and day. It pulled at her legs and shoulders and tear ducts, always there and ready to consume her, because how could anyone think rationally about a spouse in a war zone?[4]

Meg, the protagonist of the first short story in Siobhan Fallon's collection *You Know When the Men Are Gone*, is a contemporary waiting wife whose psychological experience might resonate with anyone who has endured the emotional strain that accompanies a loved one's absence on active service. The story, like the others in the collection, is informed by Fallon's own experience as a military spouse; the author draws on the realities of life for the partner left at home when a serving soldier is away on active duty. The constant worry, and the physical impact which it has, is a recurring presence in stories told by spouses who have endured similar separations; Fallon's description of Meg could apply equally to the mythical Penelope. As I will explore in this section, the 'waiting wife' of the *Odyssey* is plagued too by worries which are ever-present, day and night, and which take a physical and emotional toll.

We first meet Penelope in the opening book of the *Odyssey*, twenty years after Odysseus' departure for Troy. At this point, Odysseus has spent ten years fighting at Troy and a further ten years on a meandering journey home, the story of which occupies much of the poem's narrative. Meanwhile 108 suitors have taken up residence in the palace, disregarding the respectful behaviours expected of guests in Homeric poetry as they consume and destroy Odysseus' possessions while each of them attempts to persuade

---

[4] Fallon (2011, p. 22). This first story in the collection shares its title, 'You Know When the Men Are Gone', with that of the book.

Penelope to marry him. In the scene where Penelope first appears, the bard
Phemius is entertaining the suitors by singing of the difficult return home of
the Greeks from Troy (1.325–7). On hearing the song, Penelope descends
from her rooms upstairs and asks Phemius to sing of something else. Her
son Telemachus responds by instructing her to allow the bard to sing on,
and to return to her own rooms, separate from the men. As Penelope's first
appearance in the poem, the scene is enlightening for the way in which it
condenses several aspects of the representation of Penelope throughout the
poem, each of which I will discuss in turn: the image of her as an ideal wife;
her own description of the emotions she experiences in response to
Odysseus' absence; and ultimately the silencing which results from her dismissal by Telemachus.

From the outset, Penelope is framed in the poem as the ideal wife, with a
reputation for the prudence, fidelity, and resourcefulness which are illustrated by her actions in the course of Odysseus' absence. The epithet used to
describe her when we first meet her (1.329), and frequently throughout the
Odyssey, is περίφρων, which can be translated as 'thoughtful', 'circumspect',
or 'wise'.[5] In this initial passage, she is also described, as elsewhere in the
poem, as δῖα γυναικῶν (1.332, cf. 21.42, 21.63), a phrase whose possible
translations all imply that she is set apart in some way from other women.
The Greek words here can be rendered as 'illustrious/glorious among
women' but may also suggest that she is 'divine among women'.[6] Penelope is
renowned as a model wife for her fidelity—which I will discuss at greater
length in Chapter 4—as well as for her 'skill in beautiful handiwork, her
good character and intelligence' (ἔργα τ' ἐπίστασθαι περικαλλέα καὶ φρένας
ἐσθλὰς / κέρδεά θ', in the words of the suitor Antinous at 2.117–18). It is this
combination of characteristics which makes her deserving of the *kleos*
(honour, glory, or fame—the Greek term is more usually applied to male
heroes than to women) on which Odysseus compliments her on his return

[5] The adjective περίφρων can be taken to mean 'very thoughtful' or 'very careful'; translators
use a variety of synonyms to render this into English. Wilson (2017) chooses 'intelligent' or
'wise'; Lattimore (1967) and Verity (2016) favour 'circumspect'; Rieu (1946) uses 'wise'.
[6] Verity (2016) translates this as 'glorious among women' and Lattimore (1967) 'shining
among women'; Rieu (1946) refers to Penelope here as 'the great lady'; and Wilson (2017) takes
the phrase when it appears in Book 1 to refer to Penelope's appearance as 'looking like a goddess', later translating it in Book 21 as 'the queen'. For the sense that Penelope is superior to
other women, and that this is what makes her so desirable to the suitors, see also the suitor
Eurymachus' words extolling both her beauty and her mind at 18.245–9, and Telemachus'
description of her at 21.106–10, where he asserts that there is no other woman like his mother
throughout Greece. The shade of Agamemnon, in the underworld, also extols Penelope's
virtues as wife and mother at 11.445–6, and later at 24.192–7.

home (19.108, cf. 2.125). Yet, as Penelope herself suggests, her own identity is bound up with that of the husband on whom she depends; his absence, she remarks, has had an impact on both her appearance and her status. In response to the suitor Eurymachus' comments on her beauty and intellect, she reflects at 18.251–3 that 'the gods destroyed all my excellence (aretē), both in beauty and form [ἐμὴν ἀρετὴν εἶδός τε δέμας τε], when the Argives, and with them my husband Odysseus, set out for Troy'. In that scene, she then goes on to say, 'If he were to come and look after my life, my kleos would be greater and lovelier' (εἰ κεῖνος γ᾽ ἐλθὼν τὸν ἐμὸν βίον ἀμφιπολεύοι, / μεῖζόν κε κλέος εἴη ἐμὸν καὶ κάλλιον οὕτως, 18.254–5).[7] This sense that Penelope's identity is subsumed to that of Odysseus calls to mind the experiences of some of the modern-day military spouses whom we met in the previous chapter.

If, however, we view Penelope only as the model spouse for the man whose story dominates the Odyssey, we risk overlooking central elements of her psychological experience as waiting wife of an absent warrior husband. Further examination of the poet's introduction to Penelope already reveals some insights into the impact of the separation and the way in which she expresses her emotions. It is 'through tears' (δακρύσασα, 1.336) that she addresses the bard. In asking him to stop singing she also describes her personal response to his song (1.340–4): 'stop with this mournful song, which always wears away the heart in my chest (ἥ τέ μοι αἰεὶ ἐνὶ στήθεσσι φίλον κῆρ / τείρει) as an extreme and unforgettable grief (πένθος ἄλαστον) touches me. For, always remembering [him], I long for the man who is so dear and whose fame (kleos) is widespread through Hellas and mid-Argos.' Even in this brief description, we gain an impression of a grief which has an impact that is both physical and mental. The notion that Penelope's heart is worn away is accompanied by an acknowledgement that she is unable to forget either her sadness (it is πένθος ἄλαστον, 'unforgettable grief') or Odysseus himself. The sense of this ever-present sorrow, and the physical sensations associated with it, is echoed by contemporary depictions of military spouses such as Siobhan Fallon's Meg, with whom I opened this section.

Penelope's appearance at this point in the poem is brief, as her request for the bard to choose a different song is rejected by her son Telemachus, who asserts that the song is one which the audience wants to hear (1.345–52). He then instructs her, 'Bolster your heart and spirit to listen' (σοὶ δ᾽ ἐπιτολμάτω

---

[7] Penelope repeats the same formulaic phrase when talking to the disguised Odysseus at 19.124–8.

κραδίη καὶ θυμὸς ἀκούειν, 1.353), reminding her that Odysseus is not the only man who has not returned from Troy. While acknowledging that other wives have lost husbands, Telemachus' words appear to dismiss the feelings which Penelope has just expressed, perhaps suggesting too that she ought to be able to bear her grief without complaint. He then goes on to send her from the room entirely, instructing her (1.356–9): 'Go back to your quarters and take up your own work, the loom and the distaff, and order your women slaves to go about their work. For talking shall be the men's concern (μῦθος δ' ἄνδρεσσι μελήσει), and especially mine; for the power in the house is mine.' The formulation in Greek echoes the words spoken by Hector to Andromache in the *Iliad*, where it is πόλεμος, war, rather than 'talking', or 'speech' (μῦθος) which is said to concern the men (*Iliad* 6.492).[8] Like Andromache in the *Iliad*, Penelope is reminded by a man of the role— indoors, attending to domestic tasks—to which her gender confines her.

Telemachus' rebuke of Penelope also has the effect of quite literally hiding Penelope away and silencing her attempt to describe her own experience and emotions. Having emerged from her seclusion in the women's part of the house (at 1.328–31, she was described as descending the stairs from her rooms) she is swiftly sent back again.[9] This silencing when Penelope attempts to speak of her own emotions surrounding the absence of Odysseus perhaps anticipates the invisibility of the experiences of the spouses of soldiers even today; three army wives interviewed for one small-scale study variously described the silencing which they had experienced as 'no one understands' (Holly), 'no one is listening' (Nicole), and 'we are forgotten' (Amy).[10] When Penelope—along with her grief—is now out of sight of the men in the household, we as the audience of the poem follow her as she returns to her rooms, and we witness how she behaves in that more private moment. In the seclusion of her room, we are told, 'she wept for Odysseus, her dear husband, until grey-eyed Athena put sweet sleep on her eyes' (1.363–4). On this occasion, sleep brings temporary respite from her grief. The formula used by the poet here is repeated much later in the poem

---

[8] See above, p. 1 and p. 30.

[9] Telemachus dismisses Penelope to her rooms twice more in the poem: once at 17.45–51, after he has returned from his mission to find news of Odysseus; and again at 21.350–3, where the Greek text repeats the formula used at 1.356–9, although on this occasion (just prior to the contest with Odysseus' bow) it is 'the bow', rather than 'talking', which is said to be men's concern. In each case, the effect is to delineate male and female spheres of influence. See Rousseau (2015).

[10] Davis et al. (2011, p. 58).

too, when at the end of Book 19 Penelope falls asleep after she has conversed with the still-disguised Odysseus (19.603–4).[11]

This initial brief encounter with Penelope in the *Odyssey* already reflects key elements of this waiting wife's life in her husband's absence. The sense, reinforced by Telemachus' reproach, that her difficult thoughts and emotions relating to the absence of Odysseus should either be suppressed, or at the very least be expressed only in private, is particularly striking. Her grief, and the accompanying tears, are—just like the domestic, female, tasks to which she is instructed to attend—to be hidden away from the men who form the poem's internal audience at this point. In a story where attention is already predominantly on the adventures of the absent partner, this might encourage us too, as the external audience of the epic, to overlook the impact that the situation has on Penelope. Close attention to the text reveals, however, that there are further clues elsewhere as to her emotional responses. Penelope uses a range of vocabulary to describe her emotional pain: at 18.256–71 and 19.129 she uses the Greek verb ἄχομαι, 'I grieve' or 'I mourn' as she reflects on the troubles sent to her 'by a god'; elsewhere she says 'I am sorely/deeply troubled' (πυκινῶς ἀκάχημαι, 19.95); and later she reflects, 'my heart is melting away in longing for Odysseus' (ἀλλ' Ὀδυσῆ ποθέουσα φίλον κατατήκομαι ἦτορ, 19.136). The sense that the situation has an impact on her body as well as on her mind is reflected too when she confesses that she has trouble sleeping, and that her worries are magnified as she lies in bed at night: 'By day I indulge in lamenting and weeping (τέρπομ' ὀδυρομένη, γοόωσα), as I look to my own tasks and those of the servants in the house, but when night comes and sleep takes everyone else, I lie in my bed as bitter worries swarm my throbbing heart and torment me in my sorrow (πυκιναὶ δέ μοι ἀμφ' ἀδινὸν κῆρ / ὀξεῖαι μελεδῶναι ὀδυρομένην ἐρέθουσιν)' (19.513–17).[12]

The most obvious physical manifestation of Penelope's anxiety and grief is her tears; she is frequently seen weeping throughout the poem, although it is important to note that the tears of grief brought on by Odysseus' absence are produced by emotions which differ from her tears of relief

---

[11] The Greek text at both 1.363–4 and 19.603–4 reads as follows: κλαῖεν ἔπειτ' Ὀδυσῆα, φίλον πόσιν, ὄφρα οἱ ὕπνον / ἡδὺν ἐπὶ βλεφάροισι βάλε γλαυκῶπις Ἀθήνη. On sleep as bringing Penelope respite, see also 18.201–2 (where she wishes too that death could be so gentle) and 23.17–18.

[12] This last example comes as part of Penelope's reflection on the multiple practical challenges that she faces in Odysseus' absence, while also dealing with her grief. I discuss these challenges further below, at pp. 90–96.

during the reunion process (23.207; cf. 23.33 where she weeps with joy when Eurycleia reports on Odysseus' return).[13] When Odysseus encounters his mother Anticlea in the underworld, she reports to him that his wife 'waits with enduring heart in your halls; and always the miserable nights and days wear her down (φθίνουσιν) as she sheds tears' (11.181–3). This report of Penelope's actions is repeated partially by Athena when Odysseus first arrives back on Ithaca (13.337–8), and later word for word by the swineherd Eumaeus (16.37–9). It seems intended primarily on each occasion to reassure Odysseus of his wife's fidelity, yet at the same time it offers the audience an insight into Penelope's mental state during his prolonged absence. Elsewhere, once to Telemachus and later to the disguised Odysseus on his return to Ithaca, Penelope herself describes her bed as 'made mournful for me, always wetted with my tears (μοι στονόεσσα τέτυκται, / αἰεὶ δάκρυσ᾽ ἐμοῖσι πεφυρμένη), since the time when Odysseus went to Troy with the sons of Atreus' (17.102–4; cf. 19.595–7).[14] The reference to her bed as the place where she weeps, rather than the scene of an adulterous liaison, again seems intended to hint at her faithfulness; the image of her at night, restless and crying, also highlights once more the endless worrying caused by Odysseus' absence.[15]

As will become apparent in the rest of this chapter, the mythical Penelope shares some of her experience—and her tears—with military spouses whose partners are in a war zone. The twentieth-century American poet Edna St Vincent Millay drew on these similarities in her 'An Ancient Gesture', first published posthumously in 1954.[16] The speaker whose voice we hear in the poem recognizes that, in drying her own tears, she performs a gesture mimicking that of Penelope before her, then goes on to recall the long sleepless nights which she shares with her mythical predecessor:

[13] See Seaford (2017) for an exploration of the ways in which tears of grief and tears of joy are often indistinguishable from one another in early Greek literature. I present a detailed discussion of the process of reunion for Penelope and Odysseus in Chapter 5 below.

[14] In the second of these two occurrences, the ending of the phrase is altered to read, '…since the time when Odysseus went to set eyes on Evil-Troy, never to be named'.

[15] Note that Odysseus too is frequently seen weeping: 4.556, 5.82–3, 5.157, and 7.260, when trapped on Calypso's island and longing to return home; 8.86–95 and 8.521–31, on hearing the bard Demodocus sing tales of Troy; 10.497–9, when Circe tells him that he must visit the underworld; 11.55, 11.87, and 11.395, when he sees the souls of his unburied comrade Elpenor, his mother, and Agamemnon in the underworld; 16.191–2, when he reunites with Telemachus; 17.304, when he sees his old dog Argus in a pitiful state; and 23.231–41, upon his reunion with Penelope. The parallels between his actions and those of his wife might be seen as a manifestation of their *homophrosunē*, 'like-mindedness', or as the poet's emphasis on the shared elements of their experience. On this, see further below, p. 113 and p. 153.

[16] Millay (1954, p. 65).

And along towards morning, when you think it will never
    be light,
And your husband has been gone, and you don't know
    where, for years.
Suddenly you burst into tears;
There is simply nothing else to do.

Millay's poem highlights a key aspect of the waiting wife's experience—the sense of uncertainty as to whether a loved one will return home safely— which sets this apart from other kinds of separation. This lack of certainty, and the emotions which it generates, is sometimes referred to by psychologists as 'ambiguous loss'; it is this concept on which I will focus in the next section.

Ambiguous loss and the wait for news

The hardest thing is not knowing if he's okay...not knowing if you're going to get somebody at your doorstep saying that he's passed....I want my husband here; I don't want my husband to die.[17]

The sense of nagging anxiety described here by 'Jamie', a contemporary military spouse, echoes Penelope's constant doubt as to whether her husband will return home safely from war. This is a theme which recurs time and again in the personal reflections of military spouses on their own experiences, as they report their fear of a dreaded knock at the door which will bring news of their partner's injury or death. The absence of a military partner on active service brings for those who remain at home fear for their loved one's safety along with a perpetual sense of uncertainty.[18] The experience of those left behind under such circumstances has been described by psychologists as 'ambiguous loss': that is, a loss where there is no clear resolution. In this section, I will outline the concept of ambiguous loss in the

---

[17] Quoted in Davis et al. (2011, p. 56) (ellipses in original).
[18] De Burgh et al. (2011) provide an overview of the literature published from 2000 to 2010 on the impact of deployments to Iraq and Afghanistan on the partners of service personnel. Wilson and Murray (2016, p. 110) summarize the evidence of studies into waiting spouses' experiences of deployment. See also Easterling and Knox (2010: sections entitled 'Deployments in the 21st Century' and 'Feelings').

context of military separations and explore how it relates to Penelope's situation. I will then go on to examine how those who wait at home—as described both in ancient texts and in contemporary situations—experience an internal conflict between the desperate need to hear news of their absent loved ones and the fear of the horrors which that news might reveal.

The theory of 'ambiguous loss' was first proposed and developed by psychologist and sociologist Pauline Boss, who gives the example of Penelope waiting for Odysseus as an illustration of the theory; Boss does not, however, elaborate on this reading of Penelope.[19] There are two key types of ambiguous loss: one in which a person is physically present but 'psychologically absent' (for example, suffering with dementia or another form of cognitive impairment), and the other where a person is physically absent but 'psychologically present' in the minds of those who love them.[20] Boss applied the term 'ambiguous loss' to situations where there is ambiguity surrounding a person's absence, often after an event such as war or a disaster, where there has been no definite confirmation of a death. The lack of certainty as to whether or when their loved one will return, Boss pointed out, adds to the stress of family members. Later proponents of the theory recognized that it can also be applied in cases where military families are dealing with a loved one's deployment, even without the exceptional additional stress of a missing in action/prisoner of war situation.[21] Boss summarizes one of the impacts of ambiguous loss as follows:

> ...uncertainty or a lack of information about the whereabouts or status of a loved one as absent or present, as dead or alive, is traumatizing for most individuals, couples, and families. The ambiguity freezes the grief process (Boss, 1999) and prevents cognition, thus blocking coping and decision-making processes. Closure is impossible. Family members have no other option but to construct their own truth about the status of the person absent in mind or body. Without information to clarify their loss, family members have no choice but to live with the paradox of absence and presence (Boss, 2006). For example, when family members are separated by

---

[19] Boss (1999, p. 5).
[20] See Boss (1999) for a detailed discussion of different ways in which the two types of ambiguous loss manifest.
[21] See Huebner et al. (2007) and Easterling and Knox (2010, section titled 'Theoretical Framework—Ambiguous Loss Theory').

deployment, they of course hope to be reunited again but also know that they will never be the same as they were before the separation.[22]

In circumstances where a serving partner is away for a lengthy period, the evidence points—unsurprisingly—to heightened anxiety and more complex disruption to normality than over the period of short-term deployments. One study of families with a service member missing in action (MIA) or held as a prisoner of war (PW) conducted after the Vietnam War concluded that 'normal patterns of coping with father/husband absence were disturbed by the unprecedented and indeterminate length of his absence, and that much of the social acceptance, stability, and continuity which are taken for granted in the intact family was lacking or severely taxed in the PW/MIA family'.[23] This sense of ambiguous loss is dramatized particularly effectively in the story of one of the women on whom Donna Moreau focuses in *Waiting Wives*.[24] Early on in Moreau's narrative, 'Bonnie' receives a telegram that her husband Bruce is missing in action, yet she remains utterly certain that he is alive, and spends much of her time in the years which follow going to great lengths in her quest to find information about his whereabouts.

For the majority of the *Odyssey*, Odysseus is in a situation that might today be classified as 'missing in action'. It is his father Laertes who perhaps best sums up the sense of ambiguous loss felt by Odysseus' family: in the final book of the poem, before he learns that Odysseus has returned, Laertes reflects, 'His father and mother, who bore him, could not weep over and shroud him. Nor could his richly-dowered wife, thoughtful Penelope, close his eyes and lament her husband on his bier, as is fitting' (24.292–6). Penelope has no way of knowing whether Odysseus is dead or alive, and, if he has survived, in what state he might eventually return to her: this mythical couple's scenario, in which it has been almost twenty years since Odysseus left for the war at Troy, is a particularly extreme manifestation of the story of separations undergone by soldiers and their spouses in conflicts the world over. One study of the impact of separation on non-serving members of a military family during the first Gulf War outlines responses common to many spouses during the deployment of a loved one to a war zone. The authors suggest that during the first six weeks of deployment the partner at home experiences 'emotional confusion', which can manifest itself

---

[22] Boss (2007, p. 105).   [23] McCubbin et al. (1975, p. 95).
[24] On the context of Moreau's fictionalized memoir, see above, p. 28, with n. 31.

through 'crying, loss of sleep, loss of appetite [and] keeping busy'.[25] Penelope, as we observe her in the *Odyssey*, has been suspended in this state for an exceptionally long period, and, as discussed in the previous section, she still displays some of these behaviours long after Odysseus' departure. I will return to discuss the 'keeping busy' aspect of this pattern later in this chapter.

Despite his physical absence, however, Odysseus is very much 'psychologically present' in the minds of his family. The first four books of the poem (sometimes referred to as the 'Telemachy'), which focus primarily on the situation on Ithaca and Telemachus' journey in search of news of his father rather than on Odysseus' own story, make this clear. Odysseus' name is frequently on the lips of the members of his family and household, as well as of the suitors and those who knew him at Troy: Nestor, Menelaus, and Helen tell tales of their shared history with Odysseus, and, as we saw earlier, Penelope still weeps for him (1.363). Meanwhile Telemachus—in accordance with the Homeric tendency to use patronymics to identify characters—is repeatedly described as 'Odysseus' son' (1.207, 2.2, 2.35, 2.415, 3.352, 3.398), and other characters often remark upon his resemblance to his absent father.[26] The palace too is still referred to as belonging to Odysseus—it is the 'house of Odysseus' at 4.674 and 4.715, and when Athena visits, she appears on 'Odysseus' porch' (1.103)—and his weapons are still stored there long after he departed (1.128–9). This 'absent presence' of Odysseus in the minds of his family is wholly consistent with the theory of ambiguous loss.

As noted, the experience of those left behind is characterized by uncertainty, and as a result waiting spouses can have an ambivalent relationship with their desire for news from the front line. At the same time as being desperate for information, they are very often fearful of what such news might reveal. In the modern world, the anxiety brought on by hearing news from the front line can be exacerbated by media reporting on conflict: twenty-four hour rolling news, the accessibility of online media, and the presence of embedded reporters in the field with troops mean that those waiting at home can have continuous access to a stream of information about events in the theatre of war. Since Vietnam, which was the first war to

---

[25] Norwood et al. (1996, p. 171).
[26] The disguised goddess Athena comments on Telemachus' likeness to Odysseus (1.207–8) and refers to the qualities which he has inherited from him (2.270–80); Nestor comments on how Telemachus' speech resembles that of Odysseus (3.123–5); and Helen and Menelaus remark on his similarity to his father (4.141–54).

be televised,[27] the availability of footage from the front line to viewers back home has steadily increased. One study carried out in the US on a small group of army wives whose husbands were deployed during Operation Iraqi Freedom in 2003 examined the impact of exposure to television news on their well-being, and reported that some had revealed that they would avidly watch the television for six hours or more a day in their hunger for news. Some compulsive viewers would even sleep with the rolling news channels switched on, sometimes waking instinctively when hearing the voice of a reporter they knew to be embedded with their husbands' unit.[28] Some spouses report that regular contact with their deployed partner is an important element of their coping mechanisms, and that this is often enhanced by the use of modern technology.[29] Many, however, also report problems stemming from modern-day rumour networks which can spread false stories—about the nature of a mission, injuries, or the timing of a unit's return—with alarming rapidity.[30]

Today, when the worst happens on the front line, the British and US military operate a system whereby serving troops are prevented from communicating with home, to avoid the situation in which a family receives news of a loved one's death by social media or email.[31] Names are anonymized in news reporting immediately after a fatality, which results nonetheless in a state of heightened anxiety for all those at home: as one reporter who spent time with the families of servicemen at Fort Campbell, Kentucky, related after the news that a roadside bomb in Afghanistan had killed five of their company, 'In moments of crisis, the connectivity can make the looming possibility of death seem almost suffocating. The spouses jump with each phone call. Ringing doorbells spark tremors of terror.'[32] This kind of communications blackout after a fatality is a recurring feature of stories told by and about contemporary military spouses. Siobhan Fallon, for example, explores this in one of her short stories, 'Inside the Break': 'Ten and a half

---

[27]   Note, for example, Moreau (2005, p. 114) on the effect of watching, for the first time, television reports from the field of battle on the Vietnam soldiers' wives: 'The Vietnam War had infiltrated our living room.' On television coverage of the Vietnam War, see also Steinman (2002).

[28]   Ender et al. (2007).   [29]   Wilson and Murray (2016, pp. 112–13).

[30]   Easterling and Knox (2010: section entitled 'Challenges of Deployment').

[31]   The British military refers to this procedure, by which all communications are closed down until the families of the dead have been informed, as 'Operation Minimise'. Hyde (2015, p. 124–7) provides an illustration of how this plays out for the families waiting at home. See also Lester (2015), outlining the procedure followed by the British military when informing a family of a service member's death.

[32]   Jaffe (2010).

months into the deployment was marked with a long and ominous silence, longer than any other.'[33] In Fallon's story, the absence of email or telephone contact for any of the waiting wives for three days is the precursor to the news that a member of their husbands' company has been killed in an explosion. For the wives of servicemen in Vietnam, long before the ubiquity of mobile phones and the internet, such fear could be sparked by the presence in the neighbourhood of a slow-moving military sedan, carrying the chaplain and personnel who would break the awful news to one waiting wife. Donna Moreau's memories of her own childhood evoke the dread which the arrival of such a vehicle would instil in every household, and the palpable sense of relief of those whose loved ones had been spared, accompanied by shared grief for the newly widowed woman: 'When the women felt it was safe to breathe, after the soldiers had entered their neighbor's home, it was like a wail of silent voices responding to the devastation of another lost life.'[34]

It is, then, an agonizing paradox of the situation of the 'waiting wife' that the constant hunger for news can also be fraught with the fear of hearing that news. The *Odyssey* too provides us with an insight into this paradox. For Penelope, who must rely on tales told by bards or passing travellers, of course communication with the 'front line' takes a very different form from that used by military couples today.[35] While Penelope is desperate to hear of Odysseus, at the same time any related news reawakens her grief, as in her distressed response early on in the *Odyssey* to Phemius' song of the Achaeans' homecomings. She has had no form of direct contact with Odysseus since his departure, and she knows that stories about him can be flawed, whether as a result of deliberate distortion, or simply as a result of messages becoming twisted over long distances and timespans. She reports that she has been tricked by visitors who have told false tales of Odysseus (14.126–30), and when she and Odysseus are finally reunited she tells him that in his absence she was always fearful of being deceived by a story told by someone in pursuit of personal gain (23.313–18).

Perhaps the most memorable image that lends an insight into Penelope's emotional state, and her response to information about his potential whereabouts, comes in Book 19 of the *Odyssey*. Here the disguised Odysseus, on

---

[33] Fallon (2011, p. 105).
[34] Moreau (2005, p. 142). Later in the same volume (pp. 225–30), Moreau recalls the moment at which one wife received news of her husband's death.
[35] Easterling and Knox (2010, section titled 'Challenges of Deployment').

his return to Ithaca, weaves a tale of an encounter that he says he has had with her husband. The description of Penelope's reaction to this story reflects the grief that accompanies the sense of ambiguous loss with which this warrior's wife has lived for so long:

> And as she listened her tears flowed and her face melted [ῥέε δάκρυα, τήκετο δὲ χρώς]. As the snow melts on the lofty mountains, the snow which Eurus thaws when Zephyr has poured it down, and as it melts the streams of the rivers flow full: so her lovely cheeks melted as she lamented for her husband, who even then was sitting by her side [ὣς τῆς τήκετο καλὰ παρήϊα δάκρυ χεούσης, / κλαιούσης ἑὸν ἄνδρα παρήμενον].
>
> (*Odyssey* 19.204–9)

This extraordinary simile, which likens Penelope's tears to mountain streams of meltwater formed from thawing snow, conveys an impression of what happens when inner feelings surface, and thus allows the poet and his audience to imagine this physical response to the emotional weight that Penelope has been carrying for so long. Repeated use of forms of the verb τήκω in the description convey a sense of both melting or dissolving, and overflowing, which is difficult to replicate accurately in an English translation. Here Penelope's protective shell melts away, while the feelings that she has tried to bury within herself bubble to the surface and spill over as tears. It is here that perhaps for the first time she opens herself fully to the possibility that her husband may be alive and may return to her. Penelope's refusal until now to believe that Odysseus will come home seems to have been a defence mechanism, which prevents her from being buoyed by false hopes. Shortly after she has finished weeping, she insists on testing the veracity of the 'stranger's' account by requesting a detailed description of Odysseus' clothing and appearance (19.215–19). Soon, however, we see her descend once more into pessimism—or perhaps self-protection, having allowed herself this brief moment of hope—as she asserts, 'I shall never again welcome him back, returning home to his native land' (19.257–8, cf. 19.312–16). Her ambivalent response here encapsulates the impact of ambiguous loss, and the uncertainty surrounding Odysseus' return, on her state of mind.[36]

---

[36] Penelope's doubts about whether Odysseus will return safely surface elsewhere in the poem too: see, for example, 4.724 and 4.814, where she reflects 'I have lost my noble, lion-hearted husband', and 19.559–69 where she cannot accept an interpretation of the dream she has had (in which an eagle kills her flock of geese) as meaning that Odysseus will return to slaughter the suitors.

Intense fear of the arrival of bad news is also an element of the mythical Penelope's experience which the Roman poet Ovid, writing in the late first century BCE, captured with particular insight. His *Heroides*, imagined letters written from the perspectives of well-known female mythological characters, open with a letter from Penelope to her husband in which she recalls how, when hearing every tale of another Greek warrior's death, she envisaged instead the death of Odysseus: 'In short,' Ovid's Penelope writes, 'whoever it was in the Argive camp that was pierced and fell, the heart of the one who loves you became colder than ice' (*denique, quisquis erat castris iugulatus Achivis, / frigidius glacie pectus amantis erat*, *Heroides* 1.21–2). In the extant Greek literary tradition, however, the waiting wife who voices most clearly this sense of foreboding is not Penelope but Clytemnestra. In Aeschylus' *Agamemnon*, first performed in Athens in 458 BCE as part of the *Oresteia* trilogy, this quite different archetypal soldier's spouse articulates clearly the situation of the wife at home, as she hears the steady stream of rumours from the battlefield:

> First, it is a dreadful evil for a woman to sit at home, deserted, separated from her man, and hearing many rumours. One person, then another, would come and report on terrible and still more terrible events. If this man here [Agamemnon] had suffered as many wounds as were reported to the house, he'd be pierced more times than a net! And if he had died as often as the reports claimed, he'd have been triple-bodied, a second Geryon.[37]
>
> (Aeschylus, *Agamemnon* 861–70)

Clytemnestra's description of this recurring ordeal is extracted from her welcome speech to the returning Agamemnon, and as such is part of the 'dutiful wife' persona which she fabricates for herself while plotting the murder of her husband.[38] Nonetheless, the insight which she (disingenuously) gives into her emotional responses would doubtless seem convincing here precisely because it evokes the state of mind of a woman overwhelmed by the strain under which she has been placed by her husband's absence.

While wives like Penelope, and her modern counterparts, wait and hope for their partners' safe return, life on the home front must go on. Along with the emotional difficulties these waiting spouses face, the absence of a

---

[37] Geryon appears in various ancient texts as a giant with either multiple heads or multiple bodies.
[38] For a detailed discussion of the various ancient versions of Clytemnestra's response to the return of Agamemnon, see below, pp. 119–35 and pp. 139–63.

military partner also brings with it other challenges. The practical elements of managing a household and perhaps raising children alone must be tackled, and often waiting spouses find themselves taking on a dual role in which they occupy the gap left by the serving partner. In some cases, this can also challenge the traditional division of gendered labour which has long been perpetuated by the military. In the next section, I turn to focus on these aspects of the experience of the waiting wife.

Pressures on the spouse left behind

The feminist work of Cynthia Enloe on militarism and international relations examines, among other issues, the gendered nature of military relationships. In *Maneuvers: The International Politics of Militarizing Women's Lives* (2000), Enloe set out a series of criteria which she had identified as meeting the ideal of the 'Model Military Wife'—as perpetuated by patriarchal military institutions—in the twentieth century. This ideal spouse is expected to be accepting of the demands placed by the military on the serving partner, including the need to be away from home for long periods of time. She (for, as Enloe points out, it was at the time her work was published, just as it remains today, most often a woman in the role of the civilian partner)[39] will also tackle periods of separation in a particular way:

> She has become a very competent occasional single parent and head of household when her soldier-husband is off on a training tour or deployed to a war zone. She knows how to handle the checkbook, fix the plumbing, renew the car insurance.

> Still, she does not take inordinate pride in her competence. The weeks when he is away are, to her, an inevitable but 'unnormal' time; a happy, 'normal' time resumes when he returns. She is pleased to relinquish the head-of-household mantel [*sic*] when her husband is home.[40]

The points that Enloe sets out reflect the way in which the traditional division of gender roles perpetuated by military institutions—which I discussed in Chapter 1 as asserting themselves particularly during departure scenes—can become temporarily suspended when the serving partner is

---

[39] See above, p. 1 n. 2, for statistics on the gender divide in modern armed forces.
[40] Enloe (2000, p. 163). On Enloe, see also above p. 9.

deployed away from home. A key feature of the experience of those who remain behind when their partners are away on military service is the need to take on additional responsibilities including, for some, parenting alone as well as tasks relating to managing the household.[41] Aducci et al. suggest that women in this situation assume 'androgynous roles'; their choice of phrasing here reflects the outdated gender binary, and traditional ideas about marital relationships, which are still to a large extent embedded in the ideology of military organizations.[42] As one woman summarized her own experience:

> I'm responsible for everything from paying the bills on time to getting the kids out of bed to getting the kids home and everything in between. Every pipe in our backyard had to be dug up in the middle of winter and I had our new pipes replaced while he was in Iraq...That was fun, yea, I'm responsible for all of those things. I've kinda been a carpenter while he's been gone. I don't know crap about carpentering (laughter). Things went wrong, I didn't like how it looked. I've painted the house while he was gone. I do all kinds of things.[43]

For this military wife her experience of her husband's deployment reflects clearly her sense that she took on tasks that would normally fall outside her own area of responsibility. She appears to have internalized a set of assumptions about traditional gender roles within the household; this is a narrative that is often reinforced by the military itself. As Enloe describes the situation:

> ...conventions [on military bases] lower wives' expectations of paid work and careers of their own, encourage them to derive their own sense of self-worth from their husbands' accomplishments, and suppress wives' stories of depression and physical abuse for fear that they might damage their husbands' chances of promotion. Base commanders also need beliefs about femininity that encourage wives to take charge of family affairs

---

[41] Wilson and Murray (2016, p. 114) summarize some of the many ways in which twenty-first-century military spouses assume different responsibilities in their partners' absence.

[42] Aducci et al. (2011, p. 238). See also Sahlstein et al. (2009, pp. 430–1). The notion that during earlier conflicts—notably the World Wars of the twentieth century—women took up roles that had been traditionally those of men is well documented. See, for example, Braybon and Summerfield (1987) and German (2013, pp. 1–73).

[43] Quoted in Aducci et al. (2011, p. 238).

when their husbands are away on maneuvers yet gladly relinquish any authority that comes from such responsibilities when the husband returns.[44]

I will return to discuss in more detail the eventual relinquishing of these temporarily assumed responsibilities in Chapter 5, where I explore the reunion process between returning soldier and waiting wife.

In Penelope's case, the reversal of traditional roles is highlighted by the disguised Odysseus in another striking Homeric simile (19.107–14). Odysseus' very first words to Penelope compliment her on her *kleos* ('honour', 'glory', or 'fame'), which he says 'reaches the broad sky'. Odysseus compares this to 'the *kleos* of some blameless king who, with the fear of the gods in his heart, is lord over many valiant men, upholding justice' (19.108–11) in a prosperous land. This is one of several similes in the poem which invert traditional gender roles, and which Helene Foley has described as 'reverse similes', where a woman is compared to a man, or vice versa. Foley shows how these are used to explore the interdependence and like-mindedness of Odysseus and Penelope in the build-up to their eventual reunion.[45] As well as highlighting Penelope's responsibility for assuming the role usually occupied by Odysseus, this particular simile also draws our attention to what is lacking on the island in the absence of its rightful king. The image of abundance and prosperity, and the sense of justice being upheld, in the world described within the simile, contrasts with the situation on Ithaca, where the suitors are consuming Odysseus' resources in his absence.

The responsibilities which Penelope, as wife of an absent soldier, must assume in the *Odyssey* manifest in particular and extreme ways. She must handle alone the challenging situation with the unruly suitors—household management on a grand scale—as well as acting as sole parent to Telemachus, who is now on the brink of adulthood. When her husband was present, gender roles within this marriage—as elsewhere in Homeric poetry—were clearly defined and separate.[46] Now, with Odysseus absent, the pressure to perform simultaneously, as best she can, the traditional roles of both husband and wife is constant and relentless. For her, however, much

[44] Enloe (2014, p. 72).
[45] Foley (1978). Other 'reverse similes' appear at 8.523–31, in which Odysseus is compared to a woman weeping over the body of a husband killed in battle, and 23.233–40 where Penelope, in her relief at the return of Odysseus, is compared to a shipwrecked sailor on first sighting land. On the latter, see below, pp. 153–54.
[46] On gender roles in the *Odyssey*, see Felson and Slatkin (2004, pp. 103–13).

more is at stake than the successful completion of practical tasks around the house. In a conversation with the suitor Eurymachus, Penelope recalls Odysseus' words when he departed for Troy (18.259–71). He told her, 'You must take care of everything here' (σοὶ δ' ἐνθάδε πάντα μελόντων, 18.266), and instructed her to look after his mother and father. In addition, should Odysseus not return home, she should marry a man of her choice and leave the house behind when she sees her son beginning to grow a beard.[47] The implication seems to be that once Telemachus reaches maturity Penelope should seek to allow her son to take over the running of Odysseus' household; at the point at which we meet Penelope and Telemachus in the poem, that moment is drawing near.[48]

Penelope expresses elsewhere too the pressure which she is under in Odysseus' absence. We witnessed earlier how she described herself as lying awake at night tormented with worry and sadness (19.513–17). In this same scene, she expresses her doubts as to what she should do for the best (19.524–34):

> My heart is stirred to and fro in doubt; am I to remain with my son and keep all things safe [ἠὲ μένω παρὰ παιδὶ καὶ ἔμπεδα πάντα φυλάσσω]—my possessions, my slaves, and my great, high-roofed house—respecting the bed of my husband and the voice of the people, or go now with whoever is best of the Achaeans, a man who woos me in the halls and offers countless gifts? My son, when he was a child and still thoughtless, would not allow me to marry and leave my husband's house; but now that he is grown and has reached the measure of his youth, he implores me to go back home from the palace, anxious for his property, which the Achaeans are eating away.

Penelope's dilemma as to whether she should remain in the palace or leave with one of the suitors is phrased in terms which echo those used by Odysseus in his conversation with Anticleia in the underworld in Book 11, where he asks, 'Does she remain with her son, and keep all things safe

---

[47] At 4.112 and 4.144, Menelaus, and then Helen, suggest that Telemachus was a newborn when Odysseus left for Troy. I discuss in further detail above (pp. 33–4) the instructions given to Penelope by Odysseus before his departure.

[48] At 19.158–61, Penelope says that Telemachus is now a man able to care for the household. For a detailed treatment of the character of Telemachus in the *Odyssey*, see Petropoulos (2011), Heitman (2005, pp. 50–62, on the question of his maturity), Felson (1994, pp. 67–91, discussing in particular Telemachus' relationship with Penelope), and Olson (1995, pp. 65–90).

[ἠὲ μένει παρὰ παιδὶ καὶ ἔμπεδα πάντα φυλάσσει]? Or has someone already married her, whoever is the best of the Achaeans?' (11.178-9). Zeitlin explores the meanings of ἔμπεδα (translated here as 'safe', but literally meaning 'grounded in the earth') as a characteristic often attributed to male heroes—including Odysseus—in the Homeric epics. She suggests that the term also alludes to Penelope's steadfastness and her fidelity to Odysseus. In her husband's absence, this waiting wife has had to assume responsibility for ensuring that Odysseus' reputation, his status as king of Ithaca, and his material possessions remain intact.[49] Although her husband's quest to return home is the main focus of the narrative, she too undertakes what might seem to be an insurmountable challenge, yet—unlike Odysseus, whose story remains at the forefront throughout—she does so from the relative seclusion of her home, largely hidden from view.

Her relationship with her son Telemachus also presents Penelope with further challenges. It would, of course, be a stretch too far to suggest that there are any clear comparisons to be made between Penelope's story and those of contemporary military spouses insofar as raising children in the absence of a serving partner is concerned.[50] We see little evidence in the poem of Penelope's role in parenting Telemachus since infancy, and high status women like her would be supported by the domestic labour of enslaved women. Nonetheless, the Odyssey does offer an insight into the problematic relationship that Penelope has with Telemachus as he is on the brink of adulthood and independence; her concern for her son's well-being adds to the pressure which she is under. Prior to his departure to seek news of his father in the second book of the Odyssey, Telemachus asks the nurse Eurycleia not to alert Penelope to his absence in case this causes her to weep (2.372-6; cf. 4.746-9); later, she learns of the suitors' plot to kill her son (4.696-705). Once again, however, Penelope's emotions remain hidden from public view: we find her secluded in her rooms, with no appetite for food or drink, and compared to a trapped lion beset

---

[49] Zeitlin (1996, pp. 29-30). For a detailed discussion of the motivation of the suitors in the Odyssey, and what is at stake if one of them is successful in his pursuit of Penelope, see Scodel (2001).

[50] Creech et al. (2014) review the literature on parenting in relation to military deployments. The story of 'Lorrayne' in Moreau's Waiting Wives (2005; see especially pp. 96-105) provides a case study of some of the challenges faced by a woman parenting solo in the absence of a serving partner. In this case, Lorrayne, whose situation is exacerbated by a cancer diagnosis, bears alone the stress of her son's anxiety-induced behaviour in his father's absence, choosing not to confide in her husband about their child's refusal to eat or speak.

by hunters as she dwells on the thought of Telemachus' death at the hands of the suitors (4.787–90).[51]

Elsewhere, Telemachus colludes in the silencing of his mother. As we saw earlier, when Penelope first appears, he sends her away when she asks Phemius to change the subject of his song (1.345–59). Upon his return from his visits to Nestor and Menelaus in search of news of his father Telemachus, having evaded the suitors' plot against him, sends a message to alert her that he is safe, in order to spare her tears (16.328–32; cf. 17.6–9, where he acknowledges that his mother will be unable to stop weeping until she sees him for herself). When mother and son are reunited, however, he once again dismisses her, refusing to respond to her question about where he has been in case he himself might be moved to tears, and then sending her back to her rooms to wash and to promise an offering to the gods (17.36–51). The pattern is repeated again, prior to the contest with Odysseus' bow which Penelope initiates: in formulaic lines which echo his words to her in the first book of the poem, Telemachus rebukes her as he sends her back to her rooms, 'For the bow shall be all the men's concern [τόξον δ᾽ ἄνδρεσσι μελήσει / πᾶσι], and especially mine; for the power in the house is mine' (21.352–3).[52] The events of the poem illustrate, however, that in the absence of Odysseus, however, neither his wife nor his son has had the power to take full control of the situation.[53]

As well as silencing Penelope by sending her to her private rooms, Telemachus also misinterprets her emotions at a critical point in the poem. When his mother is reluctant to approach Odysseus after his return, Telemachus rebukes her and accuses her of 'having a harsh heart' (ἀπηνέα θυμὸν ἔχουσα, 23.97); he goes on to say (23.100–3), 'No other woman would have been so stubborn (τετληότι θυμῷ) as to stay away from her husband who, after suffering so much, has returned to his homeland after twenty years. Your heart is always harder than stone [σοὶ δ᾽ αἰεὶ κραδίη στερεωτέρη ἐστὶ λίθοιο].' It is possible to suggest that Telemachus' negative judgement of

---

[51] For a detailed discussion of this lion simile in relation to Penelope's character in the *Odyssey*, see Turkeltaub (2015).

[52] In the earlier lines, at 1.358–9, it is speech/talking (μῦθος), rather than the bow, which is said to be the men's concern. On the formula and its relationship to Hector's lines in the *Iliad* asserting that 'war will be the men's concern', see above, pp. 78–9.

[53] For example, Telemachus expresses his feeling of powerlessness to protect the household in Odysseus' absence at 2.45–61. At 18.215–25, Penelope rebukes Telemachus for failing to protect the 'beggar' (the disguised Odysseus) from abuse at the hands of the suitors. At 19.308–16, she voices her concern for the lack of proper hospitality in Odysseus' absence.

Penelope stems both from a feeling that she has led on the suitors rather than dismissing them (as suggested by the suitor Antinous at 2.91–2), and his own concern as to how to handle the situation in Odysseus' household.[54] Whatever the reason, as Marquardt suggests, Telemachus' 'readiness to criticize Penelope demonstrates the gulf of misunderstanding between them'.[55] Part of the accusation levelled by Telemachus towards his mother at 23.100–3 is repeated too by Odysseus shortly afterwards (23.168–70). In accusing Penelope of harshness, both men appear to misinterpret the complexity of her emotions surrounding the reunion, and the reasons for her hesitation. Her wariness stems at least in part from an uncertainty that Odysseus is who he says he is; as I will discuss at length in Chapter 5 it is also part of the complex process of recognition which the couple must undergo at the point of reunion. When the primary focus is, as so often in war narratives, the experience of the male adventurer it is perhaps no surprise that the waiting wife's emotions are rendered invisible or incomprehensible even to those close to her.

Penelope—like every other spouse left at home by a military partner—must find ways of dealing with the challenges she faces while Odysseus is away. This ancient mythical military wife is, like the 'Model Military Wife' described by Enloe, commended for the resourcefulness on which she draws in the absences of her husband. The approach that Penelope takes in the *Odyssey*, and for which she has become famous, is one which on several levels reinforces her own status as the ideal wife for the poem's male hero: this waiting wife devises a unique plan in order to hold off the suitors and maintain her own marital fidelity. In the final section of this chapter I consider how the ruse with which Penelope occupies her time—weaving and unweaving a shroud for her father-in-law—compares with coping strategies used by contemporary military spouses, as well as exploring how Penelope's actions both reinforce the gender divide and perpetuate the limbo of her existence in Odysseus' absence.

[54] See, for example, 16.30–5 where, on his return home, Telemachus expresses doubt as to whether Penelope may already have married one of the suitors. His concern relating to her potential second marriage is doubtless exacerbated by Athena's warning at 15.18–23, in which the goddess suggests that this would pose a threat to his inheritance (since his mother would take some of his possessions with her to the home of her new husband), and that Penelope would forget both Telemachus and his father were she to marry someone new.
[55] Marquardt (1985, p. 39).

'Keeping busy': Penelope's loom

Tomorrow Jeremy would be home. That interminable waiting, waiting, waiting for her life to continue—such a long, gray nothingness between departure and return, huge chunks of existence she filled up and pushed through as if it were a task rather than a stretch of her young life—would be over. There was such unreality to the waiting, such limbo; sometimes she didn't even know what she was waiting for. So much wasted time. Time was the enemy, waking her up alone at night and ticking so slowly, each minute mocking her.[56]

For Meg, the central character of Siobhan Fallon's short story 'You Know When the Men Are Gone', whom we met earlier in this chapter, her husband's detachment on military operations brings with it an overwhelming inertia as she awaits his return. The sense that life is on hold while a serving partner is away is common to many military spouses' reflections on their experiences of deployment. As one woman, Nicole, described her situation, 'We're a family on hold because he's gone...Yes, I am living life every day. But I'm still waiting and waiting and waiting...Although he did not stop for me when he left, when he comes home we have to pick up the last time we saw each other.'[57] This short-term suspension of normal life while a partner is deployed is also accompanied for many spouses by the longer-term sense of life on hold imposed by the military lifestyle, which disrupts careers, relationships, and personal ambitions, and which I discussed in Chapter 2.[58] Few studies have been made relating to the strategies that contemporary military spouses use to help them cope during time apart, although there is some published research which suggests that the various methods employed include, for example, finding comfort in religious beliefs, venting emotions and drawing on support networks. For some the stress of separation can also lead to self-medication using alcohol or prescription drugs, substance abuse, or complete withdrawal from normal activities. Many spouses also report, however, that they use self-distraction techniques: absorbing

---

[56] Fallon (2011, p. 31).   [57] Quoted in Davis et al. (2011, p. 57) (ellipses in original).
[58] On the suspension of aspects of the lives of military spouses, see also Dimiceli et al. (2009, p. 361), Booth and Lederer (2012, p. 371), and Easterling and Knox (2010, section titled 'Uniqueness of Military Families').

themselves in work, hobbies, or other tasks in order to take their mind off the difficulties of their situation.[59] Online support networks, blogs and news sites aimed at military spouses are littered with advice about 'keeping busy' to pass the time and provide distraction from the stresses associated with deployment. As mythical predecessor to these modern-day military spouses, Penelope has her own very specific method of 'keeping busy'; yet, as I will discuss, the task with which she occupies herself is not merely a distraction technique. Instead, the 'shroud trick' is a strategy which itself reveals a great deal about expectations placed upon this waiting wife. It reinforces conventional gender roles, acts as another mechanism by which Penelope is kept secluded and invisible, and ultimately perpetuates the sense of a life on hold for her too.

In introducing her ruse, Penelope tells the disguised Odysseus, 'I spin out deceptions' (ἐγὼ δὲ δόλους τολυπεύω, 19.137); the metaphorical connection between spinning or weaving and female cunning recurs frequently in Homeric poetry.[60] Penelope describes at 19.138–56 how, inspired by a god, she set up a huge loom on which she wove a burial shroud for Odysseus' father Laertes.[61] She told the suitors that she would not choose which of them to marry until the shroud was complete, yet, 'by day I would weave at the great loom, but by night, with torches set beside me, I would unravel it' (19.149–50). The plan went undetected for three years until, with the help of one of the enslaved women of her household, the suitors discovered the trick. The ruse is one which has become an enduring symbol of Penelope's resourcefulness, her femininity, and her fidelity to her husband; the loom is the image which recurs most frequently in later artistic depictions of Penelope. Many of these images are closely related to the name vase of the so-called 'Penelope painter', a red-figure skyphos (drinking cup) dating from around 440 BCE which depicts Penelope seated before a huge loom and accompanied by a standing male figure who is identified as Telemachus.[62]

In turning to her loom, Penelope conforms to ancient Greek societal expect-ations for respectable women of high social status. Cloth production—which

---

[59] On coping strategies used by the partners of deployed personnel, see Figley (1993), Dimiceli et al. (2009), and Easterling and Knox (2010).

[60] On the connection between weaving and cunning (particularly as associated with women), see Bergren (1983).

[61] The speech is formulaic; the words used by Penelope to describe the shroud trick also appear at 2.93–110 (where the suitor Antinous reports it to Telemachus) and at 24.126–50 when the shade of the suitor Amphimedon tells the story to Agamemnon in the underworld.

[62] Buitron-Oliver and Cohen (1995, pp. 43–8) discuss the representation of Penelope in Greek art. See Hall (2008, p. 115) on the reception of the loom image.

played a key role in the domestic economy—was an emphatically female occupation in ancient Greece. In the Homeric poems, both mortal women and goddesses are often shown engaged in spinning and weaving. These are tasks which usually take place indoors, within spaces primarily occupied by women, thereby reinforcing the sense of seclusion from the public domain which is inhabited by men. As Pantelia observes, this work within the home also 'symbolizes the normal order of life, in which women take care of their households while men defend the city'.[63] In this respect, Penelope fulfils a role similar to that which is still today expected of military spouses: to keep the 'home fires burning' by attending to domestic tasks while a serving partner is occupied elsewhere.[64] Penelope's weaving also, however, has a very particular function in preserving the proper domestic order; it is the means by which she protects Odysseus' status and position at the head of his household. Not only, then, does she conform to gendered expectations in terms of the activity that occupies her, but she also uses that activity to preserve the traditional family structure. Even the object which she weaves—a funeral shroud for her husband's father—cements her place within the gendered hierarchy of the family: Pantelia notes further that 'Penelope's weaving of a shroud for Odysseus' father reflects her commitment to her husband's family and symbolizes her loyalty to the patrilinear order which she is determined to protect'.[65]

The success of the shroud trick relies on the fact that domestic labour undertaken by women remains largely unnoticed by the male characters. Penelope's weaving takes place in the upper part of the house (15.517), in the seclusion of the women's quarters, and away from the male domain. The unweaving of the shroud is also a nocturnal pursuit; this serves to conceal Penelope's activities and reinforce her seclusion further. The plan highlights the invisibility of women's labour, and is a product of a social structure in which female pursuits—like the emotions experienced by Penelope—are unseen by the men of the household. Penelope's actions ultimately confine her to the traditional role of Enloe's 'Model Military Wife', and even the method by which she achieves this—the nightly process of unweaving—is

---

[63] Pantelia (1993, p. 494).
[64] Houppert (2005, pp. 55–65) discusses at length one twentieth-century 'how-to' manual for the military wife, Nancy Shea's *The Army Wife*, which was first published in 1941 and reprinted many times. The manual emphasizes in particular the importance of attention to domestic tasks as part of the military wife's duty. Houppert's work on military marriages—which, in a nod to the ideal of domesticity for soldiers' spouses, she titled *Home Fires Burning*—illustrates how such gendered expectations still endure in military circles even today.
[65] Pantelia (1993, p. 496).

in itself an act of erasure which might be seen as a metaphor for Penelope's own invisibility. As Carolyn Heilbrun pointed out in her path-breaking essay, 'What was Penelope unweaving?', the Homeric Penelope is restricted within the limited plots traditionally reserved for women, whose 'destiny was to be married, circulated; to be given by one man, the father, to another, the husband; to become the mothers of men. Theirs has been the marriage plot, the erotic plot, the courtship plot, but never, as for men, the quest plot.'[66] Ultimately, then, despite her resourcefulness, Penelope has little agency. The control which she is able to exert over her own part in the story—and the means she adopts to do so—is limited by her gender and her subordination to the hero husband whose story has always been the primary focus of attention.

Penelope's weaving and unweaving also comes to represent a life on hold. As Foley points out, 'To keep open a place for Odysseus she has symbolically stopped change on Ithaca.'[67] Until either the return of Odysseus or her choosing of a new husband, Penelope is suspended in a state of inertia. As we saw at the opening of this section, the absence of a soldier husband still now has the capacity to induce this sense of the postponement of 'normal' life; this is often accompanied by a sense of powerlessness induced by the various uncertainties that accompany periods of deployment.[68] For Penelope the sense of ambiguous loss she experiences in Odysseus' absence is accompanied by acute uncertainty regarding her own future within a patriarchal society; should her husband not return home, she must become the property of another man. The incomplete shroud defers for a time her selection of the man who will control Penelope's future. As the means by which she is able to exercise some control over her situation, it also denies her any possibility of moving forward in Odysseus' absence. For Penelope, the point at which her ability to delay the decision to move on has become impossible—because of the suitors' discovery of her ruse—is also the time when her husband returns home, and when the *Odyssey* reaches its dramatic climax. Prompted by Athena, she appears before the suitors and announces her intention to remarry, unaware that Odysseus himself is already back in the palace, in disguise (18.158–303). She announces a contest, with herself as the prize: the man who successfully strings Odysseus' giant bow and shoots an arrow through the axes will become her husband (19.572–81, cf. 21.67–79). This chain of events leads ultimately to Odysseus'

---

[66] Heilbrun (1991, p. 108).   [67] Foley (1978, p. 10).
[68] Davis et al. (2011, pp. 56–7).

revelation of his true identity, the slaughter of the suitors, and finally the couple's reunion, a process which I will discuss in detail in Chapter 5.

The *Odyssey*'s depiction of Penelope during her long wait for her husband bears many of the hallmarks of the experiences of separation endured by soldiers' spouses ever since. She exemplifies the emotional toll which deployment so often exerts on the waiting partner, endures the strain of living with ambiguous loss, and tolerates the suspension of normal life during Odysseus' absence, managing the situation in which she finds herself as best she can. This mythical 'model military wife' also represents the idealized image of how a woman in a highly patriarchal society ought to behave. She has far fewer opportunities than her husband to articulate her thoughts and experiences for herself; in fact the final assessment of Penelope's character in the poem is voiced by a man. The shade of Agamemnon, speaking to the suitor Amphimedon in the underworld (24.192–7), compares Penelope to his own wife (and, in moral terms, Penelope's opposite) Clytemnestra. He praises Penelope's 'great virtue' ($\mu\epsilon\gamma\acute{a}\lambda\eta\ \acute{a}\rho\epsilon\tau\widehat{\eta}$, 24.193), her 'good sense' ($\acute{a}\gamma\alpha\theta\alpha\grave{\imath}\ \varphi\rho\acute{\epsilon}\nu\epsilon\varsigma$, 24.194) and her fidelity to her husband ($\acute{\omega}\varsigma\ \epsilon\mathring{\upsilon}\ \mu\acute{\epsilon}\mu\nu\eta\tau'$ $\grave{O}\delta\upsilon\sigma\widehat{\eta}os,\ /\ \acute{a}\nu\delta\rho\grave{o}s\ \kappa o\upsilon\rho\iota\delta\acute{\iota}o\upsilon$—'how well she remembered Odysseus, her wedded husband', 24.195–6). This ideal waiting wife, then, is used to set a moral standard against which other women are measured. A core element of this idealized image is her ability to remain faithful to her husband despite the length and uncertainty of their separation. Anxieties relating to spousal infidelity are a recurring theme of narratives relating to military marriages; this will be the focus of my next chapter.

4

Infidelity: Clytemnestra in Homeric poetry and Athenian tragedy

In her 2010 collection of poetry, *Stateside*, American poet and academic Jehanne Dubrow—whose own husband served for twenty years in the US Navy—uses the figure of Penelope to explore the experiences and emotions of a modern-day military spouse. The ancient tales and themes of the *Odyssey* recur throughout these poems, whose setting is emphatically contemporary, as they trace one woman's emotional journey before, during, and after her husband's deployment abroad. Dubrow's poems reflect on the stress under which a military marriage is placed by the absence of the serving partner, as her Penelope-figure deals with her own versions of farewell, separation, and reunion. In the poem 'Ithaca', Dubrow reflects directly on one key issue which is central to the portrayal of Penelope in the *Odyssey*: will she remain faithful in her husband's absence? The issue of potential infidelity is equally relevant to Dubrow's waiting wife:

> At PTA meetings, she's chased
> by divorcés and other glum
>
> suitors. Nobody seems to care
> that she still wears a wedding ring.
> Odysseus is gone—same thing
> as being dead.[1]

In another poem in the collection, Dubrow again touches on the issue of sexual fidelity. 'In Penelope's Bedroom' finds her subject in the room which still echoes with the memories of her absent husband, their marital bed with an empty space where he used to lie:

---

[1] Dubrow (2010, p. 27).

Warriors' Wives: Ancient Greek Myth and Modern Experience. Emma Bridges, Oxford University Press.
© Emma Bridges 2023. DOI: 10.1093/oso/9780198843528.003.0005

> The right side of the bed must stay
> his side. She slips into her negligee,
> as if she's still dressing for him.[2]

Dubrow's words sit within a tradition stretching back to the *Odyssey* in which, alongside the idealized image of the archetypal faithful spouse, there exists the possibility that every waiting wife has both the opportunity and the potential motivation to be unfaithful. This anxiety around possible infidelity surfaces frequently in ancient mythical narratives of the Trojan War, and it endures today both in the first-hand accounts of military couples and in fictionalized versions of such relationships.

This chapter addresses the issue of spousal infidelity by focusing first on the figure of Penelope in the *Odyssey*. Despite cementing her reputation as an exemplar of wifely virtue the epic acknowledges that Penelope's fidelity is by no means assured; I consider how this relates to enduring anxiety around female adultery in the context of modern conflicts. This anxiety is connected both with the question of the reliability of the waiting wife herself and with concerns about 'predatory' men who, like the suitors of the *Odyssey*, may seize the opportunity to seduce an absent soldier's wife. In both modern and ancient contexts, however, there exists a gendered double standard around the issue of infidelity, and I consider how this influences the representation of soldiers—including Odysseus—who betray their wives. The remainder of this chapter focuses predominantly on the character of Clytemnestra in the ancient mythical tradition. Often represented as Penelope's opposite, Clytemnestra is not only sexually unfaithful to her husband Agamemnon but commits the ultimate betrayal by killing him on his return home. I examine Aeschylus' tragic representation of Clytemnestra's infidelity, which is just one aspect of her failure to adhere to appropriate gendered norms for the respectable wife of an absent soldier. I then briefly consider the characterization of Clytemnestra by later tragedians, and the ways in which they frame her adultery as a motive for the murder of Agamemnon. The double standards which existed in ancient representations of male and female infidelity have proved to be astonishingly tenacious; I identify in the course of my discussion the persistence of the

---

[2] Dubrow (2010, p. 35). On the significance of the bed as a symbol in the *Odyssey*, see below, p. 150.

Clytemnestra-figure in modern-day misogynistic stereotypes of unfaithful military wives, and in the worries which serving soldiers still carry concerning their partners' potential infidelity.

To stay or to stray? Penelope's dilemma

> We made vows and he didn't keep them. He loved me but he didn't honor me. How could he? He barely noticed me. That's what drove me to it. I cheated on him while he was deployed, while he was serving our country, blah blah blah. It's all I ever heard about, honestly. When he was home, that's all anyone wanted to talk about, his career. When he was gone, it was even worse. He was *always* the hero. Even though I took care of everything in our lives it was always, *always* about him.[3]

In this extract from an anonymous blogpost with the title 'I'm A Woman Who Cheated On Her Deployed Husband, This is Why I Did It', the author shares her thoughts on her own infidelity. This reflection on the subordination of her own identity to that of a heroized soldier husband calls to mind the stories of some of the women—including the mythical Penelope—whom I introduced in my earlier chapters. The anonymous author's own feelings of invisibility in her relationship with a military 'hero' are clear throughout the blogpost; she concludes by saying that it was not the distance between them, or the fact that he was away for so long, which led her to be unfaithful, but instead, 'It was that he took my identity away from me. He made me into His Wife instead of my own person.' The affair seems to have provided her with the opportunity to reclaim a part of herself. Of course this highly personal account of the writer's own relationships reflects just one woman's experience; the motivations for being unfaithful may vary considerably between individuals. There has been little research into the prevalence of infidelity among contemporary military couples as compared with the population at large, and uncovering the first-hand stories of either unfaithful partners or the spouses on whom they have cheated can be very difficult given the culture of silence which often surrounds the topic in

---

[3] Anonymous (2014).

military communities.[4] However, just as in ancient literary texts, modern fictionalized representations of military marriages often draw on deep-seated fears of serving soldiers that their place in the marital bed will be usurped in their absence.[5]

Anxieties concerning infidelity have been a recurring element of discourse surrounding solders' wives ever since the Homeric epics were composed. As discussed at length in the Chapter 3, Penelope is immortalized in the *Odyssey* as the faithful partner of Odysseus and protector of his household and his good name during his long absence. Yet there is also a recognition in the ancient mythological tradition that the loyalty of even this exemplary wife was not guaranteed.[6] The persistent presence of the suitors in Odysseus' palace also reminds the audience that a wife rendered temporarily husbandless by a military campaign has ample opportunity and, particularly in the case of Penelope—ignorant as she is of her husband's fate—the potential incentive to be unfaithful. In Penelope's case there is also a social imperative to remarry, as the patriarchal structure of her society expects that a household will have a man at its head. Indeed, it is likely that alternative versions of the story of Odysseus' homecoming existed in which the hero returned to discover that his wife had been unfaithful, and that the *Odyssey* hints at these traditions; several later references to the figure of Penelope also allude to this possibility.[7]

The suggestion that Penelope might imminently succumb to one of the suitors is present throughout the poem, and never more so than when she (as yet unaware that Odysseus is back on Ithaca) announces her intention to marry whichever man is able to string Odysseus' bow. When she appears

[4] Kachadourian et al. (2015), London et al. (2012), and Snyder et al. (2012) are rare recent examples of scholarly work focusing specifically on infidelity in couples where at least one partner is, or has been, a member of the military. See also Boorstein (2012) and Fisher (1997).
[5] One recent example of this preoccupation is the US television drama *Army Wives*, which aired over seven series from 2007 to 2013, and which delves several times into the theme of spousal infidelity. See Vavrus (2013) and Cohler (2017). Thematically, the opening season of the drama *Homeland* (first aired in 2011) plays out a scenario similar to that envisaged in the *Odyssey*, where the wife of the central character is unsure whether her husband is alive or dead. *Homeland*'s central character, Marine Sergeant Nicholas Brody, has been missing in action for eight years; when he returns home his wife Jessica has begun a relationship with his friend and fellow Marine, Mike Faber.
[6] Zeitlin (1996, pp. 19–52) remains the most detailed and eloquent analysis of the theme of fidelity in the *Odyssey*; she notes (p. 29), however, that 'There are no precise terms in Homer either for sexual adultery or for marital fidelity.'
[7] See, for example, Apollodorus, *Epitome* 7.38. Gilchrist (1997) discusses at length alternative versions of Penelope's story and provides at pp. 329–32 a list of ancient references to her infidelity.

before the suitors to make this announcement, we are told, 'Their knees gave way, their hearts were bewitched with desire [ἔρῳ δ' ἄρα θυμὸν ἔθελχθεν], and they all prayed that they might lie in bed with her' (18.212–14). Penelope uses the suitors' lust for her in order to extract from them the promise of gifts as compensation for devouring the resources of Odysseus' household (18.274–303). Paradoxically, her desirability enables her to increase the wealth of the *oikos* (household) yet at the same time it brings the threat that Odysseus' rightful place at the head of his *oikos* will be usurped.[8] The poem as a whole is also haunted by the shadow of another infamous Trojan War homecoming, that of Agamemnon, which I will discuss at length later in this chapter and further in Chapter 5. The very first speech of the *Odyssey*, relayed by an authority no less powerful than Zeus, father of gods and men, refers to this infamous example, in which Aegisthus, despite warnings from the gods, had seduced Agamemnon's wife Clytemnestra and later paid the price when Agamemnon's son Orestes took revenge (1.35–43).

Throughout the poem there is a tension between Penelope's desire to remain faithful to Odysseus—as illustrated by the lengths to which she goes with the shroud trick—and the possibility that she might embark on a new relationship in his absence. This tension is also reflected in repeated allusions which connect Penelope with the goddesses Artemis and Aphrodite. In the Homeric poems and elsewhere, Artemis is associated with chastity and Aphrodite with sexuality, and the two often operate in conflict with one another.[9] Immediately prior to Penelope's appearance before the suitors in Book 18, the poet tells us that Athena beautified her, using an immortal balm like that used by 'fair-crowned Cytherea' (18.193). The term refers to Aphrodite, named as such after her legendary birthplace off the shore of the island of Cythera. Yet, only a few lines later, Penelope, on waking from the sleep induced by Athena, offers a short prayer to Artemis in which she expresses her wish that the goddess would bring her death, rather than a life spent 'longing for my dear husband, who was excellent in all virtues, and

[8] This paradox is also highlighted at 18.161–2 where the poet suggests that her appearance before the suitors will make Penelope 'become more honoured than before in the eyes of her husband and son'.

[9] The polarizing of the two goddesses' spheres of influence in relation to chastity and sexuality would later be exploited to great effect in the plot of Euripides' *Hippolytus*. As with all elements of Greek religious belief there is, however, far greater complexity in the representation of any divinity than drawing a straightforward dichotomy between these two figures might imply. For a wider-ranging insight into the figure of Artemis, see Budin (2016); on the representation of Aphrodite, see Cyrino (2010).

who was outstanding among the Achaeans' (πόσιος ποθέουσα φίλοιο, /
παντοίην ἀρετήν, ἐπεὶ ἔξοχος ἦεν Ἀχαιῶν, 18.204–5). In a scene where the
waiting wife is set up to play the seducer to her would-be lovers, this explicit
reference to her marital fidelity—reinforced by the association with the
goddess of chastity—reminds us of the dilemma with which she continues
to wrestle. The conflicting association of Penelope with both Artemis and
Aphrodite appears elsewhere in the poem too. Twice she is referred to as
'looking like Artemis or golden Aphrodite' (Ἀρτέμιδι ἰκέλη ἠὲ χρυσέη
Ἀφροδίτῃ), once when she greets Telemachus on his return from his fact-
finding voyage (17.37), and again shortly before she has her first conversation with the disguised Odysseus in the palace (19.54). She later prays again
to Artemis (20.60–90), asking once more for death, this time as a way of
avoiding remarriage. This invocation, however, also refers to the mythical
tale of the orphaned daughters of Pandareus, in which Aphrodite plays a
key role (the goddess attempts unsuccessfully to intercede with Zeus in
order to secure marriage for Pandareus' daughters).[10]

Within the wider context of the Trojan War narrative, audiences familiar
with the story would also recall the role which Aphrodite played in the
adulterous liaison which sparked the chain of events leading to the conflict.
Aphrodite's bribe of the Trojan Paris with the promise of Penelope's cousin
Helen (who was already married to Menelaus) as a prize for declaring her
the fairest goddess led to perhaps the most well-known act of adultery in
the ancient Greek mythic repertoire. Thus, while Penelope herself seems
keen to align herself with Artemis, allusions to Aphrodite also draw attention to the fact that her fidelity to Odysseus is not yet assured.[11] Penelope
herself also seems to acknowledge this, if somewhat indirectly. After
her eventual reunion with Odysseus—which I will discuss at length in
Chapter 5—Penelope reflects on the story of Helen, whom she says would
never have taken a foreign lover (Paris) if she had known that the Achaean
warriors would eventually bring her back home (23.218–24). Penelope
remarks that Helen's transgression was incited by a god, reminding the
audience once more of the instrumental role of Aphrodite, goddess of sexual desire, in the overarching plot of the Trojan War narrative. The potential

[10] For an analysis of this prayer which considers it in relation to the interplay of Artemis
and Aphrodite in the character of Penelope, see Felson-Rubin (1996, pp. 179–82). See also
Felson (1994, pp. 36–7).
[11] The *Odyssey* tells a tale too of Aphrodite's own adultery with Ares, and the humiliating
revenge carried out by her husband Hephaestus, in the song sung by Demodocus among the
Phaeacians (8.266–366).

comparison between Penelope and Helen is heightened if the audience recalls that when we first meet Helen in the *Odyssey* she, like Penelope, is compared by the poet to Artemis (4.122), although Helen herself recalls the role of Aphrodite in tempting her to stray from her home and her husband to be with another man (4.261–4).[12] Helen's story—like that of her sister Clytemnestra, whom I will discuss in more detail later in this chapter—casts Penelope's fidelity into sharp relief.

Penelope's situation in the *Odyssey* highlights two key sources of unease for a soldier who might be concerned about his wife's potential infidelity. One is the presence of the suitors, predatory males who are poised to take the absent husband's place in his bed and in his household. The other is the question of the trustworthiness of the waiting wife herself. It is this latter which predominates in ancient representations of mythical waiting wives, and which will occupy the majority of my discussion in this chapter. However, the threat posed by men who might seize the opportunity to seduce lone wives and appropriate the material possessions of troops on active duty is also a concern which modern discourse relating to armed conflict has in common with ancient war narratives. In the Second World War, for example, large numbers of women were left behind in Britain as their partners departed to serve abroad at a time when attitudes towards sex were gradually becoming more permissive. Anxiety about the presence of predatory men back home—in this case, other servicemen, stationed in Britain from the US—peaked during this time. As Sokoloff reflects:

> A veritable epidemic of worry about the fidelity of wives and sweethearts swept British society in 1943 and 1944 as the size of the US forces in the United Kingdom grew before D-Day. Rumour had it that the D-Day invasion was welcomed by British soldiers in the Middle and Far East not because it brought the defeat of Germany nearer but because it removed predatory foreign servicemen from British shores.[13]

Relatedly, a recurring character in US military marching chants (which are sometimes known as 'Jody calls') is the generic figure known as 'Jody',

---

[12] On the representation of Helen and her relationship with Menelaus in the *Odyssey*, see in particular Suzuki (1989, pp. 62–70), Doherty (1995, pp. 130–5), and Worman (2001).

[13] Sokoloff (1999, p. 38), discussing worries about infidelity in the wider context of the effect of the Second World War on marriage and gender roles. On the effect of the war on marital relationships, see also Braybon and Summerfield (1987, pp. 205–18).

who represents men who prey on the wives and girlfriends of absent soldiers:

> Ain't no use in callin' home.
> Jody's on your telephone.
>
> Ain't no use in lookin' back.
> Jody's got your Cadillac.
>
> Ain't no use in goin' home.
> Jody's got your girl and gone.
>
> Ain't no use in feelin' blue.
> Jody's got your sister too.[14]

In recent popular culture, the 'Jody' trope recurs particularly memorably in the 2005 movie *Jarhead*, which follows a US Marine during the Gulf War. In one scene the troops assemble to watch a VHS tape of the Vietnam movie *Deer Hunter*; a few seconds in, the tape cuts to a home movie in which the wife of one of the Marines is seen having sex with his neighbour. *Jarhead* is notable for its dearth of female characters and its focus on the male perspective throughout, so it is no surprise that this is a one-dimensional portrayal of the unfaithful wife. The movie dwells elsewhere too on the theme of spousal infidelity; the protagonist Anthony 'Swoff' Swofford's girlfriend cheats on him while he is away, and the troops also set up a bulletin board, or 'Jody wall', detailing their partners' infidelities. Like Penelope's suitors in the *Odyssey* (and, as I shall discuss later in this chapter, Clytemnestra's lover Aegisthus), the Jody-character represents a persistent fear that a soldier on detachment away from home cannot be assured of his partner's fidelity. As Burns notes in his discussion of military marching chants, however, a deployed soldier 'is every bit as likely to cheat on his sweetheart as she is to cheat on him, [so] perhaps Jody calls function not just as laments but also as projections, that is, transfers onto another of one's own sins'.[15] Yet in the discourse surrounding infidelity in military couples, soldiers who stray when on active duty tend to be judged far less harshly than unfaithful waiting wives. In the next section I examine the persistence of these gendered double standards, considering soldiers' infidelity as exemplified by the exploits of Odysseus.

---

[14] Quoted by Burke (1989, p. 431).   [15] Burns (2012, p. 87).

Unfaithful soldiers and sexual double standards

Although in contemporary society the domestic relationships of military couples rarely attract the attention of the wider public, occasionally a news story breaks which turns the spotlight onto the home lives of soldiers and their partners. One such high profile case in 2002 revolved around a series of brutal murders of army wives killed by their husbands on a US military base at Fort Bragg in North Carolina. Journalist Tanya Biank conducted a detailed investigation of the cases and subsequently spent time researching the lives of women who were married to US Army personnel. Reporting on the murder of Jennifer Wright by her soldier husband, Bill Wright, who had suspected her of infidelity, Biank drew attention to the sexual double standard by which adultery was judged. She observed that sympathy among the military community lay overwhelmingly not with the murdered woman but with the husband on whom she was alleged to have cheated:

> More than a few soldiers who either knew the Wrights or had heard about the case later told me, 'She got what she deserved.' Or 'She had it comin'.' These quick-trigger outbursts (they were never said casually) always caught me off-guard. To understand the root of such venom, I had to take a step back and realize that these men identified more with Bill Wright the patriot, Bill Wright the war vet and family man, than they did with his supposedly cheating wife. An unfaithful Army wife might as well be a terrorist, soldiers hate them that much. Soldiers tend to consider infidelity a personal slight on their own manhood. When a woman cheats on a buddy, she is desecrating not only her husband but also the flag and all those in uniform. Of course none of this applies when soldiers cheat on their wives.[16]

Biank's reflection here that military personnel are judged by different standards than those applied to their wives when it comes it infidelity is striking. One recent study of a small group of military wives suggests that in some cases the women themselves internalize such double standards, with some

---

[16] Biank (2006, pp. 2–3). The Fort Bragg killings led to much speculation in the media as to the psychological effects of service in a war zone and the higher rate of domestic violence among military as compared with civilian populations. See, for example, Lutz and Elliston (2002).

seeing unfaithful husbands as absolved of guilt, and instead seeing the men as 'victims of women's promiscuity'.[17]

The notion that male soldiers should be exonerated for infidelities committed when stationed away from home has also been perpetuated historically by military institutions themselves. As Hopkins observes in a study of the legal implications of infidelity in the US military, in some cases the military has encouraged a culture in which infidelity on operational detachment is an accepted part of life:

> Historically, the military has been anything but a haven of chasteness and virtue. The sexual exploits of service men when on leave overseas are legendary. Particularly when overseas, but also in some officers' clubs, the use of 'comfort women', prostitutes, 'hospitality girls', and strippers was and continues to be typical. The military hierarchy both officially and unofficially encouraged this practice as a way of diverting and fulfilling the sexual impulses of sailors.[18]

While military culture permits, or even endorses, a non-condemnatory approach to the infidelity of male service members, it demands that their wives will maintain a different set of moral standards, yet may also be expected to turn a blind eye to their husbands' indiscretions. Key features of the 'Model Military Wife' identified by Enloe are that 'She is sexually faithful', but that, at the same time, 'She accepts that soldier-husbands do not tell their wives everything, so she would think it neither worthwhile nor appropriate to ask her husband about clandestine missions or about any sexual activity he might engage in while away from home'.[19]

This sexual double standard relating to spousal infidelity plays out in the ancient narrative of the *Odyssey* too. As we saw earlier, the question of Penelope's loyalty to her absent husband is a key concern throughout the text, and there is a clear sense that she will be judged by posterity as a shining example. In heaping praise upon her for her fidelity to Odysseus, the

---

[17] Murray (2011, p. 51).

[18] Hopkins (1999, pp. 248–9). Hopkins goes on to note that, for example, during wars in Vietnam and Korea, it was not unusual for men with spouses back home to have ongoing relationships with women (referred to as a 'temporary duty wives') while abroad. The euphemistic term 'comfort women' originated during World War II with the Japanese imperial army's system of enforced prostitution that was intended to bolster soldiers' morale. See Enloe (2014, pp. 160–1).

[19] Enloe (2000, p. 164). On Enloe's 'Model Military Wife' see also p. 9, p. 48, and p. 90 above.

ghost of Agamemnon declares that 'the fame (*kleos*) of her virtue will never die' (τῷ οἱ κλέος οὔ ποτ᾽ ὀλεῖται / ἧς ἀρετῆς, 24.196–7).[20] By contrast, when the Ithacan islanders are led to believe that Penelope has succumbed to marrying one of the suitors, they had judged her to be 'merciless' or 'unflinching' (σχετλίη) for failing to hold out until her husband's return (23.149–51). In contrast, Odysseus' own infidelities pass without judgement in the text. Throughout the poem he is repeatedly tempted by the various women whom he encounters in the course of his journey home. He is detained en route by Calypso and Circe, both of them divine characters endowed with magical powers.[21] Calypso rescued Odysseus from a shipwreck before he became her lover and, after his seven-year stay with her on Ogygia, we find him becoming increasingly eager to resume his journey. From our first encounter with Odysseus in the poem he is frequently described as longing for home, weeping and looking at the sea (1.13–15, 4.555–60, 5.13–17, 5.81–4; cf. 17.142–6 and 23.333–7), and later he relates to the Phaeacians that, despite the promise of immortality, Calypso was unable to win him over (7.255–60). The poet confirms, however, albeit only in passing, that, even if he is no longer willing, there was once a time when Odysseus did desire his divine captor. When Calypso goes to deliver the news that, on Zeus' orders, she will help Odysseus on his way, the poet reports that she finds him lamenting, 'since the nymph no longer pleased him' (ἐπεὶ οὐκέτι ἥνδανε νύμφη, 5.153). The force of the Greek οὐκέτι, translated here as 'no longer', implies that Odysseus was once receptive to her passion for him, and suggests too that there was a willingness on his part to be unfaithful to his wife. Similarly, the nymph Circe enchants men with sensory pleasures, beguiling them with the sound of her voice, food, wine, and the drugs she administers in order to transform them into pigs (10.220–43). While Odysseus is initially able to resist these temptations because of a preventative drug, moly, which was supplied to him by Hermes, Circe nonetheless tempts him into her bed. He rejects her advances only until she swears not to do him harm (10.333–47), then enjoys the comfort of her bed and her hospitality for a full year until he asks for her to fulfil her promise to help him on his way.

---

[20] I discuss the comparison which is made with Agamemnon's wife Clytemnestra here in more detail below at p. 118.

[21] Shay (2002, pp. 65–75) suggests that the *Odyssey*'s depiction of Odysseus' relationships can be used as a way of thinking about Vietnam veterans' mistrust of women; at pp. 113–19 he considers the Calypso episode in relation to the sexual promiscuity of some veterans.

When Odysseus recounts his own version of his journey, first to the Phaeacians (9.28-36, referring to Circe as well as Calypso) and later to Penelope (23.333-7, reported as indirect speech by the poet), he makes no mention of having succumbed to desire. Instead he glosses these episodes and absolves himself of any responsibility for infidelity by emphasizing the scheming nature of the goddesses (23.321: 'he told of Circe's trickery and supreme cunning', καὶ Κίρκης κατέλεξε δόλον πολυμηχανίην τε), and relating that he was held against his will by Calypso, who 'was never able to persuade the heart in his breast' (ἀλλὰ τοῦ οὔ ποτε θυμὸν ἐνὶ στήθεσσιν ἔπειθεν, 23.337; the language here echoes his description to the Phaeacians of his resistance to Circe at 9.33). On recounting to the Phaeacians his liaisons with Circe and Calypso, Odysseus describes his yearning to return to Ithaca, citing a desire to see his own land and his parents as being at the root of his longing for home (9.28, 9.34-6), yet omitting to mention his wife and child. It is possible that this is also a way of leaving the door open for a relationship with the Phaeacian princess Nausicaa, daughter of Alcinous and Arete.

Nausicaa represents the final temptation of infidelity for Odysseus on his journey home. In need of her help to continue with his journey, when he first meets the princess he flatters her with comments on her attractive appearance; in fact he suggests at 6.150-2 that she looks like the goddess Artemis, to whom Penelope is, as noted earlier, also compared. He also reflects on Nausicaa's marriageability (6.158-60) before expressing a wish that the gods grant her 'all that your heart desires; may they give you a husband and a household and great likemindedness' (ὅσα φρεσὶ σῇσι μενοινᾷς, / ἄνδρα τε καὶ οἶκον καὶ ὁμοφροσύνην ὀπάσειαν / ἐσθλήν, 6.180-2). The description, with its emphasis on homophrosunē (translated here as 'likemindedness') is one which might well apply to Odysseus' own marriage to Penelope. Nausicaa later confides to her slaves that she wishes she could marry a man like him (6.244-5) before suggesting to Odysseus that, if they see her with him, the locals may gossip that he must be her future husband (6.273-84). Later her father also suggests that, should he wish to stay, Odysseus would make a fine husband for Nausicaa (7.311-15). On this occasion Odysseus resists in order to continue with his quest for home, and to return to his own wife, yet the story acts as another reminder in the poem that opportunities for infidelity present themselves to a husband unaccompanied by his wife, just as they do for the wife who is left behind.

When Odysseus returns to Ithaca, there is no direct indication from Penelope that she suspects him of having had lovers during their long separation. After all, she cannot know what the audience of the poem knows.

Penelope fulfils the role of Enloe's 'Model Military Wife' by not asking about her husband's sexual relationships, and in turn Odysseus is selective in what he tells her about his exploits.[22] The poem does, however, allow for multiple interpretations of Penelope's inner thoughts, with the result that many writers since Homer have sought to imagine what her emotions might be in relation to Odysseus. Consequently it is often in the later receptions of her character (from Ovid's first-century-BCE *Heroides* on, up to present-day reworkings, including Margaret Atwood's 2005 novel *The Penelopiad*, one of the most in-depth recent fictional explorations of Penelope's psychology) where we find Penelopes who express their suspicions, and often their anger or sorrow, at the thought of Odysseus' infidelity.[23] If, however, Odysseus remains uncensured in the *Odyssey* for his indiscretions while his wife's loyalty is subject to scrutiny, nowhere are the sexual double standards applied to soldiers and their wives more apparent than in the story of Clytemnestra and Agamemnon. Clytemnestra becomes, in the ancient mythical tradition from Homer on, the ultimate unfaithful spouse, acting as a warning about what might happen at home when a man departs for war. It is the relationship of Clytemnestra and Agamemnon—first in the *Odyssey*, and then in the tragic dramas of fifth-century-BCE Athens—which is my main focus for the remainder of this chapter.

Wives who will not wait

> Nick stopped at the threshold. There was his wife and there was a stranger sleeping next to her. Trish's face was tilted toward the door, a bare arm trailing off the bed, the toes of one pale foot poking out from the sheet, just as Nick had imagined her, night after night. The man was turned away, his back a wall, his head half hidden by a pillow, anonymous.[24]

Siobhan Fallon's short story 'Liberty', one of the pieces in her 2011 collection *You Know When the Men Are Gone*, tells the story of Nick, who suspects that his wife has been unfaithful while he has been serving in Iraq. In an elaborate deception, Nick returns home on leave without telling his wife

---

[22] On Enloe's 'Model Military Wife', see above, p. 9, p. 48, p. 90, and p. 111.
[23] See further Hall (2008, pp. 120–9) for a discussion of some of these later literary reinterpretations of the character of Penelope.
[24] Fallon (2011, p. 186).

so that he can hide out in the basement of their home for several days until he is able to confirm his suspicions. The story ends with the scene above, with Nick holding a knife, having discovered his wife and her lover in bed together; the reader never finds out whether he will use the knife on one or both of the adulterous partners, or if he will instead turn it on himself. The story is just one of countless examples of the theme of the 'cheating wife' which surfaces time and again in fictionalized retellings of military relationships. The protagonist of the opening short story of Phil Klay's collection *Redeployment*, for example, reflects on the fact that for some of his comrades there was no happy reunion on their return home from Iraq: 'I saw Lance Corporal Curtis's wife back in Jacksonville. She spent all his combat pay before he got back, and she was five months pregnant, which, for a Marine coming back from a seven-month deployment, is not pregnant enough.'[25] Unfaithful wives such as these—appearing in works of fiction, yet derived from the authors' lived experiences as, respectively, an army wife and a US Marine—play out the fears of modern-day military personnel about what might occur at home while they are deployed elsewhere.

The ancient mythical predecessor to these unfaithful contemporary military spouses is the figure of Clytemnestra who, as the 'the extreme case of the wife who will not wait',[26] would become notorious for her transgressions. In the *Odyssey* Clytemnestra, wife of the Greek military commander Agamemnon, acts as the most powerful counter-example to the faithfulness of the waiting Penelope. Like Penelope, Clytemnestra was left behind by her husband when he departed for the Trojan War; unlike Penelope, however, she took another man into her bed. As noted earlier, a comparison between the two wives—as the ideal and her antitype—is made at the very start of the *Odyssey*, where Zeus muses on the betrayal and murder of Agamemnon (1.35–43). Clytemnestra is not yet named, but Zeus reflects that 'Aegisthus courted—beyond his destiny—the wife of Atreus' son, and killed him when he returned home' (1.35–6); he goes on to say that these actions were later avenged by Orestes' killing of Aegisthus. In Zeus's version, the blame for the transgression is placed on the shoulders of Aegisthus, who plays the part of the wife-stealing 'Jody-figure' whom we encountered earlier as a despicable character in modern-day military idiom.

The story of Agamemnon's homecoming as it is told in the *Odyssey* seems to serve primarily to uphold Orestes, Agamemnon's avenging son, as a positive example for Odysseus' son Telemachus to follow, and to illustrate

---

[25] Klay (2014, pp. 9–10).   [26] Felson and Slatkin (2004, p. 108 n. 52).

the dangers which Odysseus may face on his return home.²⁷ As a result, the *Odyssey* spends far less time on Clytemnestra's role than the retellings in Athenian tragedy which I will discuss in subsequent sections of this chapter. Clytemnestra is mentioned again in the third book of the *Odyssey*, when Telemachus, visiting Pylos to seek news of his father, hears from the aged warrior Nestor tales of the return of the Achaeans from Troy. Nestor's account again suggests that Aegisthus, Clytemnestra's lover, was responsible for Agamemnon's murder. He focuses on the vengeance wrought by Orestes, with the implication that this is an example for Telemachus to follow: 'Aegisthus paid terribly. So it's good for a man who has died to leave behind a son, as [Orestes] took revenge on his father's killer, crafty Aegisthus, who killed his renowned father' (3.195–8). There is no mention yet of Clytemnestra's involvement in the betrayal of Agamemnon, although shortly afterwards Athena places the blame for Agamemnon's murder equally upon both the unfaithful wife and her lover, describing Agamemnon as having been 'destroyed by the plot/trick (δόλῳ) of Aegisthus and of his own wife' (3.235). It is in Nestor's subsequent and more detailed account of the return of Agamemnon (3.254–312) where Clytemnestra is first named (3.266); she is said by Nestor initially to have resisted Aegisthus' advances, in part 'because she had good sense' (φρεσὶ γὰρ κέχρητ' ἀγαθῇσι, 3.266). The vocabulary used here is later echoed by the ghost of Agamemnon in his description of Penelope, when he praises her 'good sense' (ἀγαθαὶ φρένες, 24.194) as well as her virtue and her loyalty to Odysseus;²⁸ there is a reminder, then, that any waiting wife might have the potential to be unfaithful. Nestor recalls too that Agamemnon had left a bard in the palace to watch over her (3.266–7).²⁹ Nonetheless, in accordance with 'the gods' fate' (μοῖρα θεῶν, 271) Clytemnestra did yield 'willingly' (ἐθέλουσαν, 3.272) when Aegisthus removed the guardian to a remote island. In this case the adultery was only the start of a disastrous outcome for Agamemnon; subsequently Aegisthus would plot his murder (3.303). The internal narrators of the *Odyssey* do not give one consistent view of the extent to which Clytemnestra was to blame for the death of Agamemnon; in contrast with later texts produced by the Athenian tragic dramatists, her role as his killer is not at the forefront here.³⁰

---

²⁷ Goldhill (1992, pp. 46–53).

²⁸ On Agamemnon's description of Penelope here see also p. 101 above.

²⁹ This detail calls to mind accounts of absent husbands charging other male relatives with keeping an eye on their wives during the Second World War: see Sokoloff (1999, p. 42).

³⁰ Like Nestor, Menelaus—in the account of Agamemnon's homecoming which he says was related to him by Proteus, Old Man of the Sea—suggests that the plan was all Aegisthus', making

What does become significant in the *Odyssey*, however, is the way in which—just as Penelope becomes the supreme example of a virtuous wife—Clytemnestra is upheld as a negative exemplar. Moreover, there is a clear message that the example set by Clytemnestra will affect how other women will be judged in future. When Agamemnon's ghost relates to Odysseus the story of his own murder at the hands of Aegisthus 'with my accursed wife's help' (σὺν οὐλομένῃ ἀλόχῳ, 11.410),[31] he reflects, 'There is nothing more horrible nor more shameless [αἰνότερον καὶ κύντερον] than a woman who can plan deeds like this in her heart, like this shameful deed that she plotted: the murder of her wedded husband' (11.427–30). Agamemnon concludes his account by saying that, with her extreme wickedness, Clytemnestra 'has poured shame not only on herself but also over all future generations of women, even those who are virtuous' (οἵ τε κατ' αἶσχος ἔχευε καὶ ἐσσομένῃσιν ὀπίσσω / θηλυτέρῃσι γυναιξί, καὶ ἥ κ' ἐνεργὸς ἔῃσιν, 11.432–4). There appears to be an awareness here on the part of the poet that mythical narratives shape ideology; the notoriety of this one extreme paradigm will, Agamemnon suggests, tarnish the reputation of all women. Penelope remains here as the counter-example to Clytemnestra's wickedness, although even she becomes an object of suspicion in light of Agamemnon's experience. Agamemnon urges Odysseus to proceed with caution on his return home, suggesting that he should not be overly kind to his wife, and should hold back from disclosing all of his thoughts to her (11.441–3). This warning might be seen, in part, to lie behind Odysseus' initial reluctance to reveal his true identity to Penelope on his return home.[32] Agamemnon does go on, however, to note that Penelope is unlikely to murder Odysseus, 'for the daughter of Icarius, thoughtful Penelope, is exceedingly loyal, and knows only good thoughts in her heart' (λίην γὰρ πινυτή τε καὶ εὖ φρεσὶ μήδεα οἶδε / κούρη Ἰκαρίοιο, περίφρων Πηνελόπεια, 11.445–6).[33]

---

no mention at all of Clytemnestra (4.518–37); by contrast, however, the ghost of Agamemnon seems to suggest that both Clytemnestra and her lover were equally responsible for his death (11.409–10, 11.429–34, 24.96–7). On the ways in which the varying stories of Agamemnon's death function in the *Odyssey*, see Olson (1990). Sommerstein (2012, pp. 136–45) compares the variant versions of this story as it is told in other surviving textual sources.

[31] This is also the only point in the *Odyssey* at which Agamemnon mentions Cassandra, whom he says Clytemnestra also killed (11.421–3). It is only in the later surviving versions of the story where more detail about the role and death of Cassandra—newly enslaved and brought back from Troy by Agamemnon as a war captive—is provided.

[32] I discuss the reunion of Odysseus and Penelope in depth in Chapter 5.

[33] Note, however, Felson-Rubin (1996), demonstrating that the representation of Penelope in the *Odyssey* is more complex than the description given by Agamemnon's ghost would suggest. On the complexities of Penelope's character, see also Marquardt (1985).

Agamemnon's ghost also reiterates this comparison between the virtuous, loyal wife and her opposite in the poem's final book, where he heaps praise on Penelope before declaring that 'the fame (*kleos*) of her virtue will never die, and the immortals will make for mortals a beautiful song for prudent Penelope' (τῷ οἱ κλέος οὔ ποτ' ὀλεῖται / ἧς ἀρετῆς, τεύξουσι δ' ἐπιχθονίοισιν ἀοιδὴν / ἀθάνατοι χαρίεσσαν ἐχέφρονι Πηνελοπείη, 24.196–8).[34] By contrast, Clytemnestra 'killed her wedded husband' (κουρίδιον κτείνασα πόσιν, 24.200) and as a result her 'song among men will be hateful, and she will leave women with a terrible reputation, even those who are virtuous' (στυγερὴ δέ τ' ἀοιδὴ / ἔσσετ' ἐπ' ἀνθρώπους, χαλεπὴν δέ τε φῆμιν ὀπάσσει / θηλυτέρῃσι γυναιξί, καὶ ἥ κ' εὐεργὸς ἔῃσιν, 24.200–2). His concluding line here is an exact repetition of his earlier words at 11.434 about Clytemnestra's effect on how other women will be perceived in future. Subsequent ancient retellings of Clytemnestra's story would cement her notoriety, reinforcing the negative image of the unfaithful waiting wife, and feeding into—or drawing on—fears about what warriors' wives might be getting up to while their husbands are away from home. Pindar's eleventh Pythian ode of 474 BCE (composed to celebrate a victory at the Pythian Games in that year),[35] for example, hints at the public censure which women who stray from their marriage beds might attract for their misdeeds, and wonders whether Clytemnestra was motivated by her own infidelity or by Agamemnon's killing of their daughter to murder her husband. The poet asks:

> Was it the slaying of Iphigenia at the Euripus, far from her fatherland, which provoked her to raise the heavy hand of her anger? Or was she led astray by nightly lovemaking, seduced by another's bed? That is the most hateful mistake for young brides, and impossible to conceal because of others' tongues.
>
> (*Pythian* 11.22–7)

It was the tragic dramatists of fifth-century-BCE Athens, however, who would explore in the greatest depth the transgressions of this notorious character. The rest of this chapter will focus on these staged versions of Clytemnestra, as retold by Aeschylus, Sophocles, and Euripides.

---

[34] See above, pp. 77–8 and p. 92, on the ways in which Penelope's *kleos* is referred to elsewhere in the *Odyssey*.

[35] For a discussion of the possible reasoning behind the poet's choice of the Clytemnestra myth here, see Instone (1986).

Aeschylus' Clytemnestra

The story of Clytemnestra has enjoyed a particularly rich afterlife, thanks largely to the attention which Aeschylus gave to her relationship with Agamemnon in his 458 BCE trilogy, the *Oresteia* (comprising the tragedies *Agamemnon*, *Choephoroi*, and *Eumenides*). As discussed in Chapter 2, Agamemnon's sacrifice of his and Clytemnestra's daughter Iphigenia for the sake of pursuing war against Troy might represent metaphorically the challenges faced by couples when the demands of the military take precedence over those of a soldier's partner and family. This mythical marriage, as scrutinized by Athenian tragic dramatists, can also be read as an extreme manifestation of the fears of troops on active service that their place at home might be filled by another man in their absence. In Chapter 5 I will analyse in detail the representation of Agamemnon's return as a distortion of the normal processes of reunion between returning husband and waiting wife; there I will explore further Clytemnestra's refusal to relinquish her role as head of the household, and consider how this relates to her transgression of gendered norms. For now, however, I consider the way in which infidelity is represented in the *Agamemnon*, and in particular how Aeschylus draws here on the Homeric comparison between Clytemnestra and Penelope. In this play—in contrast with tragedies by Sophocles and Euripides, which I will discuss briefly later in this chapter—Clytemnestra's relationship with Aegisthus is given less weight as a motive for murder than her desire to take revenge for Agamemnon's sacrifice of their daughter Iphigenia. For Aeschylus, Clytemnestra's infidelity is just one element of this waiting wife's transgression of societal norms, and of her failure to behave as a warrior's wife should. I will also consider in this section what the *Agamemnon* suggests about Clytemnestra's perspective on her husband's extramarital relationship with Cassandra, the war captive with whom he has returned home.

Although infidelity is not cast here as the primary motivation for the murder of Agamemnon, the shadow of Clytemnestra's adultery is present throughout Aeschylus' *Agamemnon*. The watchman comments in his opening speech that Agamemnon's house is 'not tended very well as in the past' (οὐχ ὡς τὰ πρόσθ' ἄριστα διαπονουμένου, 19; cf. 36–7, where he suggests that he is unable to speak out about the house's troubles); this appears to be an oblique reference to Clytemnestra's behaviour. In his representation of Clytemnestra Aeschylus plays with the image of the good and faithful waiting wife, drawing on the Homeric precedent which sets her up as Penelope's opposite. For example, Clytemnestra's opening words in the play, and her exchange with the chorus, where she expresses joy at the news of Troy's fall (264, 266–7), are duplicitous; the listening chorus cannot yet know that her delight stems from the fact that she can now carry out her plan to kill Agamemnon.[36] She later articulates a response to her husband's homecoming which combines all of the elements that her listeners (the chorus as internal audience, and the spectators in the theatre) might expect from a loyal wife (601–12):

> I'll rush to receive my honoured husband as well as possible on his return. For what dawn is sweeter for a woman to see than when she opens the gates for a man, saved by a god from battle? Take this message to my husband: tell him to come swiftly, his city's darling, come to find at home his loyal wife exactly as he left her [γυναῖκα πιστὴν δ' ἐν δόμοις εὕροι μολὼν / οἵανπερ οὖν ἔλειπε], watchdog of his house, faithful to him, enemy to those who wish him harm, and the same in all other things, having destroyed no seal in all this time. I know no pleasure, nor scandalous rumour, from another man, any more than I know of dipping bronze.

In stressing a waiting wife's joy at seeing her husband arriving home, as well as her eagerness to welcome him back into the palace, Clytemnestra presents an outward image of herself as virtuous wife, a persona which evokes the idealized figure of Penelope. She insists that she has remained faithful to Agamemnon as well as watching over his house and possessions: she is 'exactly as he left her'. Meanwhile the claim that she has 'destroyed no seal' (σημαντήριον / οὐδὲν διαφθείρασαν, 609–10) seems to be a metaphorical reference to chastity, as well as perhaps a reference to not having broken into any of his valuables. Commentators have suggested too that the ambiguous reference to 'dipping bronze', while ostensibly a craft of which she knows nothing, could convey an allusion to her plan to 'dip' a bronze sword in the blood of her husband.[37]

---

[36] See McClure (1999, pp. 70–104), and Foley (2001, pp. 207–34) for detailed discussions of Clytemnestra's use of language, and the ways in which this relates to representations of gender by Aeschylus. Goldhill (1986, pp. 1–32) considers in depth the emphasis placed on the power of language in the *Oresteia*.

[37] There has been much debate among translators and critics as to the precise interpretation of the phrasing here: see Holm (2012) for a detailed discussion. It seems reasonable to infer, with Raeburn and Thomas (2011, commenting on lines 611–12) that 'Agamemnon is to assume that Clytemnestra, like a normal wife, is equally *ignorant* of adultery and metallurgy. But we and the Chorus know about Aegisthus, and thus receive a hint to confirm our suspicion that she has plans for a weapon to be dipped in Agamemnon's blood.'

In contrast with the persona that Clytemnestra creates for herself here—faithful, submissive, eager to welcome back her husband as head of the household—she is revealed in the course of the play as having transgressed the gender boundaries which would be familiar to an audience of fifth-century-BCE Athens. She is the wife who will not wait for her husband to return, not only by failing to remain sexually faithful, but also by taking up, in Agamemnon's absence, the role traditionally reserved for the male head of the household. As a woman Clytemnestra has assumed control because of Agamemnon's absence, and she can now only retain that control by dispensing with him. Ultimately she challenges the established order, both in the domestic sphere and in relation to the wider politics of the city.[38] Our attention is drawn to the reversal of ancient Greek gendered norms from the start of the play, where the watchman reflects that Clytemnestra 'rules thus, (with) a woman's hoping heart which thinks like a man' (ὧδε γὰρ κρατεῖ / γυναικὸς ἀνδρόβουλον ἐλπίζον κέαρ, 10–11). Later, the chorus also point to her assumption of power 'when the throne is empty of a male' (ἐρημωθέντος ἄρσενος θρόνου, 260). Despite the chorus' obvious scepticism that a woman can be relied upon to provide accurate information (they doubt the news of Agamemnon's return, believing women to be susceptible to dreams or rumours, 274–6; cf. 483–7 and 590–4), they also draw attention to Clytemnestra's 'masculine' conduct after she has related the course of the beacon signal which she had arranged as a means of conveying the news of Troy's fall (281–316): 'Woman,' they comment, 'you speak as wisely as a man of good sense' (γύναι, κατ' ἄνδρα σώφρον' εὐφρόνως λέγεις, 351).

Throughout the play, Clytemnestra's deployment of persuasive language, particularly in her interactions with the chorus, as well as in convincing Agamemnon to tread on the garments which she has spread out before him (a scene which I will discuss further in Chapter 5), repeatedly marks her as behaving in a masculinized way. For an audience in ancient Athens, where persuasive rhetoric and public speech (for example, in court or on the political stage) were the preserve of male citizens, this behaviour would run counter to expected norms about women's public discourse.[39] Later too, Cassandra's description of Clytemnestra highlights her 'masculine' behaviour. Cassandra recalls how, when Agamemnon returned home,

---

[38] See Komar (2003, p. 49), suggesting that as she moves from the domestic to the political and public sphere, Clytemnestra 'becomes a distinct liability to all men who would rule'.

[39] McClure (1999, pp. 70–111) discusses in detail the connections between gender and language in the *Oresteia*. See also McClure (1997, p. 140) and Foley (2001, p. 103).

Clytemnestra 'shouted in triumph, the all-daring one, like when the battle turns; yet she seemed to be joyful at his safe return' (1236–8).[40] By using a simile alluding to warfare—a traditionally male sphere of activity—this short description captures concisely the contradiction between the (feminine) persona which Clytemnestra assumes, as the joyful waiting wife, and her contravention of conventional gender boundaries. The Greek term which I have translated as 'the all-daring one' (ἡ παντότολμος) adds to the impression of gender reversal as, while the playwright uses the feminine definite article (ἡ) to refer to Clytemnestra, the ending of the adjectival noun in Greek is masculine, perhaps suggesting that her breed of daring is characteristically male behaviour.[41]

While Clytemnestra is marked out as violating moral and social boundaries, in relation both to her assumption of a traditionally male role and her infidelity to her absent husband, she is at pains in the play to present an image of herself as a Penelope-figure which is at odds with these transgressions. This contrast between the morally upright ideal and her degenerate counterpart becomes particularly apparent when Clytemnestra and Agamemnon meet face-to-face for the first time in the play. The welcome scene is carefully orchestrated by Clytemnestra in such a way as to demonstrate that she now has full control over the situation. Agamemnon's entrance—on a chariot, accompanied by Cassandra[42]—is marked by a speech (810–54) in which, having summarized the destruction of Troy, he outlines his future plans as ruler of Argos (plans which will soon, of course, be thwarted by his wife). He then makes it clear that he expects that he will now enter into the house ('now I will go into the palace hall and household hearth', 851–2); instead, however, it is Clytemnestra who comes out of the palace to greet him. In stepping out of the private domestic space in order to receive Agamemnon in public, Clytemnestra demonstrates that, unlike Penelope, this waiting spouse will not be confined within the traditionally female domain. Clytemnestra then begins her speech not with the affectionate greeting which her husband might expect but with an address to the chorus which suggests that she is performing a political rather than a domestic role: her opening words are, 'Citizen men, elders of Argos'

---

[40] The wording also recalls the chorus' earlier description of Agamemnon as he prepared to sacrifice Iphigenia, when he is described as carrying out τὸ παντότολμον (a thing of 'utmost daring' 221).

[41] For a reflection on some of the ways in which, similarly, contemporary military wives take on roles traditionally conceived of as 'masculine', see above, pp. 90–1.

[42] On the staging of the entrance of Agamemnon and Cassandra, see Taplin (1977, pp. 302–6).

(ἄνδρες πολῖται, πρέσβος Ἀργείων τόδε, 855). She goes on to say that she is not ashamed to talk about her 'man-loving ways' (τοὺς φιλάνορας τρόπους, 856), an ambiguous phrase which might be interpreted either as referring to her love for Agamemnon (the Greek could also be translated as 'husband-loving') or her adulterous relationship with Aegisthus. The speech simultaneously advertises her assumption of power and promotes an image of her as a dutiful wife who has behaved in accordance with convention during her husband's absence. Here Clytemnestra casts herself as a waiting wife tormented by rumours that Agamemnon has come to harm, to the extent that she has considered suicide (859–76).[43] The image is one which mirrors the anguish felt by Penelope in the absence of Odysseus; indeed, Clytemnestra talks of her own weeping as she has lain awake waiting for news of Agamemnon's return (887–94).[44] Of course Clytemnestra's words can be interpreted on two levels: she intends that Agamemnon and the chorus will see her anticipation of news as stemming from concern for her husband's safety, yet of course it will soon transpire that her eagerness for him to come home is a result of her desire to kill him.

That Aeschylus intended his audience to perceive a direct comparison between his Clytemnestra and the Homeric figure of Penelope is reinforced in what follows. Towards the close of this long speech Clytemnestra reports on her relief at Agamemnon's return and makes a series of comparisons which present him as a saviour-figure. There is clear irony in the manner in which Clytemnestra draws attention to Agamemnon's role as protector when all the while she is harbouring long-held resentment over his failure to protect their daughter and his role in her death (895–903):

But now, having endured all these things, my heart free from grief [ἀπενθήτῳ φρενί], I would call this man here the watchdog of the fold, the forestay, preserver of a ship, firm-fixed pillar of a high roof, sole child and heir to a father, and land appearing before sailors past hope, fairest day to see after a storm, the rushing stream to a thirsty traveller—how delightful it is to escape from stress. Such are the greetings with which I honour him.

Here Clytemnestra adopts the role of the very model of a commander's wife, telling Agamemnon what he expects or wants to hear—that he is provider

---

[43] See above, p. 89, on Clytemnestra's report of her wait for news in relation to Penelope's waiting in the *Odyssey*.
[44] On Penelope's sleeplessness and nocturnal weeping, see above, pp. 80–1.

of stability and support—and reinforcing the sense that his absence has left a void in the household. References here to the home (both in terms of its physical structure and family relations) and allusions to images relating to sailing (the sight of land, and respite from a storm) or travelling, are also appropriate for any *nostos* (homecoming) scenario. More than that, however, Clytemnestra's choice of metaphors hints strongly at a direct comparison with Odysseus' return home to Penelope.[45] In particular, the reference to land sighted by sailors calls to mind the reverse simile at *Odyssey* 23.233–40 by which Homer compares Penelope's relief to that of shipwrecked sailors as they reach dry land;[46] and the comparison of Agamemnon to a pillar supporting the roof of a house also perhaps evokes a suggestion of the olive-tree bed, around which Odysseus builds the roof and walls of his bedchamber, so that it forms the focal point both of his home and his relationship with Penelope.[47] There is also, however, a clue that all is not as it seems: Clytemnestra's description of Agamemnon as 'watchdog of the fold' (τῶν σταθμῶν κύνα, 896) reminds us of her earlier reference to her own role as 'watchdog of the house' (δωμάτων κύνα, 607) in Agamemnon's absence. The echo might remind an audience once again that Clytemnestra has usurped the traditional role of the male head of the household.[48]

Even for an audience member not attuned to such allusions to Penelope, her virtuous opposite, with this speech Clytemnestra performs the role of dutiful wife welcoming her husband home from war. The image she presents—of the faithful and emotionally fragile spouse, anxious for news of her absent husband—is one which belies the power which Clytemnestra has assumed in Agamemnon's absence, and her transgression of traditional gender roles within the household. Her words as she welcomes Agamemnon home also call to mind advice given to contemporary military spouses to

---

[45] Betensky's discussion of this passage (1978, pp. 16–17) explores in detail the imagery used here, and also highlights the connection between this passage and the *Odyssey*, pointing out in particular that the reference to an only child is more suited to the figure of Odysseus than to Agamemnon.

[46] I consider this simile in more detail in my discussion of Penelope's reunion with Odysseus below, at pp. 153–4.

[47] Note, however, that Aeschylus' vocabulary in Greek here does not echo precisely that of the *Odyssey*; for Homer the pillar to which Odysseus compares the olive tree is a κίων (23.191), where for Aeschylus it is a στῦλος (898). Clytemnestra's later use of a metaphor comparing Agamemnon to a tree, offering protective shade to the house (963–5) might also, however, reinforce the Homeric allusion. On the olive-tree bed and its role in the reunion of Penelope and Odysseus, see further p. 150.

[48] Raeburn and Thomas (2011, pp. lxvi–lxviii) explore the use of dog imagery in the *Agamemnon*, and note in commenting on line 607 that 'female dogs were also a symbol of shamelessness'.

provide reassurance that their husbands are needed even though they have coped at home while they have been away: one twenty-first-century US Department of Defense guide, for example, offered the following suggestions for women welcoming a returning partner: 'Reassure your spouse that they are needed, even though you've coped during the deployment', and 'Be calm and assertive, not defensive when discussing decisions you have made, new family activities and customs, or methods of disciplining children. Your spouse may need to hear that it wasn't the same doing these things alone...'[49] As discussed in the previous chapter, Enloe's 'Model Military Wife' is one who is 'pleased to relinquish the head-of-household mantel [sic] when her husband is home';[50] Clytemnestra, by contrast, holds on fiercely to her newly acquired role as head of the household.

The mismatch between the submissive and traditionally feminine persona which Clytemnestra assumes and her desire for the kind of power usually reserved for men is also apparent in what follows. Clytemnestra now speaks to Agamemnon directly for the first time, as she invites him to step down from his chariot and calls on her attendants to spread out rich purple fabrics for him to walk on as he enters the house. Here Clytemnestra performs the role of affectionate wife and subordinate, addressing him with the affectionate φίλον κάρα ('darling', or more literally 'dear head', 905) and then the formal ὦναξ (literally 'oh lord', although 'your majesty' might best convey the sense in English, 907). Yet the invitation which she extends, while presented as part of a loving welcome and honour for a returning hero, is in fact intended to provoke divine envy and bring Agamemnon closer to his demise. By treading on the luxurious cloths, Agamemnon will appear to behave in a manner fit only for a god, rather than for a mere mortal; as well as being hubristic, and thereby provoking divine wrath, this wasteful use of extortionately expensive fabrics would also represent, for an ancient audience, a shocking display of reckless arrogance.[51] In orchestrating this scene Clytemnestra demonstrates her control of the situation, as Agamemnon— despite his initial reluctance to do so, and his recognition that he risks angering the gods (921-4)—eventually yields to her authority.[52] Where for

[49]   Cited by Houppert (2005, pp. 131–2).

[50]   Enloe (2000, p. 163). See also p. 90 above.

[51]   On the extraordinarily costly process of producing purple dye, see Hall (forthcoming, commenting on line 909).

[52]   On the symbolism and staging of the 'carpet scene', see Taplin (1978, pp. 78–83). For discussions of the reasons why the reluctant Agamemnon eventually yields to Clytemnestra's request, see Meridor (1987) and Konishi (1989). George (2001) discusses Clytemnestra's assertion of her power in the Oresteia.

the Homeric Penelope, a trick involving woven cloth was a crucial part of her strategy to remain as Odysseus' faithful wife, Aeschylus' adulterous Clytemnestra subverts this image of the relationship between weaving and fidelity, instead using cloth as a key element of her deception of her own husband.[53]

Clytemnestra's lover Aegisthus has very little presence in the play; he appears onstage only in the last 100 lines, and is alluded to only briefly—and usually indirectly—before this. There is, for example, a veiled reference to his disloyalty when the chorus advise Agamemnon, 'In time you will know through careful enquiry which of the citizens who stayed at home has behaved correctly and which inappropriately [τόν τε δικαίως καὶ τὸν ἀκαίρως]' (807–9). Cassandra later refers to Aegisthus as a 'cowardly lion, a stay-at-home [οἰκουρόν] wallowing in bed' (1224–5) and then as a wolf, when she describes Clytemnestra as a 'two-footed lioness who mates with a wolf when the noble lion is away' (1258–60). After the murder of Agamemnon, Clytemnestra suggests that she derives some of her confidence from her relationship with Aegisthus, declaring that she feels no fear 'while the fire in my hearth is kindled by Aegisthus, and he is well-disposed towards me as before. For he is no small shield of confidence to me [οὗτος γὰρ ἡμῖν ἀσπὶς οὐ σμικρὰ θράσους]' (1435–6). The military reference here—to Aegisthus as her 'shield'—highlights ironically Aegisthus' failure to participate in the real military action alongside the other men of fighting age. The language used to describe him elsewhere also draws attention to a gendered role reversal: the chorus address him as γύναι (the Greek can mean either 'woman' or 'wife', 1625), and they echo Cassandra's earlier description of him as a 'stay-at-home' (οἰκουρός, 1626; cf. 1225).[54] The reminder that he did not accompany the Greeks on their mission to Troy helps to create a picture of an emasculated figure subordinated to the 'unnaturally' masculine Clytemnestra.[55] Despite his attempt to claim credit for planning the murder of Agamemnon (1604), the chorus taunt Aegisthus for not having the courage to carry out the deed himself (1635), suggesting

[53] Morrell (1997, p. 153) draws a comparison between Penelope's test of Odysseus on her first encounter with him and this scene in which Clytemnestra tests Agamemnon's character.

[54] One is put in mind here of the 'white feather movement' of the First World War, in which women attempted to pressurize men into enlisting into the British Army by handing out white feathers to those seen not wearing a uniform. Then too men who did not take part in the fighting were perceived as transgressing established gender norms. See Hart (2010).

[55] In Euripides' later Electra, Clytemnestra and Agamemnon's daughter Electra taunts Aegisthus with a similar accusation, contrasting him with her father who led the army to Troy (Euripides, Electra 916–17).

that he does not have the strength to rule Argos in place of Agamemnon (1633). Shortly afterwards they ask, 'Why were you so cowardly (ἀπὸ ψυχῆς κακῆς) as not to kill this man yourself, but with a woman?' (1643–4). Aeschylus' Aegisthus, then, is a man who lacks the qualities of courage and daring traditionally associated in Athenian society with masculinity. The shame of shirking military service is compounded by his actions back home, where he took Agamemnon's place in the marital bed. In this respect he fills, in the ancient text, the role of the cuckolding 'Jody' who represents modern-day soldiers' anxieties about what might happen at home in their absence.

As well as giving centre stage to an adulterous waiting wife, Aeschylus' *Agamemnon* also depicts, in Agamemnon himself, the figure of the unfaithful soldier who has sexual relations with other women while he is away from home. Where her own adultery is downplayed as a motive for the murder of Agamemnon in favour of emphasis on revenge for his sacrifice of Iphigenia, Aeschylus' Clytemnestra also condemns her husband's relationship with Cassandra, the forced concubine with whom he has returned from Troy.[56] It is important to note that the mythical narratives of tragic drama were—like those of Homeric poetry—produced at a time when the enslavement of human beings by other human beings was still a fundamental element of social organization.[57] As a result these texts often normalize the capture and rape of women by victorious armies as an inevitable consequence of conflict, and one which formed part of the conquering force's demonstration of its dominance over a defeated people. Therefore Agamemnon's return home with the newly enslaved Trojan princess Cassandra, daughter of Priam, to share his bed might not in itself be seen by an ancient audience as an unusual occurrence.[58] Yet in Aeschylus' *Agamemnon* Clytemnestra appears to reframe her husband's relationship with Cassandra not as the socially acceptable (in ancient Athens, that is) actions of a victor bringing home the human spoils of war but instead as adultery, to be condemned as such. Clytemnestra refers to her husband as 'abuser of his wife [γυναικὸς τῆσδ' ὁ λυμαντήριος], charmer of Chryseis at

---

[56] On the use of the term 'forced concubine' to refer to a woman captured in war, see below, p. 184 n. 59. On the representation of Cassandra in *Agamemnon*, see Debnar (2010), Doyle (2008), McCoskey (1998), and Mitchell-Boyask (2006).

[57] Hunt (2018) provides an introductory overview of key topics relating to ancient slavery. For more detailed discussions, see chapters in Bradley and Cartledge (2011, eds.).

[58] See Gaca (2015) on the representation of the wartime capture and rape of women in the Homeric poems and tragedy. I discuss the sexual violation of women in wartime in detail in Chapter 6 below.

Troy, and with him this captive, this prophet and this chanter of oracles who shared his bed, this faithful consort, this mast-rubber of the ship's benches' (1438–43). The phrasing used here perhaps implies that Cassandra prostituted herself for other sailors on the journey home;[59] Clytemnestra's contempt for her is clear. The reference here to Chryseis alludes to Agamemnon's story as it is told in the *Iliad*, in which a quarrel over the possession of a captive woman as a 'war prize' sparks the events which dominate the narrative of the Homeric epic.

In accusing Agamemnon of infidelity with Cassandra, and in using this as at least partial justification for her murder of her husband and his forced concubine, Clytemnestra enacts a reversal of the prevailing sexual double standards of fifth-century-BCE Athens. The adultery of a married woman would usually be condemned with greater force than that of a husband who had strayed. As Foley points out—noting too that, according to Athenian law, Aegisthus, as the lover of a married woman, should receive greater censure than Agamemnon, the wayward husband, for his adultery— Clytemnestra 'attributes to Agamemnon's inappropriate liaisons with women the culpability normally accorded unfaithful wives'.[60] As an ancient theatre audience would recognize, in Athenian law severe punishments applied both to men who had sexual relations with others' wives (this included the legal right of a husband or father to physically abuse or kill a man they found having sex with their wife or daughter), and to unfaithful wives themselves. A woman found guilty of extramarital sex could be barred from entering public temples, and could be beaten for ignoring this ban, yet the same laws were not applicable to men who had been unfaithful to their own spouses.[61] Aeschylus' Clytemnestra, in denouncing her husband's infidelity and taking matters into her own hands, once again challenges established gendered norms.

Anxieties relating to absent husbands' infidelity continue to resurface in narratives relating to today's military spouses.[62] Invariably individuals differ in how they react after the discovery of infidelity; responses might range from denial or choosing to ignore infidelities on a soldier's return home, to

---

[59] See Raeburn and Thomas (2011), commenting on line 1443 that the Greek ἱστοτριβής, translated here as 'mast-rubber', is an obscene pun.

[60] Foley (2001, p. 215).

[61] Carey (1995) sets out the evidence for this, based on Athenian oratorical texts.

[62] Note also, as discussed above, at pp. 43–4, that sometimes this infidelity is metaphorical, with the military itself or the conflict in which a partner has served being configured as the 'other woman'.

excusing the behaviour and seeking to rebuild the relationship, and of course in some cases infidelity might lead to relationship breakdown.[63] Stories of revenge carried out by soldiers on unfaithful partners are more prevalent in the modern world than those of military spouses themselves seeking retribution after betrayal by their husbands. Occasionally, however, narratives of wartime separation reveal a glimpse of the potentially devastating consequences of extramarital infidelity from the perspective of female partners, perhaps with a hint of the kind of wrath enacted by Aeschylus' Clytemnestra. In Donna Moreau's *Waiting Wives*, she imagines the response of a Vietnam soldier's wife to the news of one man's infidelity:

> 'If I were her,' offered the warrant officer's wife, 'I'd put out a contract on that...that...thing that was her husband. In all my born days I have never, ever, heard of anything so disgusting. If my husband ever did something like that to me, I'd castrate him with the dullest catfish knife I could find.'[64]

This imagined reprisal is a response to the extraordinary story of a soldier who, after a lengthy break in communications with his wife while he was deployed, contacted her to ask if they could adopt a 'war orphan' from Vietnam. He later returned home with the 'orphan', who was in fact a 'young woman wearing a skintight minidress, heels, and makeup',[65] then handed his wife a set of divorce papers before admitting that he had fallen in love and that the adoption was a ruse so that he could bring his lover into the country. The response of the 'warrant officer's wife'[66] to the story conjures up an image of a violent and emasculating revenge which might not have seemed out of place on the Athenian tragic stage.

The wartime separation of couples has, then, always led to anxiety about the potential for one or both partners in a military marriage to be unfaithful. Aeschylus' version of Clytemnestra's story puts this issue under the

---

[63] McCray (2015) surveys the evidence for the impact of infidelity on relationships in a US context.

[64] Moreau (2005, p. 139). Another of the wives here, 'the lieutenant's wife', offers an alternative response to the husband's infidelity, suggesting that she would have to kill herself should her husband ever do something similar. See above, pp. 28–30 and p. 48, on Moreau's book, a fictionalized memoir of the lives of women awaiting their husbands' return from Vietnam.

[65] Moreau (2005, p. 136).

[66] As in this case, many of the women in the story are anonymized and defined only in relation to the role or rank of their husband, in what seems to be intended as an unspoken comment on the way in which military spouses' identities can often become subsumed beneath those of their serving partners. See above, p. 48.

spotlight; here infidelity is one among several complications brought about by the war with Troy. As we have seen, Clytemnestra's own extramarital relationship is not represented in the *Agamemnon* as the main motivation for the murder of her husband, but instead it becomes one among several elements of the image of a transgressive waiting wife. This is a woman who in all respects does not behave as a woman should when her commander husband leaves her behind to carry out his military duty. Later tragedians would consider Clytemnestra's story, her unfaithfulness, and her murder of Agamemnon, from different angles. Both Sophocles and Euripides reflect on her infidelity, and, in contrast to Aeschylus, they suggest on occasion that this was at least a partial motive for killing Agamemnon. In what remains of this chapter, I turn to consider briefly these later tragic representations of Clytemnestra.

The Clytemnestras of Sophocles and Euripides

Elsewhere in the corpus of surviving tragic dramas, far greater emphasis is placed on Clytemnestra's adultery than on Iphigenia's death as her motive for murdering her husband. There is a noticeable increase in emphasis on Clytemnestra's adultery in the plays where her surviving children, Orestes and Electra, pass judgement on their mother: Sophocles' *Electra* (*c.* 420–410 BCE), Euripides' *Electra* (*c.* 422–413 BCE), and Euripides' *Orestes* (408 BCE). In these plays, in the eyes of her children—and often those of the choruses with whom they interact on stage—Clytemnestra becomes less the avenging mother and more the murderous adulterer. This is already hinted at in Aeschylus' *Choephoroi*, where, having killed Aegisthus, Orestes suggests to Clytemnestra that her primary motive for murdering Agamemnon was her infidelity: 'For while [Aegisthus] was alive, you thought him above my father; now sleep with him in death since you loved this man, but hated the one you ought to love' (*Choephoroi* 905–7). After he has completed his revenge by murdering Clytemnestra too, Orestes later implies that the pair's plot against Agamemnon was motivated by a desire for power (973–9); this paves the way for his justification of matricide in the *Eumenides*, the final play in Aeschylus' 458 BCE trilogy.[67] In the *Eumenides* Athena's ultimate exoneration of Orestes for the murder of his mother as revenge for

---

[67] See Allen-Hornblower (2016, pp. 199–246) for a detailed discussion of the way in which the matricide committed by Orestes and Electra is represented by the three tragedians.

Agamemnon's death emphatically reasserts the patriarchal norm which had been disrupted by Clytemnestra's actions.[68]

Subsequent tragic retellings also reflect the notion that this is 'a woman who does not act as a woman should', according to her society's patriarchal norms.[69] In Sophocles' *Electra*, for example, in which Clytemnestra's children conspire to take revenge for the death of their father, Electra suggests that it was not revenge for Iphigenia's death but Clytemnestra's lust for Aegisthus, and the pair's desire for power, which drove them to kill Agamemnon. She implies that the pair committed the crime together (Sophocles, *Electra* 97–9) and speaks of a 'marriage-bed stolen from under' (εὐνὰς ὑποκλεπτονένους, 114) Agamemnon, noting that Aegisthus even wears her father's robes as he sits on his throne and shares her mother's bed (267–74). The chorus of *Electra* also assert that 'deceit was the plotter, lust the killer' (δόλος ἦν ὁ φράσας, ἔρος ὁ κτείνας, 197). In this play too, as in Aeschylus' version, there is a sense in which Clytemnestra's adultery and assumption of power is linked with a reversal of normal gender roles; this is a woman who does not behave in accordance with what is appropriate for a woman. Accordingly, Aegisthus is described by Electra as 'wholly impotent, that utter plague who fights his battles with women's help' (ὁ πάντ' ἄναλκις οὗτος, ἡ πᾶσα βλάβη, / ὁ σὺν γυναιξὶ τὰς μάχας ποιούμενος, 301–2). His emasculation, as in Aeschylus' *Agamemnon*, parallels Clytemnestra's assumption of the power which is usually afforded only to men. Clytemnestra herself later asserts that she was motivated to kill Agamemnon because he sacrificed Iphigenia (530–2), yet in response Electra reaffirms her conviction that the killing of Agamemnon was 'unjust' (οὐ δίκῃ, 561), and that it was her mother's relationship with Aegisthus which drove her to murder: 'The persuasion of that wicked man, with whom you now sleep, drew you to it' (ἀλλά σ' ἔσπασεν / πειθὼ κακοῦ πρὸς ἀνδρός, ᾧ τανῦν ξύνει, 561–2). She also defends her father's decision to sacrifice her sister, suggesting that he was driven to do so 'under much duress and against his will' (βιασθεὶς πολλὰ κἀντιβάς, 575). Electra's defence of her father, and the implication that his killing of her sister was a lesser crime than her mother's actions, reaffirms the patriarchal order.

Euripides' *Electra*—which, like Sophocles' play of the same name, involves a plot by Orestes and Electra to avenge their father's death—also

foregrounds Clytemnestra's adultery as a motive for murder. This play finds
Electra, now in the countryside with a peasant farmer to whom Aegisthus
has given her in marriage, still mourning Agamemnon. Her laments
emphasize the stark difference between Agamemnon's actual homecoming
and what, as a returning and victorious warrior, he should rightly have
expected: 'Your wife received you not with garlands or crowns, but with a
two-edged sword; she made you the mournful victim of Aegisthus, and
took a treacherous husband (δόλιον ἔσχεν ἀκοίταν)' (Euripides, *Electra*
163–6).[70] Now, reflects Electra, 'my mother, married to another man, lives
in a bloodstained bed' (μάτηρ δ' ἐν λέκτροις φονίοις / ἄλλῳ σύγγαμος οἰκεῖ,
211–12). Later in the play, after her brother Orestes has murdered
Aegisthus, Electra reiterates her condemnation of the adulterous relationship as she addresses Aegisthus' corpse: 'Shamefully, you married my
mother [κἄγημας αἰσχρῶς μητέρ'] and killed her husband, who com-
manded the Greek army, although you didn't go to Troy' (916–17). In contrast with the Aeschylean version, Electra suggests here that Aegisthus, and
not Clytemnestra, killed Agamemnon; once again, however, Aegisthus is
cast as the cuckolding duty-dodger, like the 'Jody' figure of the modern
world whom we met earlier in this chapter. The notion that Clytemnestra's
relationship with Aegisthus reverses traditional gender roles is present here
too, as Electra reflects that it is 'shameful for the woman and not the man to
rule over the house' (καίτοι τόδ' αἰσχρόν, προστατεῖν γε δωμάτων / γυναῖκα,
μὴ τὸν ἄνδρα, 932–3). Later, Electra compares Clytemnestra with her adulterous sister Helen (1062–6), then claims that her mother was plotting infidelity as soon as Agamemnon departed.[71] Iphigenia's death becomes to
Electra merely a pretext for Agamemnon's murder (1067–8). Clytemnestra,
in her daughter's eyes, typifies the kind of woman who cannot be trusted to
behave appropriately when her husband is away: 'Write off as bad a wife she
who in her husband's absence preens herself' (1072–3); once again we can
see in Clytemnestra an early mythical antecedent of the modern-day image
of the unfaithful waiting spouse. Electra is also aware, however, that there is
a gendered double standard at play in the judgements which are cast upon
dishonourable relationships; she recognizes that it is the woman and not the
man who gains notoriety in such cases, as 'there is talk not of the man, but

---

[70] I discuss further in Chapter 5, at pp. 159–63, the way in which the stories surrounding
Clytemnestra's 'welcome' of Agamemnon—as imagined in particular by Aeschylus—invert the
idea of a traditional homecoming for a warrior.

[71] Comparisons between the two adulterous sisters recur in other versions of Clytemnestra's
story too: see above, p. 67.

only of the woman' (936-7). Nor does the sexual double standard go unnoticed by Clytemnestra herself in this play: having suggested that she would have forgiven Agamemnon for the sacrifice of Iphigenia had he not brought Cassandra into the marital home (1033-4), she points out that while men who take lovers escape censure, women who do the same are publicly blamed (1035-40). That the extramarital infidelity of a mythical waiting wife is judged more harshly than adultery committed by her serving husband, might come as no surprise to generations of military wives since. As Tanya Biank observed in her study of the Fort Bragg military community, cheating husbands seem not to attract the same condemnation and hatred as unfaithful army wives.[72]

It is in in Euripides' *Orestes*, however, where we find perhaps the clearest articulation in the surviving ancient texts as to why the infidelity of waiting wives is the cause of such anxiety among military communities. There, Clytemnestra's son justifies his matricide on grounds first that he has done a service to Greece as, if women can attract pity for murdering their husbands by claiming that they did it for the sake of their children, this may lead to further such crimes (563-70). Having declared, 'I hated my mother and killed her justly' ($\mu\iota\sigma\hat{\omega}\nu$ $\delta\dot{\epsilon}$ $\mu\eta\tau\dot{\epsilon}\rho$' $\dot{\epsilon}\nu\delta\dot{\iota}\kappa\omega s$ $\dot{a}\pi\dot{\omega}\lambda\epsilon\sigma a$, 572), he asserts that Clytemnestra, 'when her husband was away from home in battle, serving as commander for the whole of Greece... betrayed him and did not keep his bed undefiled [$\kappa o\dot{\upsilon}\kappa$ $\ddot{\epsilon}\sigma\omega\sigma$' $\dot{a}\kappa\dot{\eta}\rho a\tau o\nu$ $\lambda\dot{\epsilon}\chi o s$]' (573-5); this is what led her to kill Agamemnon. Orestes then draws on the comparison which is made between Clytemnestra and Penelope in the *Odyssey* and elsewhere by comparing himself with Telemachus, who did not kill Penelope, because 'she did not marry husband upon husband' ($o\dot{\upsilon}$ $\gamma\dot{a}\rho$ $\dot{\epsilon}\pi\epsilon\gamma\dot{a}\mu\epsilon\iota$ $\pi\dot{o}\sigma\epsilon\iota$ $\pi\dot{o}\sigma\iota\nu$, 589); unlike that of Clytemnestra, Penelope's marriage-bed remained untainted (590) in Odysseus' absence. Later in the same play, the messenger reports on the debate concerning whether Orestes should be put to death for his murder of Clytemnestra, noting that one man in the crowd defended his actions on the grounds that 'he killed a wicked and godless woman who would stop men from arming themselves and serving with the army if those left behind destroy households by seducing men's wives' (925-9).

Orestes' anger at the adultery committed by his mother and Aegisthus in the absence of his father, and the messenger's suggestion that those who do not go away to fight might seize the opportunity to steal their wives, would

---

[72] See above, p. 110.

doubtless touch a nerve with ancient audiences, for some of whom this would be an ever-present concern. By the time of the production of Euripides' *Orestes* in 408 BCE, Athens had been fighting an ongoing series of wars with Sparta for more than twenty years, and for some returning soldiers, the notion of having their place in the marital bed usurped might be a real possibility, and one which posed a threat both to the integrity of their family (and indeed questions over the parentage of any children) and the morale of the fighting force. At times when the population as a whole is under pressure, the actions of individuals, as well as affecting the immediate family, might carry wider implications for the whole military force and, as a consequence, for the security of the city. This raises broader questions too about honour and duty, and about the responsibilities which individuals have to act in the interests of wider society. Not only, then, is Clytemnestra to be condemned for her infidelity, but Aegisthus too, having escaped the responsibility of military service, commits an atrocious transgression in sleeping with her. This transgression threatens the *polis* (state) as a whole, as well as one particular *oikos* (household).[73] Even without her subsequent murder of Agamemnon, then, the infidelity is presented in this play as an unforgiveable crime.

The figure of the cheating military spouse, and the contrast which is drawn between her and the ideal loyal wife, is, therefore, exemplified in the ancient tragic representations of Clytemnestra, as compared with the Penelope-figure of Homeric poetry. Where Penelope behaves in accordance with what is expected of her, Clytemnestra subverts the traditional role assigned to a woman in ancient Greek society, not only by being unfaithful but also by assuming, and clinging to, the power which would ordinarily belong to her husband. This representation of two polarized models—one positive and praiseworthy, one negative and abhorrent—of the military spouse still persists today in conversations around military relationships, where the image of acceptable behaviour for the wife of a soldier is still largely conditioned by gendered norms and often outdated ideas about 'appropriate femininity'.[74] Even the most cursory search of online message boards, blogs and YouTube videos today will point to the persistence of a misogynistic stereotype of the unfaithful military wife; there exist groups on social media sites whose sole purpose is to identify and shame individual

---

[73] See further Silva (2010, p. 76).

[74] On the way in which this idea of 'appropriate femininity' is presented in the highly contrived public-facing image of the 'military wives' choirs' in the UK, see Cree (2018, pp. 259–61).

military spouses who are alleged to have cheated on their husbands, or women thought to have had sex with married soldiers.[75] The gendered double standard persists here, as the narratives surrounding infidelity in these cases focus on the alleged questionable morals of the women concerned. They often exonerate male soldiers who have cheated on grounds that they were mentally and emotionally vulnerable to exploitation by opportunistic women on a (clichéd) mission to have intercourse with a man in uniform. Meanwhile, contemptuous caricatures of the antitype of the model military wife abound: for example, the so-called 'Dependa' is represented as a parasite who marries her husband for his rank and pay check, while sleeping around behind his back; 'Suzy Rottencrotch' stands in for the cheating military spouse.[76] In these caricatures, there is almost always an implied or explicit contrast with the ideal attractive, devoted, and loyal wife who puts her husband and the military first.

These contemporary counterparts of the Clytemnestra-figure of ancient myth bear little similarity to the murdering adulteress represented by the Athenian playwrights, and the simplified twenty-first century stereotype allows no room for a complex backstory and individualized motivations such as those which are imagined for Clytemnestra and her family. Nonetheless, this modern-day stereotype too, it seems, is built upon ingrained fears relating to the absence of military personnel from the family home while on active service, and the opportunities which this presents for things to go awry while they are away. Of course, the mythical Clytemnestra's betrayal of Agamemnon does not stop with her infidelity, but is taken to an extreme with the murder she commits on his return home, in a reunion story which cemented her place as the most notorious waiting wife in the ancient world. In my next chapter, I turn to consider in more detail the process of reunion after the return of a soldier.

---

[75] Mindful of the risk of driving traffic to online resources which amplify hate speech and/ or target individuals, I have chosen not to provide direct citations for such sites here. On stereotypes of military spouses—including that of the unfaithful wife—as perceived by spouses themselves, see Hyde (2015, pp. 99–100).

[76] On the 'Dependa', see Marcotte (2017); on 'Suzy Rottencrotch', see Burns (2012, p. 87).

5

Reunion: Penelope, Clytemnestra, and Trojan War homecomings

In a collection of verses with the title *So Spoke Penelope*, contemporary American poet Tino Villanueva imagines Penelope's thoughts during Odysseus' absence and on his eventual return. The final poem in the volume, 'Twenty Years Waiting', is a retelling of the reunion of husband and wife which recreates, in condensed form, the events of the twenty-third book of the *Odyssey*. The joyful Penelope of the modern poem recalls the couple's long-awaited first embrace and their insatiable kisses, followed by their retirement to the bed they previously shared. In an echo of the scene described by Homer, Athena delays the onset of dawn in order to prolong a blissful night of lovemaking and conversation. In her description of the reunion, this Penelope recalls:

> And what we uttered took
> love that much higher; made it ascend to heights
>
> of delight where no sound could be heard, save
> the sound of two lovers in a room full of love
>
> where husband and wife finally arrived, moored to
> each other, at the dreamed-of, the imagined, the absolute
>
> moment of rapture, beyond words, sweet to our mortal
> taste. O astonished and exalted heart when, before it,
>
> is revealed that hoping against hope has yielded
> its reward. To him, last night, all of me I gave.[1]

Penelope's delight and relief, and Villanueva's romanticized version of the reunion of the pair—to whom he refers in the poem as 'Lovers long estranged'—perhaps reflects an idealized perception, held by some without experience of military life, of the return of a serving partner from the front

---

[1] Villanueva (2013, pp. 59–60).

Warriors' Wives: Ancient Greek Myth and Modern Experience. Emma Bridges, Oxford University Press.
© Emma Bridges 2023. DOI: 10.1093/oso/9780198843528.003.0006

line. Bolstered by the media's fondness for sharing heart-warming pictures of returning troops embracing their loved ones,[2] this uncomplicated image of a military reunion rests on the assumption that the post-deployment period is, for both partners, a time of unmitigated joy at being back together after a long separation: the worries for the serving partner's safety are over, the marital relationship can begin again where it left off, and life 'as normal' can resume.

As the narrative of the *Odyssey* suggests, however, the process of reunion is far from straightforward for Odysseus and Penelope. So too, modern-day accounts and psychological studies of the return of military personnel from deployment reveal that soldiers' homecomings are often fraught with challenges for both partners. This chapter will consider the complexities of military partner reunions, in contrast with the romantic ideal. Focusing primarily on Penelope's interactions with her husband in *Odyssey* 23, I will examine the way in which the Homeric poet presents in microcosm key aspects of the reunion process which are still present in modern-day homecomings, beginning with the emotional confusion which Penelope exhibits. I then suggest that the literal disguise assumed by Odysseus on his return to Ithaca mirrors the struggles which contemporary military couples have with recognizing one another after time spent apart, before considering how Homer represents the process of rebuilding trust and reopening communication which is necessary for a couple to undertake as they resume their relationship. Couples are not, however, always able to reconnect successfully, and this is reflected in different ways in Trojan War narratives: Hector's death in the *Iliad* means that he will never be reunited with Andromache, and—as described in Aeschylus' *Agamemnon*—Clytemnestra's reunion with Agamemnon is thwarted by her murder of her husband on his return home. I will consider briefly how the ancient versions of these stories represent these failed reunions as distorted versions of the rituals which accompany a soldier's successful homecoming.

Military homecomings: ideal versus reality

I have been home doing all things and being all the things to everyone. He's been there. Being everything to everyone. Then,

---

[2] Houppert (2005, p. 161) provides a detailed and insightful description of the way in which homecoming ceremonies have often been orchestrated by the US military as public relations exercises: 'Press attendance is encouraged... Visuals are controlled and grandly patriotic... The evening news inevitably runs shots of soldiers hugging ecstatic wives... These homecoming images are the ones the army hopes will supplant the flag-draped coffin that the public saw on yesterday's front page.'

in the blink of an eye…we are back under one roof and the shift happens instantaneously. Only, it doesn't.[3]

In a candid personal blogpost, Valli Gideons—wife of a US Marine—offers a snapshot of the challenges faced by the whole family whenever her husband returns home from deployment. The reality, she writes, is far from 'the dream of a Hollywood ending' that people around her seem to assume she is living.[4] In contrast with the imagined romantic ideal, the post-deployment period is a turbulent time punctuated by rows, tears, and misunderstandings as the couple and their children adjust to the change; each time her husband returns home the family 'pay[s] the price for months to come'. Gideons reflects that the emotional turmoil for her comes from 'the cumulative effects of a life full of loneliness and missed moments; being left behind and asked to be strong and hold it together'. In contrast, many of the images of military reunions in today's media focus on the romance and excitement of the return home, rather than on the difficulties that Gideons' account reflects. Any internet search for 'romantic military reunion' will deliver an abundance of photographs and videos of marriage proposals staged on military airfields, as well as surprise returns home which appear to radiate the joy and relief of both the waiting spouse and returning partner. Yet Gideons' account of her experiences is far from unique among military spouses.[5] The process which she describes here can be explained in psychological terms by the 'relational turbulence model', a theory which illuminates the ways in which interpersonal relationships develop and fluctuate over time.[6] Psychologists recognize that at times of transition, there is an increased likelihood of relational turbulence, and studies of relationships where at least one partner serves in the military suggest that deployment and the return home are key periods of transition which can impact both positively and negatively.[7] One feature of such transitions is the uncertainty that both

---

[3]   Gideons (2018).

[4]   An interesting comparison can be made here with an example from David Finkel's 2013 work of nonfiction journalism, *Thank You for Your Service*, which presents (pp. 20–1) from a soldier's perspective an idealized image of a joyous and unproblematic transition back to domesticity, as compared with the reality. Finkel compares the bleak homecoming of Sergeant Adam Schumann, and his shame at being invalided home on mental health grounds, with the impossibly perfect homecoming ceremonies that Schumann recalls as raucous celebrations imbued with relief and the promise of passion.

[5]   Karakurt et al. (2012) discuss the evidence for the ways in which romantic relationships are affected by wartime deployment.

[6]   For a summary of the relational turbulence model, see Solomon (2015).

[7]   See Knobloch and Theiss (2014) and Baptist et al. (2011).

partners can feel about the future of their relationship. This may manifest itself with difficulties in communication, emotional turmoil including anger and sadness, and fear about changes in the other partner's behaviour. In short, 'reentry is rife with relational uncertainty for military couples'.[8]

This relational uncertainty is apparent too in the *Odyssey*'s account of Penelope's reunion with Odysseus. Psychologists Mateczun and Holmes begin their discussion of the return of soldiers home to the US from the 1990–1 Gulf War with a brief retelling of the homecoming of Odysseus. In conclusion to their summary of the Homeric poem, they suggest that 'This timeless story serves as a reminder that there are pitfalls on the path to a successful reunion', and that it illustrates what they refer to as the 'three R's of reunion': return, readjustment, and reintegration.[9] The comparison with the *Odyssey* is not one which Mateczun and Holmes develop in detail in their subsequent discussion, however, and—in common with Jonathan Shay's book-length study comparing Vietnam veterans' experiences with those of the returning Odysseus—their primary focus rests on the psychology of the combatants themselves rather than on that of their waiting spouses.[10] Mateczun and Holmes do point out, however, that the notion that individuals in a soldier/spouse relationship are in some ways unrecognizable to one another at the point of reunion is expressed quite literally in the Homeric version of Penelope and Odysseus' story. In relation to contemporary military reunions, they observe that, often, 'The new habits of family life are most noticeable to those who have been apart. It is as if families and couples recognize each other but have a sense that the other is not really who he or she says he or she is—that the other is somehow "disguised" and not who he or she was thought to be.'[11] I will return later in this chapter to discuss the significance of Odysseus' literal disguise and the recognition process which he and Penelope, in common with modern-day military couples, must undergo on his return home.

Although the culmination of Penelope's reunion with her husband is delayed until the penultimate book of the *Odyssey*, this is the final stage of a process that has been anticipated throughout the whole poem. Odysseus' arrival on Ithaca is described as early as Book 13, when, having been transported there by the Phaeacians, he awakes on the island. Here, although he

---

[8] Knobloch and Theiss (2014, p. 45).   [9] Mateczun and Holmes (1996, p. 372).
[10] Shay (2002, pp. 132–4 and 137–8), touches only briefly on the reunion of Odysseus and Penelope, focusing primarily on Odysseus' blankness in the face of his wife's emotional responses.
[11] Mateczun and Holmes (1996, p. 378).

is now physically close, there is already a sense of the psychological distance between the returning soldier and his home.[12] He fails at first to recognize his homeland as the goddess Athena has shrouded it in mist so as to conceal him until he has taken revenge on the suitors (13.187–94); as a result, 'everything appeared unfamiliar' (ἀλλοειδέα φαινέσκετο πάντα, 13.194). He needs further reassurance from Athena that this is indeed Ithaca, and that Penelope is still waiting for him (13.333–8). Athena then facilitates Odysseus' plan to observe without being observed, giving him the disguise—the appearance of a beggar—which he maintains during his initial encounter with Penelope.[13] While the appearance of divine mediators is an aspect of the Homeric poems that seems unfamiliar to a modern reader, for an ancient audience the presence of Athena—Odysseus' protector and guide— would serve in the poem to signify the importance of an event. The goddess's appearance here, and at key moments later in the reunion of Penelope and Odysseus, perhaps indicates that the *Odyssey* offers a divinely orchestrated paradigm for the journey of a returning soldier, with all of its potential complications.[14] In this case, the threat of potential infidelity is ever-present too: Athena later inspires Penelope to appear before the suitors and inflame them with desire (18.158–62) in the presence of Odysseus, who is said by the poet to be glad that her actions allow her to obtain more gifts from the unwelcome guests (18.281–3).[15] Only in Book 19, however, does Penelope first meet her husband face-to-face. At this point he remains in disguise, acting as her confidant so that she shares with him her troubles and describes the shroud trick with which until recently she has held off the suitors. All the while, Odysseus conceals his true identity from his wife, most notably by crafting a false tale in which he claims Cretan ancestry (19.172–202).[16] There is still at this point some distance to go before the couple's reunion is fully accomplished.

[12] On the ways in which Odysseus' experience might mirror the psychology of returning veterans, for whom home and family can feel very far removed, see Shay (2002, pp. 121–37). Booth and Lederer (2012, p. 375) identify guardedness as a common behaviour of soldiers returning from combat situations.

[13] Penelope first learns of Odysseus as the 'beggar in the hall' after he has been abused by the suitors when the swineherd Eumaeus describes him as a guest-friend of the family (17.513–27). On the disguise theme more widely in the *Odyssey*, see Murnaghan (2011).

[14] I am grateful to Elton Barker for this point.

[15] For a discussion of the possible motivations behind Penelope's actions in *Odyssey* 18, in which she appears before the suitors and admonishes them for failing to bring her gifts, see Rutherford (1992, pp. 29–33), and Hölscher (1996). Foley (1995) considers in depth the question of Penelope's moral agency in the poem as a whole, but particularly with reference to her actions relating to her choice to remarry. See also Felson-Rubin (1996).

[16] I discuss aspects of the exchange between Penelope and Odysseus in Book 19 in earlier chapters, at p. 35, pp. 87–8, pp. 92–3, and p. 98.

Despite the complicated and drawn-out nature of Odysseus' homecoming, and the challenges that both he and Penelope face on this final stage of his journey, it can be tempting for contemporary readers of the *Odyssey* to romanticize the mythical couple's reunion. Tino Villanueva's poem, with which this chapter opens, is just one example of this tendency. Some scholarship too has interpreted Odysseus' return to Penelope in romantic terms; Austin, for example, describes the recognition process—which he sees as beginning in Book 19, when Penelope first meets the disguised Odysseus—as an 'overt courtship',[17] and similarly Felson sees the couple's reunion as a 'courtship dance'.[18] The resumption of Penelope and Odysseus' relationship is, however, far more fraught with challenges than the courtship which might take place at the start of a new relationship. Foley, while also referring to 'the long recourting of Penelope by Odysseus', acknowledges the accompanying emotional complexities; she describes the process as 'primarily a mature renegotiation between two potential strangers, two established powers, which ends in a recreation of trust and a mutual establishment of the limits within which their future relationship will take place'.[19] In what follows I will explore these complexities as they surface in the *Odyssey*'s narrative of reunion in Book 23—from Penelope's emotional confusion, through to her eventual recognition of her husband and the reopening of communication between the couple—and will also consider some of the ways in which they are reflected in contemporary accounts of military reunions.

Emotional confusion

It's just a lot to take in, It's like you don't know what to say. You don't know what to do. You don't know to hug them, cry, lay down and go to sleep. Start all over again, you know, you just don't know. Now he was fine but now he's here. I see his face. He's talking to me. He's telling me what he seen [*sic*], what happened to him. It's really hard.

It is... It's really hard...[20]

The description given by this anonymous military spouse of her emotional responses to the return of her husband from deployment captures a sense of

---

[17] Austin (1975, p. 214).   [18] Felson (1994, p. 61).   [19] Foley (1978, p. 16).
[20] Quoted in Aducci et al. (2011, p. 240).

her bewilderment after their reunion. Her uncertainty about how to behave towards him is palpable as she repeatedly states that she does not know what to say or do, acknowledging her own difficulties with communication in straightforward terms: 'It's really hard.' This emotional confusion, and the difficulty in adapting to the return, is a recurring feature of military couples' experiences of the post-deployment period.[21] As will become apparent in what follows, it is also clearly identifiable in the *Odyssey*'s description of Penelope's reactions to Odysseus' return.

The opening of the twenty-third book of the *Odyssey* is devoted to describing Penelope's response to the news that Odysseus is home, and her uncertainty as to how to interact with him. At this point, although Odysseus is now back in the palace and has asserted his place in the household by killing the suitors, there is still some way to go before he and Penelope are fully reunited. Having declared, towards the end of Book 19, her intention to set up the contest of the bow, Penelope had retired to her bed, weeping until Athena brought her sleep (19.602–4).[22] On waking, she began weeping once more (20.57–8) before recalling her dream that Odysseus was sleeping beside her, looking as he did when he left for Troy (20.87–90).[23] The recollection here of her husband as he once was (perhaps initiated by her earlier conversation with the disguised Odysseus describing his appearance) acts to prepare the audience for what is to come later in the poem, when the couple are finally brought back together. The poet then focuses primarily for several books on Odysseus' actions in winning the contest of the bow and then, with the help of Telemachus, brutally massacring the suitors. Penelope, removed from the scene, witnesses none of this dramatic action; the first she learns of it is when Eurycleia wakes her with the news that Odysseus has indeed returned home and has killed the suitors (23.5–9).

Penelope's emotional responses to the return of Odysseus in what follows encompass a whole range of feelings, from denial and suspicion to joy and relief; at times she switches from delight to disbelief within only a few lines of text. Her first response to the news brought by Eurycleia is an expression of complete denial, and she suggests that the old woman is not in her right mind (23.11–14): 'Dear nurse, the gods have made you mad...they have

---

[21] Knobloch and Theiss (2014).

[22] On the significance of the contest with the bow, see above, p. 100 and p. 105.

[23] On Penelope's weeping elsewhere in the *Odyssey*, see above, pp. 80–1 and pp. 87–8.

deluded you, although before you were right-minded.' She goes on to rebuke Eurycleia, asking her, 'Why are you mocking me, when my heart is so deeply mournful [πολυπενθέα θυμὸν ἔχουσαν]?' (23.15), and complaining that she should not have woken Penelope from her restorative sleep. The acknowledgement here of the depth of her continuing grief, relieved only by sleep, echoes the poem's earlier insights into Penelope's emotions.[24] On Eurycleia's insistence that she is speaking the truth, and that the 'beggar' in the hall was in fact Odysseus, Penelope's mood swiftly changes: 'she was overjoyed, and sprang from the bed, embracing the old woman, and shedding tears from her eyes' (ἡ δ' ἐχάρη καὶ ἀπὸ λέκτροιο θοροῦσα / γρηἳ περιπλέχθη, βλεφάρων δ'ἀπὸ δάκρυον ἧκε, 23.32–3). She is, however, still unsure as to whether she can believe the news, asking Eurycleia for further details about how Odysseus managed to kill the suitors. Eurycleia's account of seeing the blood-stained Odysseus amid the dead suitors in the aftermath of the slaughter in the hall is not enough, however, to reassure Penelope that her story is true. Penelope restates her disbelief, suggesting that it must be a god who has killed the suitors as punishment for their transgressions; she asserts, 'But Odysseus has lost his homecoming (*nostos*), far from Achaea, and he is lost too' (23.67–8). Her continued scepticism earns her a reproach from Eurycleia, who observes, 'Your heart was always mistrustful (ἄπιστος, 23.72).' Only when the aged nurse reveals that she herself has seen proof of Odysseus' identity, in the form of the scar on his leg (from a wound caused by a wild boar in his youth, 23.74, cf. 19.390–475), does Penelope agree to leave her room to view the dead suitors and their killer. Her initial scepticism might relate to the fact that she has been tricked in the past by visitors bringing false tales of Odysseus (14.126–30; she later reiterates her fear of deception to Odysseus at 23.313–18). However, in what follows the poet provides further insight into her state of mind and the complex mix of emotions she is experiencing in relation to her husband's return.

Homer's description of Penelope's emotional turmoil as she descends to the hall reflects her uncertainty and internal conflict at this point: 'She turned over many things in her heart [πολλὰ δέ οἱ κῆρ / ὅρμαιν'], whether to stand apart and question her dear husband or to approach him and take hold of his head and hands and kiss him' (23.85–7). Her indecision about whether or not to embrace Odysseus is strikingly reminiscent of the reflections of the anonymous military spouse whose words I quoted at the

---

[24] On sleep as bringing relief from Penelope's troubles, see above, p. 79.

opening of this section. For Penelope, however, the confusion arises in large part from a quite literal difficulty in recognizing her husband; this is, after all, the man who deliberately concealed his identity from her when she last saw him. In the event, Penelope sits opposite Odysseus, observing him from a distance: 'For a long time she sat, speechless, with astonishment in her heart (τάφος δέ οἱ ἦτορ ἵκανεν). At times she would look him full in the face, and at others she would fail to recognize (ἀγνώσασκε) him with the wretched clothes on his body' (23.93–5). As discussed in Chapter 3 (p. 95), her reticence to approach Odysseus earns her Telemachus' disapproval. He accuses her of 'having a harsh heart' (ἀπηνέα θυμὸν ἔχουσα, 23.97), a 'stubborn heart' (τετληότι θυμῷ, 23.100) and a 'heart always harder than stone' (αἰεὶ κραδίη στερεωτέρη ἐστὶ λίθοιο, 23.103), and these accusations will be echoed shortly afterwards by Odysseus himself (23.168–70). The men in the family, in their misinterpretation of Penelope's emotions, allow no space for her emotional confusion and the difficulty she has in accepting that this is indeed her husband after such a long time apart.

Penelope does respond to Telemachus with an insight into her own reasons for hesitation here. She acknowledges her own paralysis and bewilderment, saying that 'the heart in my breast is astounded' (θυμός μοι ἐνὶ στήθεσσι τέθηπεν, 23.105) and that she is 'unable to say a word to him or question him, nor to look him straight in the face' (23.106–7). This is, she suggests, because she needs certainty that Odysseus is who he claims to be. Proof of his identity will come from the 'signs we have which we both know, but which are hidden from other people' (ἔστι γὰρ ἡμῖν / σήμαθ', ἃ δὴ καὶ νῶϊ κεκρυμμένα ἴδμεν ἀπ' ἄλλων, 23.109–10). Odysseus assumes that it is because he is ragged and dirty that Penelope does not recognize him (23.115–17), and of course his outward appearance is one of the things which makes it impossible for her to be sure whether this is truly her husband. Yet there is more to the question of recognition here than looks alone. The process of reunion seen in *Odyssey* 23 also illustrates a psychological issue often experienced by those who have been apart for long periods of time, particularly when that time apart has been spent by one of them in a place which is both geographically distant from, and completely alien to, the domestic setting of the reunion. We might therefore see Odysseus' literal disguise as an outward representation of the difficulty which reuniting couples can have in recognizing one another. It is to the various ways in which 'disguise' and the recognition process operates in relation to military reunions that I now turn.

Disguise and the problem of recognition

> I think they [military] put him in a different state of mind cause
> he's not himself, he's not who he used to be. I can still see it in
> him but he's not exactly who he used to be…cause he spaces
> out sometimes…you try to reach him and he's just so far and
> when he's like that, that makes me distant. He's probably, you
> know, got something on his mind and it's probably bothering him,
> which bothers me…You have to get to know each other all over
> again. It's like you're walking up to this person in an airport and
> you're like, 'Hi, I'm ____, and you are?' Before he left, he would
> dance, and you know, just have a good time and everything when
> he came back he was quiet…always pacing…weighing more than
> he used to…I think that really hurt him.[25]

The words of one anonymous military wife describing the return of her
husband from deployment during Operation Iraqi Freedom in 2003
provide an insight into some of the issues which many military couples
must navigate at the point of reunion. Her assertion that 'he's not who he
used to be', the acknowledgement that she struggled to recognize the person he
had become, and her suggestion that both his appearance and his behaviour
had changed on his return all create the impression that her husband had
become something of a stranger to her over the course of his absence. While
many military spouses report experiencing this feeling that the serving
partner has changed during deployment, there is also often a sense that
things back at home might not be as they once were. 'In retrospect,' reported
one spouse interviewed for a 2010 study of the experiences of wives whose
husbands had been deployed, 'one of the most difficult parts of deployment
for us was the post-deployment. We had a baby right before my husband
left, and by the time he came home, things were dramatically different in
our home.'[26] Children will have grown (or even been born) and changed in
their parent's absence, and the civilian partner has had to take on new tasks
and responsibilities, with the result that home and the people in it may
appear very different from how they were when the initial separation took

[25] Quoted in Aducci et al. (2011, p. 240).
[26] Quoted in Easterling and Knox (2010, section titled 'Perceptions of Stages of Deployment').

place.[27] This might mean that the fantasy of homecoming which a couple has held in mind during their time apart is far removed from what actually transpires.[28]

The distance between partners can be even more pronounced where trauma is present; this is a particularly striking element of the accounts of Vietnam veterans and their families.[29] The first-hand accounts of waiting wives often reflect on the transformation of veterans' physical appearance alongside inner psychological changes. The recollections of one Vietnam wife, Patience Mason, are instructive here. Mason's *Recovering From the War*, first published in 1990 as a guide written to help the wives and families of Vietnam veterans, is interspersed with her memories of her husband Bob. Reflecting on the moment of reunion, and the dramatic difference in Bob's appearance as compared with the photograph she took on the day of his departure, Mason writes:

> When he went to Vietnam, Bob was an optimistic, idealistic person who could do anything, work any job…I still have a picture of him I took the day he left, with one-year-old Jack tucked underneath his arm, both of them smiling. His face is young and enthusiastic. He's skinny but handsome, carried about 140 pounds on his five-foot-eleven frame.
>
> In August 1966, I ran across the parking lot of the Greyhound bus station into his arms. I couldn't believe it was over. He'd *lived*. I had him *back*. Incredible joy swept through me and tears poured down my face. As I hugged him, I could feel every bone in his body.
>
> When he got back, Bob weighed 119 pounds. As a combat helicopter pilot flying almost every day, toward the end of his tour he had been given tranquilizers, quite illegally, to help him sleep. He flew combat assaults up to the last day. He had lost *15 per cent* of his body weight. He'd always been thin, but now he looked as if he'd been in a death camp. His wrists looked enormous. His eyes glittered. He was honed down.
>
> 'See, Jack, this is *Daddy!*' We'd been kissing that picture goodnight every night for a year.[30]

---

[27] On the ways in which waiting spouses might take on new roles within the household in the absence of a serving partner, see above, pp. 90–2 and p. 121.

[28] On the 'fantasy of homecoming' as compared with the reality, see Yerkes and Holloway (1996, p. 31). Bowling and Sherman (2008, pp. 452–3) summarize some of the changes which often take place at home while a partner is deployed overseas. On the reintegration of military families after a long separation, see also Gober (2005).

[29] See, for example, Mason (1990, pp. 163–86) and Matsakis (1996, pp. 54–81).

[30] Mason (1990, pp. 173–4) (italics in original).

Mason's description captures some of her own emotions surrounding reunion, as her joy and relief mingle—as for Penelope in her own initial reactions to Odysseus' return—with disbelief that Bob actually made it home. At the same time, as the couple reconnect physically with an embrace, this is the point at which the realization begins to dawn that not only is his appearance different from before, but that he is also psychologically changed. Now dealing with the trauma brought on by his experiences, Bob was in many ways unrecognizable from the man who left for war, with the sleepless nights as he relived the horrors of combat, and his new habit of chain-smoking which later developed into other types of substance abuse.[31] As for many military couples, there is a profound sense of unfamiliarity which goes far deeper than any superficial changes to Bob's appearance.[32]

Unfamiliarity is a defining feature of the reunion of Penelope and Odysseus too. As noted earlier, during Penelope's first encounter with the returning Odysseus (in Book 19 of the *Odyssey*) he remained deliberately in disguise; this exacerbates the difficulties which she has in recognizing him when he is ready to reveal his true identity. The eventual restoration of his physical appearance—with a bath and fresh clothing prepared by the enslaved attendant Eurynome, and Athena's help to enhance his looks (23.153–63)—is not in itself enough for Penelope to be certain about who he is. On returning from his bath, Odysseus addresses his wife as δαιμονίη (23.166), 'strange,'[33]

---

[31] The foreword of Patience Mason's book is written by Bob himself (Robert Mason), who reflects on his own responses to combat trauma—anxiety, mood swings, and self-medicating with drugs and alcohol—and their impact on his relationship with his wife. See Mason (1990, pp. ix–xv).

[32] The sense of unfamiliarity is also present in returning soldiers' accounts of the moment of reunion with their partners. Phil Klay's fictionalized retelling of the return home of one US Marine in his short story 'Redeployment' (from his collection that is also titled *Redeployment*) captures this well. The Marine recalls, 'She was skinnier than I remembered. More makeup, too. I was nervous and tired and she looked a bit different. But it was her.' He reflects when hugs his partner that 'Her body was soft and fit into mine…I hadn't felt anything like her in seven months. It was almost like I'd forgotten how she felt, or never really known it, and now here was this new feeling that made everything else black and white fading before color' (Klay (2014), pp. 7–8). I am put in mind here of Odysseus' confession that the hardships he has endured in his absence have made him uncomfortable with the luxuries associated with home (19.336–48). Klay's story also carries other echoes of Odysseus' homecoming—the soldier is, like Odysseus, met on his return by an aged dog who is near death. In this case, in a detail which allows the author to explore the psychological effects of combat on the soldier for whom death is an inextricable part of his experience, Klay's protagonist takes it upon himself to shoot the dog.

[33] δαιμόνιος can be translated in various ways and might also be rendered as 'marvellous' as well as 'strange' in some contexts. The use of the adjective here might have a note of ambivalence: Russo et al. (1992) point out at lines 166–7 that Odysseus 'may be as much taken aback by admiration for the exceptional cunning of his wife as disappointed by her reaction'. Nonetheless, Odysseus' apparent criticism of Penelope's hard-heartedness would suggest that it is less than complimentary here. On the use of the term in the *Iliad*, see above, pp. 23–4.

before accusing her of being stubborn and hard-hearted in an echo of Telemachus' earlier words (23.167–70, cf. 23.100–3). Again Penelope offers her own interpretation of her response to Odysseus. In a detail which reminds the audience that both parties are still struggling to understand one another, she mirrors the description which Odysseus use of her, addressing him too as δαιμόνι(ε), 'strange' (23.174; cf. 23.166 and 23.264, where Odysseus again uses the feminine form of the adjective to address Penelope). She goes on to defend herself against his accusations, saying that she is not arrogant or scornful (οὔτ᾽ ἄρ τι μεγαλίζομαι οὔτ᾽ ἀθερίζω, 23.174) before asserting that she remembers what he looked like when he left Ithaca for Troy (23.175). The gap in this scene between Odysseus' interpretation of Penelope's behaviour and his wife's own expression of her thoughts provides the audience with a glimpse of the gulf of understanding which can lie between partners who once knew each other well yet have been apart for an extended period of time. In order to re-establish intimacy and trust in their relationship, and as part of the reintegration of a returning soldier into domestic life, this mythical couple, like so many real-life couples, needs to engage in what Mateczun and Holmes refer to as 'an active process of communication', without which relationships can flounder.[34]

For Penelope and Odysseus, this active process of communication can begin only after Penelope has assured herself of Odysseus' identity. This assurance comes with her use of the 'bed trick', which cements her trust in the man who says he is her long-absent husband; I will discuss this in more detail shortly. It is first worth noting, however, that the question of the point at which Penelope actually recognizes that the 'beggar' is in fact Odysseus has been the subject of much scholarly debate. These discussions reveal individual scholars' attitudes towards Penelope and Odysseus' relationship and the process of reunion; they remind us that the lens through which each new reader perceives the *Odyssey* is influenced by their own experiences and the context within which they encounter the text. Philip Harsh first set out in detail, in 1950, the view that Penelope sees Odysseus for who he really is when he is still in disguise in *Odyssey* 19, arguing that this early recognition leads first to Penelope's testing of her husband by confiding in him her dream in which an eagle killed her pet geese and then declared that

---

[34] Mateczun and Holmes (1996, p. 383). The re-establishment of communication is not always straightforward, however: Sahlstein et al. (2009, pp. 433–6) note that problems can arise in some cases if one party is unwilling either to talk or to listen. On the reintegration process after deployment, see also Andres et al. (2015).

it was her husband come to slay the suitors (19.535–50).[35] Harsh suggested that in what follows, the audience witnesses covert 'teamwork' between husband and wife in setting up the contest of the bow and the subsequent slaying of the suitors.[36] The view expressed by Harsh is one which rests on the notion that Odysseus' and Penelope's is a model marriage, guided by the principle of *homophrosunē*, or 'like-mindedness', which Odysseus suggests is a key feature of the ideal husband/wife relationship in his conversation with Nausicaa at *Odyssey* 6.180–5.[37] This interpretation reads today, however, as though it may well have been a projection of Harsh's own ideas midway through the twentieth century about what an ideal marriage should look like, and it is perhaps reflective of tendencies towards romanticizing the reunion process which I identified earlier in this chapter.[38] Subsequent modifications proposed by scholars to Harsh's 'early recognition' theory, including that of Anne Amory (1963), argued that the recognition occurs at first in Book 19 on a subconscious level for Penelope, but that this only progresses to become a conscious realization in Book 23 after she has tested Odysseus to ensure that he is not an impostor.[39] Irrespective of the varying interpretations of the text, the point at which it is made explicit that Penelope has recognized Odysseus comes only after she has been able to test him in connection with one of the shared 'signs' to which she alluded at 23.110; this is where the 'bed trick' comes in.[40]

---

[35] Felson (1994, pp. 31–3) considers the possible reasons behind Penelope's sharing of her dream with Odysseus here. For an interpretation of the meaning of the dream, see Marquardt (1985, pp. 43–5 with n. 12).

[36] Harsh (1950).   [37] See above, p. 113.

[38] Margaret Atwood's 2005 reception of Penelope, her novel *The Penelopiad*, played on this interpretation from a feminist perspective. Atwood (2005, p. 137) emphasizes the shrewd perspicacity of her Penelope, who declares, 'I didn't let on I knew. It would have been dangerous for him. Also, if a man takes pride in his disguising skills, it would be a foolish wife who would claim to recognise him; it's always an imprudence to step between a man and the reflection of his own cleverness.'

[39] Amory (1963). Doherty (1995, pp. 31–56) provides a comprehensive overview of the scholarly discussions of the question of the point at which Penelope recognizes Odysseus, offering a critique which is grounded in feminist criticism and which considers the textual issues surrounding the debate. More recently, an entire special issue of the journal *College Literature* (2011, vol. 38.2) has been devoted to papers discussing the question of Penelope's recognition of Odysseus; for a brief summary, see Myrsiades' (2011) introduction to that issue.

[40] Note that—as pointed out by Emlyn-Jones (1984, pp. 6–7)—the recognition scene between Penelope and Odysseus in Book 23 is one of several moments of recognition: that between Odysseus and Telemachus (16.186–219), which foreshadows elements of Penelope's reunion with Odysseus, including Telemachus' denial that this is his father (16.194–200), their tearful embrace (16.213–19), and the exchange of news (16.226–57); Odysseus' 'reunion' with the old dog Argos who, lying neglected and filthy, wags his tail in recognition and then dies shortly afterwards (17.290–327); Eurycleia's recognition of Odysseus when, on washing his feet, she notices the familiar scar from a wound caused by a wild boar in his youth (19.390–475);

Like Patience Mason, whose account of her post-Vietnam reunion I quoted earlier, Penelope has a clear idea of what her husband looked like when he left for war (23.175). As discussed, however, the restoration of his external appearance alone is not enough to prove that this is really Odysseus. After so long apart she needs a flawless method of knowing that the man before her is the same person she once knew, and that the shared understanding on which their marriage was founded is still there. Penelope's method of assuring herself of Odysseus' true identity involves the bed, carved from a single olive tree, which is literally at the centre of their household both in spatial terms and in its symbolic place at the heart of their marriage.[41] Her test of Odysseus here shows Penelope as at least her husband's equal in intelligence and—like the shroud trick—highlights her own resourcefulness. Penelope asks that Eurycleia move their bed outside the bedroom to make up a place for Odysseus to sleep (23.177–80). Her husband's enraged reaction (he is described as $\dot{o}\chi\theta\dot{\eta}\sigma\alpha s$, 'angered', at 23.182) to the suggestion that their bed—which he carved from an ancient olive tree with his own hands—has somehow been moved is the proof she needs that this is really her husband.[42] Odysseus points out the impossibility of moving the bed for a mere mortal (23.184–9) before describing in detail the process by which he constructed it, and the room around it (23.190–201). This, he says, is the $\sigma\hat{\eta}\mu\alpha$ ('sign', 23.202) which he shares with Penelope; the choice of word here harks back to Penelope's declaration at 23.110 that the couple had signs known only to the two of them and which could be used as proof of Odysseus' identity. The immovability of the bed also acts here as a metaphor for Penelope's sexual fidelity, as emphasized when Odysseus retorts, 'I do not know if my bed is still standing firm ($\check{\epsilon}\mu\pi\epsilon\delta ov$) or if some man has now cut through the base of the olive tree and put it elsewhere' (23.203–4). The use of the adjective $\check{\epsilon}\mu\pi\epsilon\delta os$, which I have translated here as 'standing firm', but which can also be used to mean 'safe', 'sure', or 'steadfast', echoes earlier reflections on Penelope's character and responsibilities,

---

Odysseus' divulging of his identity to the cowherd Philoetius and swineherd Eumaeus (21.207–25); and (after Odysseus' reunion with Penelope), the reunion with his father Laertes, whom Odysseus tests with a false story before revealing himself (24.315–48). Gainsford (2003) examines the formal structure of these recognition scenes. Such scenes are not unique to Homer, and are also identifiable as part of a wider folk-tale motif involving the return of an absent husband to a waiting wife: see Clark (1990).

[41]   On the symbolism of the olive-tree bed, see Katz (1991, pp. 177–82) and Zeitlin (1996).

[42]   In discussing the outcomes of the *Ancient Greeks/Modern Lives* program, in which US military veterans watched readings of *Odyssey* 23 as well as performances of Athenian drama, Meineck reports that soldiers watching were particularly moved by this moment of recognition: one veteran was 'struck at how much this scene resembled how he and his wife had to reconnect each time he came home, over a simple, intimate "shared experience"' (Meineck 2012, p. 19).

where both she and Odysseus refer to her role at home as 'keeping everything safe' (ἔμπεδα πάντα φυλάσσει, 11.178, cf. 19.525).[43] As I discussed at length in Chapter 4, worries about a partner's potential infidelity can very often be a barrier to the resumption of a relationship after time apart.

It is in the moments after Odysseus has at last proved his true identity that Penelope's emotional and physical reaction perhaps best mirrors the joyful reunion scenes which modern-day news reporters are so fond of broadcasting. The poet's description of her response captures the sense of elation and relief at this delayed reunion (and the reference to the 'sure signs'—σήματ'...ἔμπεδα—which Penelope recognizes once again echoes earlier vocabulary relating to steadfastness):

> As he spoke, her knees and heart loosened as she recognized the sure signs which Odysseus had shown her. Then, bursting into tears, she ran straight towards him, and flung her arms around Odysseus' neck, and kissed his face and spoke to him. (ὣς φάτο, τῆς δ' αὐτοῦ λύτο γούνατα καὶ φίλον ἦτορ, / σήματ' ἀναγνούσῃ τά οἱ ἔμπεδα πέφραδ' Ὀδυσσεύς· / δακρύσασα δ' ἔπειτ' ἰθὺς δράμεν, ἀμφὶ δὲ χεῖρας / δειρῇ βάλλ' Ὀδυσῆϊ, κάρη δ' ἔκυσ' ἠδὲ προσηύδα·, 23.205–8)

The embrace which Penelope and Odysseus share at this moment is a gesture recognizable from many reunion moments, including those recounted by military spouses earlier in this chapter. For Penelope it brings the physical connection over which she had hesitated earlier in the reunion scene, where she wondered whether to 'approach [Odysseus] and take hold of his head and hands and kiss him' (23.87). The embrace also marks the point at which verbal communication between the couple starts to become more open. The poet explores in further detail this process of reopening communication in the remainder of the twenty-third book of the *Odyssey*; this will be the focus of my next section.

Reopening communication

> I packed that ruck
> I loaded those bags
> I, you know

---

[43] See above, p. 93, on the use of this adjective at 19.525 and 11.178, and its various connotations.

> I walked the walk
> I shed the tears
> I think at the end
> I said, you just come home to me
> I met him on that soldier level
> I wasn't the pitiful wife[44]

This poem, composed by a recently reunited military spouse, captures the sense that, although the writer's own experiences were in many ways far removed from those of her absent husband, she too lived through the deployment and had her own story of suffering to tell. Her words render visible the experiences of the waiting spouse and propose a way of developing mutual understanding between this woman and her returning partner; in declaring, 'I met him on that soldier level' she suggests a need to find some shared insight despite the gap between their experiences. Psychiatrists Yerkes and Holloway, in discussing the transition from deployment to home for military personnel, acknowledge the distance that can exist between the returning soldier and the waiting family: 'The family's experiences at home, coping with society and the local community, differs dramatically from the veteran's experiences. With few shared deployment experiences between them, each is seen as a stranger in the other's world.'[45] The unfamiliarity to which Yerkes and Holloway allude is a feature of some of the personal accounts of reunion highlighted earlier in this chapter and, as discussed, is particularly striking in the *Odyssey*'s description of Penelope's relationship with Odysseus and the literal disguise which he assumes.

For a successful reunion, like many military couples Penelope and Odysseus need to be gradually reacquainted with one another, and, like the anonymous military spouse whose poetry I have quoted above, to find ways for each to comprehend the other's perspective. Penelope's acknowledgement that the person before her is Odysseus, and that no other man could know the shared secret of their marriage-bed, enables her to begin speaking to him as her husband rather than as a stranger. Yet, as Homer recognizes, there are still challenges and obstacles to overcome as the couple need to reach a shared understanding of one another. The pair, like many reuniting couples, must find ways to bridge the gap between their individual experiences during the time they have spent apart. As I will discuss in this section,

---

[44]   Quoted in Aducci et al. (2011, p. 242).   [45]   Yerkes and Holloway (1996, p. 37).

the *Odyssey* explores the couple's reopening of communication through both the conversations and physical connection—beginning with their first embrace—which Penelope and Odysseus share. In describing their reunion, the poet also uses a unique extended simile which acknowledges the trials which both partners have undergone.

In the moments after her embrace with Odysseus, Penelope initially seems to fear that all may still be swept from under her: twice she pleads with Odysseus not to be angry with her for her reticence (23.209 and 23.213). She then explains her reasoning, saying that she was afraid that another man might try to deceive her for his own advantage (23.215–17). She also blames the gods for their long separation (23.210–12), and goes on to compare this with a god's luring of Helen away from her home before the Trojan War (23.218–24).[46] Now, however, Odysseus has shown her 'clear signs' (σήματ᾽ ἀριφραδέα, 23.225) with his knowledge of their bed. With these explanations Penelope also answers the accusations levelled against her earlier by Telemachus: echoing the vocabulary used by her son at 23.97, where he refers to her as 'having a harsh heart' (ἀπηνέα θυμὸν ἔχουσα), she concludes that 'you persuade my heart, although it is very harsh' (πείθεις δή μευ θυμόν, ἀπηνέα περ μάλ᾽ ἐόντα, 23.230). Her words move Odysseus to tears as he holds Penelope to him (23.231–2); this outward expression of his emotions mirrors that of his wife. It is impossible to be certain what these tears signify—whether joy and relief at their reunion, grief over time spent apart, or a combination of these emotions—but the image of husband and wife crying together as they embrace reflects their progress towards mutual understanding.[47]

This development of mutual understanding is also highlighted by an extended 'reverse simile' which inverts traditional gender roles and frames Penelope's experiences in a way which relate them to those of Odysseus.[48] In describing their reconciliation and the embrace which they share, the poet reflects (23.233–40):

As welcome is the appearance of land to swimmers, whose well-built ship, beset by winds and heavy seas, Poseidon has wrecked in the ocean; and

---

[46] I discuss the significance of this reference to Helen, and the contrast between Helen's infidelity with Paris and Penelope's faithfulness to Odysseus, above at p. 107.

[47] On Penelope's and Odysseus' weeping elsewhere in the poem, see above, p. 80 with n. 15.

[48] In Book 19, Odysseus uses a 'reverse simile' to compare Penelope to a king; see above, p. 92, and Foley (1978).

only a few have escaped the grey sea by swimming to shore, their skin thickly covered with brine. Joyous, they set foot on land, having escaped their troubles. So welcome was her husband to her as she looked at him, and she could not altogether release her white arms from his neck.

By comparing Penelope's relieved reaction to the joy of shipwrecked sailors as they reach dry land, the poet confounds the expectations of an audience who might instead assume that such a description would more naturally be applied to Odysseus himself. After all, much of the poem has been dedicated to his travels at sea, and we have witnessed him experience shipwrecks of his own, most notably in the account of his arrival on Scheria, land of the Phaeacians, in Book 5. In reversing conventional gender roles, the simile draws attention to the fact that Penelope too, as the waiting wife, has been through a distressing ordeal of her own in Odysseus' absence. While Penelope's trials are markedly different from those which her husband has undergone, the Homeric simile of the shipwrecked sailor transports her symbolically to the realms of Odysseus' experience. Just as her husband has re-entered the domestic sphere from which he has been absent for so long, the comparison which is evoked also allows Penelope to step beyond the domain to which she has been limited by her position as the waiting wife, and to find a degree of shared understanding of the trials which he has undergone. The Homeric simile seems too to give due credit to the waiting spouse for the role which she has played; in doing so it offers the couple the opportunity to move beyond the stage of reunion in which each is, as Yerkes and Holloway describe it, a 'stranger in the other's world' towards being able to communicate with one another once more.[49]

In what follows, Penelope and Odysseus are able to progress further towards the restoration of their marital relationship through conversation and physical intimacy. For this they once again receive supernatural assistance from Athena, who delays the arrival of the dawn to give them time to reconnect (23.241–6). Odysseus reveals that there are still further trials ahead; in common with many a returning soldier, he has not yet made his last trip away from home. Initially he gives only a brief hint of the prophet Teiresias' prediction for his future (23.249–53) before inviting Penelope to bed 'so that we can both enjoy sweet sleep' (23.254–5). Penelope is, however, insistent that he shares more with her about what lies ahead; bed, she says, can wait (23.257–62). Odysseus once again refers to her as δαιμονίη, 'strange'

---

[49] Yerkes and Holloway (1996, p. 37).

(23.264), before giving further details about the expedition prophesied for him. His final journey is not to be a military mission, but a trip to appease the sea god Poseidon by dedicating an oar and an offering to him in a place where the inhabitants know nothing of the sea.[50] There is still a sense of distance between the pair: Odysseus' reluctance to share full details of the prophecy, and the repetition of his earlier description of Penelope as strange, suggests a continuing gap in his understanding of her perspective. Penelope gives only a brief response to the news of his departure, saying 'If the gods make your old age better, there is still hope for an escape from your troubles' (23.286–7). Her emotions here are hard to decipher as she says so little, and, as is so often the case, an interpretation might depend on the audience's personal experience and perspective. Her response might be read as an expression of acceptance and even optimism for the future, or it may perhaps conceals some deeper worry or resentment.[51]

The bed, now firmly established as a symbol of Penelope and Odysseus' marriage and their return to one another, continues to dominate in this scene as the couple restore their connection further. In just eight lines of text after Penelope's response to Odysseus' revelation (23.289–96), different Greek words meaning 'bed' ($\epsilon\dot{\upsilon}\nu\dot{\eta}$, $\lambda\acute{\epsilon}\chi\sigma$, and $\lambda\acute{\epsilon}\kappa\tau\rho\sigma\nu$) occur four times, as the poet shows Eurynome and Eurycleia preparing the couple's bedroom, then reports that Odysseus and Penelope 'went gladly to the place of their old bed' ($\dot{\alpha}\sigma\pi\acute{\alpha}\sigma\iota\sigma\iota$ $\lambda\acute{\epsilon}\kappa\tau\rho\sigma\iota\sigma$ $\pi\alpha\lambda\alpha\iota\sigma\hat{\upsilon}$ $\theta\epsilon\sigma\mu\dot{\sigma}\nu$ $\ddot{\iota}\kappa\sigma\nu\tau\sigma$, 23.296).[52] Their familiar bed now becomes the site of physical connection and verbal communication. The poet glosses over their sexual reconnection in customarily brief and euphemistic fashion before recounting the conversation that they share: 'When they had both enjoyed their lovemaking, they took pleasure in talking' ($\tau\dot{\omega}$ δ' $\dot{\epsilon}\pi\epsilon\dot{\iota}$ $\sigma\dot{\upsilon}\nu$ $\phi\iota\lambda\acute{\sigma}\tau\eta\tau\sigma$ $\dot{\epsilon}\tau\alpha\rho\pi\acute{\eta}\tau\eta\nu$ $\dot{\epsilon}\rho\alpha\tau\epsilon\iota\nu\hat{\eta}s$, / $\tau\epsilon\rho\pi\acute{\epsilon}\sigma\theta\eta\nu$ $\mu\acute{\upsilon}\theta\sigma\iota\sigma\iota$, 23.300–1).

---

[50] The text here (23.267–84) is largely a formulaic repetition (altered so that it reads as a first-person narrative) of the prophet Teiresias' words to Odysseus in the underworld at 11.122–37.

[51] My own experiences of military life have led me in the past towards reading Penelope's response here as an expression of resigned acceptance that another period of separation is inevitable. The performer and theatre-maker Caroline Horton pointed out in a conversation I had with her some years ago that 'maybe she's resigned, or maybe she just operates on two different levels; there's what's on the surface, and there's also a deep pool of turmoil underneath'. See Bridges (2015a). Russo et al. (1992, at lines 286–7) suggest that 'Odysseus' words have not so much caused [Penelope] anxiety as inspired her with confidence in the future'.

[52] Scholars have debated extensively over the ending of the *Odyssey* since comments by Alexandrian critics seem to imply that 23.296, where Penelope and Odysseus retire to their bed, was considered by some in antiquity as the 'original' ending. Russo et al. (1992, at line 297) provide a summary of the scholarship relating to this issue.

In the exchange that follows, each shares their own version of the events which have taken place while they have been apart. This swapping of stories before they fall asleep, retold in third-person narrative by the poet in an edited-down version of the plot of the *Odyssey* as a whole, is the culmination of their reunion process. Odysseus tailors his narrative, however, to avoid any hints at his own infidelities: he omits to mention the year he spent sharing Circe's bed, glosses over his desire for Calypso, and makes no reference at all to Nausicaa.[53] As also noted in Chapter 3 (p. 75) the Penelope of Homeric poetry is afforded relatively little space to tell her own story. Here only four lines (23.302–5) are given over to a summary of her experiences; in comparison, the recap of Odysseus' adventures occupies thirty-two lines (23.310–41). This imbalance in the time devoted to their stories might seem an apt metaphor for the way in which women's stories have so often been overlooked in war narratives ever since. Of Penelope's response we are told only that 'she listened with delight [ἡ δ' ἄρ' ἐτέρπετ' ἀκούουσ'], and sleep did not fall on her eyelids until he had recounted it all' (23.308–9).

Aspects of the process of reconnection which Penelope and Odysseus undergo in the *Odyssey* might seem familiar to military spouses who have welcomed home a returning partner. As discussed earlier in this chapter, echoes of the challenges of recognition, and the need to find ways to reopen communication, recur in contemporary first-hand accounts of military reunions. One autobiographical insight into the moment of reunion, from the perspective of the waiting wife, which bears some striking similarities to aspects of *Odyssey* 23 can be found in the 1991 memoir of Marian Novak, *Lonely Girls with Burning Eyes*. Novak's book reflects on her experience as the wife of a US Marine who was deployed to Vietnam: she charts the couple's separation and the lengthy process of his return. The memoir opens, 'I am the wife of a man who went to war. I watched my husband train for war; I waited thirteen months for him to return from it; and then I waited another fifteen years for him to truly come home.'[54] In what I have come to think of as a twentieth-century version of the Homeric bed scene, Novak recalls in detail her first meeting with her husband David in 1967 on his return—initially only for a short period of 'R&R', rest and recuperation—after six months in Vietnam. As was customary for such reunions, the pair met for five days in Hawaii, accompanied by Jeannie, the baby with whom

<hr />

[53] Odysseus mentions only Circe's trickery (23.321) and tells Penelope that Calypso wanted him for her husband but was unable to persuade him despite her promise of immortality (23.333–7).
[54] Novak (1991, p. 3).

Marian had been pregnant when David left for the war. She describes the first night of their reunion:

> We were all three very tired that first night. But only Jeannie slept. Dave and I had 132 hours to be together, and sleep seemed such a waste of time. We held each other in the dark and talked softly. Dave had protected me from the war when he wrote, and holding me in bed that night he protected me when he spoke. We clung to each other, to feel flesh and bone, something real next to us where for months there had been only emptiness outlined in fear. Dave was real at last, but when we talked, what we kept from each other was the truth: our words skimmed over the surface of our life, ghostlike and hollow. But we talked on into the night, for the sheer pleasure of hearing each other's voice.
>
> Toward morning, we made love. I know we both expected a scene of pent-up passion, perhaps even looked forward to one. But instead it was a sweet, tender communion. We were both shy at first, uncomfortable with our intimacy, though that is strange to admit. My breasts were different from pregnancy, and I had episiotomy scars. Dave was thinner and his muscles had hardened; his skin was rough and he had infections, open sores, on his legs. And there were the new scars on his arm, the bullet scars.
>
> Perhaps more significant than the physical changes were the emotional and psychological ones, though we did not acknowledge those then. I was a mother now. Dave must have felt the new tilt of the axis of my world. As for him, he had had the responsibility for men's lives. I had seen a boy off to war, and he had come back to me a warrior.[55]

There is no olive-tree bed for Marian and David, and no supernatural assistance from a divine protector—this couple must forgo sleep in order to spend more time together—yet their reunion experience bears many resemblances to that of their mythical predecessors. Both have undergone changes to their body and mind during their separation, and these transformations, both visible and invisible, create a distance and an apprehension between the two which is overcome here by their physical closeness and their sharing of conversation, albeit an edited version of their experiences. Meanwhile, their bed—not in a palace on Ithaca but in a Hawaiian hotel room—is, like that of Odysseus and Penelope, the site of the restoration of their intimacy, and the place where they are able to reconnect after so long apart.

---

[55] Novak (1991, pp. 216–17).

The social, political, and cultural context of the two reunions described differs vastly, and as always we must be wary of the temptation to draw universal parallels across time and space. Nonetheless, the resonances of the Homeric narrative which are identifiable in Marian Novak's account act as a reminder that the ability to find ways of reopening communication after a period of separation is a crucial aspect of the path to a successful reunion. Inevitably, not all couples are able to reunite successfully, however. I now turn to consider the ways in which thwarted reunions—in particular that of Clytemnestra and Agamemnon, but also that of Andromache and Hector—are represented in ancient myth.

Homecoming rituals distorted

As discussed, the process of homecoming as it is described in the *Odyssey* features behaviour that reflects the renewed physical and emotional connection of Penelope and Odysseus: a tearful embrace and kisses, sex, and the exchange of stories. It also incorporates a series of actions which are associated with the transition of a returning soldier back home: bathing and putting on fresh clothing, and retiring to bed, which is the site of rest as well as of physical and emotional intimacy. The importance of meeting a returning soldier's basic needs as a step on the return to life outside a war zone is recognized by psychologists such as Steven Gerardi, whose work draws on his experience with veterans. Gerardi observes:

> Rather than attempt to treat the battle-fatigued soldier with elaborate psychotherapeutic interventions, he is best managed by using the management principles referred to as the four R's: rest, replenishment, reassurance, and restoration. The battle-fatigued soldier often needs rest to repay an incurred sleep debt. For severely sleep-deprived soldiers, this may amount to 14 or more hours of uninterrupted sleep. Replenishment of physiologic needs, such as food, water, and comfort needs, such as a shower and a clean set of clothes are also important. Most of us have experienced the rejuvenating effects of a good meal and a hot bath. For the battle-fatigued soldier, this revitalizing effect is significantly magnified. The combat stress casualty is also afforded the opportunity to tell his story and share his psychic trauma.[56]

---

[56] Gerardi (1999, p. 187).

Not only, then, does the fulfilment of physical needs provide refreshment after the toil and stress of combat and ease the transition from battle to home, but it can also—as in the case of Odysseus' reunion with Penelope—be an important step on the journey towards enabling the recently returned combatant to begin communicating his experience. In some narratives, however, the normal rituals connected with a soldier's homecoming are distorted, and a successful return is never accomplished.

For some soldiers, like the Trojan warrior Hector, the return to their wives and families is thwarted by death in battle: in the *Iliad*'s account of Hector's death the poet focuses on details that draw the audience's attention to a homecoming that will never be, and among these is the ritual of the bath. Immediately before she learns of her husband's death, Andromache is at home inside the walls of Troy, weaving: she has ordered her enslaved attendants to heat water for Hector's bath on his return (*Iliad* 22.442–4). Her concern to provide for Hector's physical well-being with the simple act of cleansing his body draws attention to Andromache's emotional connection with her husband. The audience's knowledge that Hector has already been killed by Achilles and will never return home also makes this a profoundly moving moment, one which immediately precedes Andromache's realization, on hearing the mourning wails of the other women of Troy, that Hector is dead. The image of bathing as a refreshing and cleansing ritual for warriors in both life and death recurs elsewhere in this poem. In life it represents the transition from the danger of the battlefield to the safety of home (or, in the case of the Greeks, to the temporary 'home' of their camp), yet in a different context, with the ritual washing of a corpse, it can also mark the point at which a soldier's homecoming has been thwarted by his death.[57]

In the later mythological tradition, it is in the story of Clytemnestra and Agamemnon where the distortion of the comforting rituals of a successful homecoming is most noticeable. As discussed at length in Chapter 4, Clytemnestra is often presented in mythical narratives as the paradigmatic example of the unfaithful waiting wife, or as the woman who oversteps conventional gender boundaries and assumes an unacceptable level of power in the absence of her husband. The reunion of Clytemnestra and Agamemnon is also an extreme example of a homecoming gone awry, and in this respect

---

[57] Examples of warriors bathing after battle include *Iliad* 10.574–9 (Odysseus and Diomedes) and 14.6–7 (Machaon). The corpses of Sarpedon, Patroclus, and Hector are washed and given fresh clothes (16.676–80, 18.343–53, 24.582–90). Grethlein (2007) explores the motif of the bath in the *Iliad*, examining its association with both death and cleansing after battle, and showing how the Andromache scene alludes to both of these types of bathing ritual.

it contrasts too with the reunion of Penelope with Odysseus. As Zeitlin first pointed out, Aeschylus' *Oresteia* trilogy repeatedly plays with the distortion of ritual actions; this is most apparent in Clytemnestra's use of language relating to ritual sacrifice to describe the death of Agamemnon.[58] There is a sense too in which the homecoming of Agamemnon is connected with the ritual of *xenia*, the proper reception of a guest by a host. This ritual is an important feature of the Homeric poems (and in particular in the narrative of Odysseus' *nostos*) and, in its focus on providing food and material comforts, it has elements in common with the welcome of a homecoming hero.[59] In Aeschylus' *Agamemnon*, however, Clytemnestra's 'welcome' of Agamemnon forms part of her plot to lure her husband to his death; it subverts familiar, and ordinarily non-threatening, aspects of the welcome of a returning soldier for sinister ends.

There are in particular three key elements of the ordinary homecoming which are distorted by Clytemnestra's actions in Aeschylus' play: clean clothes, the bath, and the couple's bed. As I discussed in detail in Chapter 4, Clytemnestra adopts the persona of the model 'waiting wife' in her initial exchanges with Agamemnon, claiming that she will provide the best possible welcome for him (600–4). Yet, as Cassandra later observes, Clytemnestra only 'pretends to be delighted at [Agamemnon's] safe return' (δοκεῖ δὲ χαίρειν νοστίμῳ σωτηρίᾳ, 1238), and the homecoming she devises is far removed from the ideal. In a ruse designed to provoke divine wrath towards Agamemnon, she invites him to walk over rich fabrics as he enters he house (*Agamemnon* 908–57).[60] The question as to what kind of fabrics these might be has been much discussed, with some commentators suggesting that they may be tapestries or carpets. However, the suggestion made by several scholars that these are instead richly decorated and expensive woven garments is convincing.[61] If this is the case, the scene becomes one in which items associated elsewhere in ancient mythical narratives with the domestic rituals of homecoming are appropriated for another purpose. Here fresh

---

[58] Zeitlin (1965). See, for example, *Agamemnon* 1385–95. At *Agamemnon* 1125–9, Cassandra also imagines Agamemnon as a sacrificial bull.

[59] On the various ways in which *xenia* is corrupted in the *Oresteia*, see Roth (1993).

[60] For further discussion of the significance of this scene, see above, p. 125.

[61] Morell (1997, pp. 155–6) with n. 21, collates the terminology used by various scholars to refer to the cloths in this scene. He argues that the fabrics are garments of some kind, and that they are symbolic of household wealth which is no longer needed for a dowry since Agamemnon's murder of Iphigenia. See also Raeburn and Thomas (2011), commenting on lines 905–11, noting that references to these items in terms derived from the Greek εἵματα suggest that they are 'large rectangular pieces of cloth used principally for cloaks and robes or occasionally as blankets, but not as carpet-rugs'.

clothing, which would more usually be offered as a replacement for a battle-weary traveller's soiled garments, is part of Clytemnestra's plan to engineer Agamemnon's demise. When viewed in conjunction with the bath as the site of her husband's murder, Clytemnestra's provision of clothes for Agamemnon sets this homecoming in contrast with that of Odysseus in the *Odyssey*, where the bath and fresh clothes were a key moment in the path towards reunion with his wife. Clytemnestra's deployment of rich woven fabrics in an unexpected—and, to an ancient audience, outrageous—manner confounds expectations as to how a wife should welcome home a returning warrior. The chorus' foreboding about what is to come (expressed in their ode at 975–1034) is reinforced by Cassandra's prophetic words that the house of Agamemnon will soon become a 'slaughter-house of men' (ἀνδροσφαγεῖον, 1092). Rather than providing sustenance and comfort, Agamemnon's home will be the site of his murder.

The distortion of the customary elements of a warrior's homecoming continues in what follows. Cassandra's prediction of the grotesque events which will take place offstage also draws attention to Clytemnestra's improper use of both Agamemnon's bed and his bath: neither of these household objects will serve the restorative purpose for which they might ordinarily be used. 'Wretched woman', Cassandra asks, 'will you really do this deed? Having washed your husband, who shares your bed, with a bath [τὸν ὁμοδέμνιον πόσιν / λουτροῖσι φαιδρύνασα]...how shall I tell the end?' (1107–9) This couple will not get as far as their marital bed, which in Aeschylus' play—unlike the bed of Penelope and Odysseus in the *Odyssey*—is neither the site of a harmonious emotional and physical reunion nor a place of rest for the returning soldier. Instead it symbolizes Clytemnestra's adultery with Aegisthus.[62] Meanwhile the bath, as the scene of Agamemnon's death, will soon be awash with his blood in a distorted version of death rituals in which the body is cleansed for burial. The chorus draw attention to this connection when they refer to Agamemnon as 'lying on the low bed of a silver-sided bathtub' (ἀργυροτοίχου / δροίτας κατέχοντα χάμευναν, 1539–40). The Greek δροίτη, translated here as 'bathtub', can also mean 'coffin'; the choice of vocabulary reinforces the sense that the bath has been reappropriated as a funerary object.[63] It is possible that the introduction of the bath as the location for Agamemnon's death was Aeschylus' innovation; it is a detail which

---

[62] On Aeschylus' representation of Clytemnestra's relationship with Aegisthus, see above, p. 119 and p. 126.

[63] See Raeburn and Thomas (2011, commenting on line 1540).

is not mentioned in earlier surviving sources.[64] This might suggest a conscious intention on Aeschylus' part to draw his audience's attention to the distortion of key elements of a soldier's successful homecoming.

Further details in Aeschylus' version of Agamemnon's murder also point to this sense of his homecoming as a warped version of the norm, as Clytemnestra reappropriates another item of clothing for sinister ends. Cassandra prophesies that Clytemnestra will trap Agamemnon 'in robes' (ἐν πέπλοισιν, 1126) before she kills him; elsewhere these robes are described by Cassandra as a 'net of Hades' (δίκτυόν... Ἅιδου, 1115; the name of the god Hades is used here as a personification of death). Later, in the unapologetically triumphant speech where she describes the murder of her husband, Clytemnestra recalls how she cast about him a 'wicked richness of robe' (πλοῦτον εἵματος κακόν, 1383) before striking him three times as he gasped his last breaths and bled out in the bath. Once more—as with the garments over which Agamemnon walked into his house—an item of clothing is used for a purpose other than that for which it was intended, and what might have been a homecoming ritual becomes instead a grotesque travesty of a funerary rite.[65] The garment used to trap Agamemnon in his final moments is also used to striking effect later in the *Oresteia* trilogy, when in the *Choephoroi* Orestes brandishes it as a prop, describing it in terms which echo those used in *Agamemnon* as a 'trap for a wild beast', a 'covering for a corpse' (the Greek here could also mean 'curtain for a bath', alluding to the manner of Agamemnon's death), a 'net for hunting', or 'robes entangling feet' (*Choephoroi* 998–1000).[66] In that play too, Aeschylus draws his audience's attention to the contrast between the proper practices of hospitality and Agamemnon's thwarted return home. When Clytemnestra welcomes the disguised Orestes and Pylades, she tells them that the house can provide to strangers 'warm baths, and beds to soothe away cares' (θερμὰ λουτρὰ καὶ πόνων θελκτηρία / στρωμνή, *Choephoroi* 670–1); the reference to bathing reminds us of the scene of Agamemnon's death, and the image of the welcoming bed might call to mind Clytemnestra's adultery.[67]

---

[64] See Gantz (1993, p. 669).

[65] Seaford (1984) considers the funerary associations of Agamemnon's bath and the robe in the *Oresteia* trilogy.

[66] The Greek at *Choephoroi* 998–1000 reads as follows: ἄγρευμα θηρός, ἢ νεκροῦ ποδένδυτον / δροίτης κατασκήνωμα; δίκτυον μὲν οὖν / ἄρκυν τ' ἂν εἴποις καὶ ποδιστῆρας πέπλους.

McNeil (2005, p. 10 n. 19) also notes Orestes' description in the *Choephoroi* of the robe as his 'mother's sacrilegious handiwork' (ἄναγνα μητρὸς ἔργα τῆς ἐμῆς, *Choephoroi* 986), drawing on the comparison between this and the virtuous weaving project of the Homeric Penelope.

[67] See Goldhill (1986, pp. 14–15).

In the *Agamemnon*, the vision of Clytemnestra as antithesis of the virtuous welcoming wife becomes complete when she rejoices not at the safe
return of her husband from war but at the successful accomplishment of the
deed she has long been plotting in revenge for the sacrifice of Iphigenia
(1374–9; cf. 1415–18, 1432). Agamemnon, rather than occupying the role of
a beloved husband welcomed with open arms after a long absence, becomes
instead a sacrificial victim whose death is his atonement for his earlier crime.
Instead of enjoying the imagined reunion at home with his waiting wife, he
will be greeted in the underworld by Iphigenia, the daughter for whose
death he was responsible (1555–6). Clytemnestra imagines that Iphigenia
'will throw her arms around him and kiss him' (περὶ χεῖρα βαλοῦσα φιλήσει,
1559). The gesture recalls that of Clytemnestra's opposite, Penelope, whose
eventual reunion with Odysseus, complete with kisses and an embrace
(*Odyssey* 23.205–8) offers a model against which to compare Agamemnon's
failed homecoming.

Clytemnestra's nightmarish 'welcome' of Agamemnon in Aeschylus' play
is thus one further element of her portrayal as the antithesis of Penelope.
While—as noted in Chapter 4—stereotypes of adulterous military spouses
persist, the image of the waiting wife as murderer of her returning husband
has not percolated through into contemporary narratives surrounding
military reunions. Actual real-life cases of murders of military personnel by
their civilian partners are today vanishingly rare, although, by contrast,
there is ample evidence of domestic violence as committed by military personnel upon their partners.[68] Aeschylus' depiction of the horrifying aftermath of Clytemnestra and Agamemnon's separation—a drastic example, in
keeping with tragic drama's ability to explore extreme scenarios—doubtless
spoke to his ancient spectators' deepest fears of what might go wrong at
home in their absence.[69] This Clytemnestra might therefore provoke audience responses of either relief that individuals' own wives were virtuous by
comparison, or alarm that leaving women at home for long periods might
breed resentment and betrayal.

---

[68] See, for example, Houppert (2005, pp. 115–40) for specific examples of spousal violence
among military populations. Cesur and Sabia (2016) is the first systematic study in a US context of the rates of domestic violence among veterans of recent conflicts. For domestic violence
in a UK military context, see Gray (2016), and Centre for Social Justice (2016, pp. 82–3).

[69] As Allen-Hornblower (2016, p. 184) points out, 'While caution is always in order regarding what we can assume the audience's reactions to a given scene might have been, it seems safe
to assume that a war hero returning to a household of adultery and betrayal is hardly likely to
have evoked a divided or uncertain response from the spectators (especially in a fifth-century,
predominantly male audience).'

Ancient stories of reunion, while very different in context from those witnessed on modern-day military bases, provide mythical paradigms for the very real challenges posed as couples deal with the complex emotions associated with the return of a soldier. As the accounts of contemporary soldiers' spouses highlighted in this chapter reveal, even in relatively straightforward situations—far removed from the horrific scenario staged by Aeschylus—there are difficulties to navigate. The notion of an 'ideal' homecoming, as often romanticized by the modern media, is as much a myth as the stories of Penelope and Odysseus. The moment of a partner's return is, as for Penelope, only the start of an often complex (and sometimes unsuccessful) process of recognition and reintegration. Moreover, as in the case of Penelope and Odysseus, such returns are usually for modern military spouses (as in the world of Homer and Aeschylus' audiences) just one part of a repeating cycle of departure, separation, and reunion. With frequent deployments still a normal part of military life, the reunion process is one which many military spouses must relive time and again. Each homecoming is in itself more than just the arrival home of an absent partner; each time the waiting spouse must, like Penelope, get to know her partner once more.

6

Aftermath: Euripides' *Trojan Women* and *Andromache*, and the Tecmessa of Sophocles' *Ajax*

Inside the hut, we found Hecuba with Polyxena kneeling at her feet. Beside them, Andromache, Hector's widow, sat staring into space. The woman standing next to me said Andromache had just been allocated to Pyrrhus, Achilles' son, the boy who'd killed Priam. Looking at her face, you could see how little it mattered to her. Less than an hour ago, Odysseus had picked up her small son by one of his chubby legs and hurled him from the battlements of Troy. Her only child dead, and tonight she was expected to spread her legs for her new owner, a pimply adolescent boy, the son of the man who'd killed her husband.

Extract from Pat Barker, *The Silence of the Girls*[1]

Narrated by Briseis, the human 'war prize' over whom Achilles and Agamemnon quarrel at the opening of the *Iliad*, Pat Barker's 2018 novel, *The Silence of the Girls*, reimagines the experiences of the female survivors of the Trojan War.[2] The reader witnesses the women being taken by force and held captive in the Greek camp while their homeland is demolished and their husbands, brothers, and sons slaughtered. Towards the end of the novel, as the women await transportation to Greece and a future as slaves of the men who have destroyed their city, the narrator paints a harrowing picture of the brutality and humiliation to which they are subjected. Herded together, they are beaten by the victorious soldiers, who strike them with the butts of their spears; some women have chosen suicide rather than enforced displacement and a lifetime of servitude. Male children, like Andromache's infant son, have been killed to prevent them from growing

---

[1] Barker (2019 [2018], p. 313).
[2] On the representation of women as war prizes in the *Iliad*, see above, pp. 25–6.

Warriors' Wives: Ancient Greek Myth and Modern Experience. Emma Bridges, Oxford University Press.
© Emma Bridges 2023. DOI: 10.1093/oso/9780198843528.003.0007

up to seek vengeance on their city's destroyers. Barker's narrative captures the range of traumatic events—bereavement, violence, rape, enslavement, and displacement—which the women of Troy suffer after the city's fall. In centring the women's experiences, *The Silence of the Girls*—along with its 2021 sequel, *The Women of Troy*—fills in some of the gaps left by the *Iliad*, where the male warriors occupy the majority of our attention. As her novel's title suggests, Barker's work breaks the silence of the women whose voices we rarely hear in the ancient epic.[3]

Although Homeric poetry alludes only in passing to the brutality to which women are subjected in wartime, some surviving ancient texts do explore more fully the fate of the Trojan women. Several Athenian tragic dramas of the fifth century BCE portray female survivors in the aftermath of the conflict. Of course, the women who suffer in war are not only the wives of soldiers, but also their daughters, sisters, and mothers. In light of the emphasis of this book, however, my focus in what follows is on tragic representations of women who are the wives of warriors. The most well-known soldier's spouse on the Trojan side is Andromache, Hector's wife. Her story, of a woman whose home is under threat from external aggressors, differs from those of women like Penelope or Clytemnestra who are left behind in relative safety while their husbands are away on military missions elsewhere. As well as appearing in the *Iliad*, Andromache is a key figure in two of Euripides' fifth-century Trojan War plays: his *Andromache* and *Trojan Women* explore her experience as a war captive after the sack of Troy.[4] Meanwhile Tecmessa, whose story is less prominent than that of Andromache in the surviving Trojan War tradition, but who features in Sophocles' fifth-century tragedy *Ajax*, also endures the profoundly distressing consequences of war. Like Andromache, Tecmessa is a survivor of enslavement and rape: she is the intimate partner of the Greek warrior Ajax who ravaged her city during a predatory raid from Troy. In Sophocles' version of her story she also witnesses at close quarters Ajax's mental breakdown and suicide. Andromache and Tecmessa endure deeply disturbing events with ongoing emotional impact; we might now refer to this as trauma, a broad term which can refer both to adverse events themselves and to the effects of those adverse events upon people who experience

---

[3] For another recent novel that focuses on the experiences of the women involved in the Trojan War, see Haynes (2019). On modern creative responses to Homer produced by women, see more broadly Cox and Theodorakopoulos (2019, eds.).

[4] On Andromache in the *Iliad*, see above, pp. 21–32.

them.[5] Both women experience primary trauma—that is, they themselves live through traumatic events including bereavement, violence, and rape. Tecmessa, through her proximity to Ajax, also experiences secondary trauma as she is exposed to his trauma as well as her own.[6]

Violence against women has always been a real and shocking feature of war. I begin this chapter by outlining the realities of wartime brutality both in ancient Greek society and in contemporary conflicts. My focus then turns to the three surviving Athenian tragedies that portray the traumatic experiences of Andromache and Tecmessa in the aftermath of the Trojan War. First I examine Euripides' *Trojan Women* and its depiction of Andromache in the moments immediately after her capture; I then consider Euripides' *Andromache*, which imagines her fate as a 'spear-won' woman long after the fall of Troy. Finally, I discuss Sophocles' *Ajax*, where, for the playwright, Tecmessa is of far less dramatic interest than his male hero. I suggest here, however, that fruitful comparisons might be drawn between his representation of Tecmessa's situation and some of the experiences reported by the partners of traumatized veterans on their return from combat. As in the earlier chapters of this book I observe too throughout the course of my discussion that the stories of women—both mythical and real—who are affected by conflict have historically been given much less attention than those of the male combatants.

Rape as a weapon of war

Representations of ancient Greek warfare in historiographical texts such as those written by the fifth-century-BCE authors Herodotus and Thucydides make it clear that the brutality experienced by the female characters of

---

[5] I use the broad term 'trauma' in both of these senses throughout this chapter. Note that trauma and its effects should not be conflated with post-traumatic stress disorder (PTSD), a clinical condition which manifests as an extreme and often debilitating response to trauma and which was first given a definition by medical practitioners in 1980. On the problematic issue of applying a retrospective 'diagnosis' of PTSD to characters—real or fictional—from the ancient past, see further below, pp. 192–3. On the evolution of the term 'trauma' to refer both to an event and its effects, see Erikson (1995, pp. 184–5). For an overview of trauma studies with specific relevance to the study of the ancient world, see Karanika and Panoussi (2020, eds., pp. 1–8). The literature on trauma is extensive; a helpful starting-point is Herman (1992). On the complexities of discussing trauma in relation to the representation of the emotional experiences of characters in ancient Greek tragedy, see Weiberg (forthcoming, Chapter 1).

[6] Shannon (2014, p. 160). On secondary traumatization of the partners of war veterans, including an overview of psychological research into the topic, see Dekel et al. (2016).

tragedy was not merely the stuff of myth; the violation and humiliation of women was a part of the routine conduct of war in the ancient Greek world. The female survivors of the Trojan War whom we meet in fifth-century tragedy are represented as enduring many of the horrors which real-life warfare brought for women on the defeated side; armed conflict often incorporated the capture, physical assault, and rape of the surviving women and children of a defeated territory. Survivors may also be forcibly removed from their native land and transported back to the victors' homeland along with the material spoils of war. As the work of Kathy Gaca has demonstrated, this practice of 'andrapodizing' (a term derived from the Greek ἀνδραποδίζω, referring to the subjugation of war captives by brutalizing and enslaving them) was the second of two phases of aggressive warfare; the first of these phases was the killing of the adult males of a defeated state.[7] For example, in the early years of the Peloponnesian War, the Athenians crushed a revolt by their former allies on the island of Lesbos, including the state of Mytilene, in 428 BCE.[8] After the surrender of the rebellious islanders, the Athenian assembly voted to execute the entire adult male population of Mytilene, and to enslave the city's women and children. The outcome of the assembly's vote was subsequently rescinded after a second debate, although around a thousand people identified as instigators of the rebellion were still put to death. This episode, just one among many such incidents, highlights the brutal reality of military action during the period when Athenian tragedy was being written and performed.[9] People captured in war were now considered to be the property of the conquerors, and could be treated as the victorious army wished; women might be expected to serve their captors sexually as well as in the performance of household tasks, and any children born as a result of these repeated sexual assaults would also now be owned by the victors.

Appallingly, the rape and brutalizing of women as a method of waging war is not safely confined to the annals of history.[10] Journalist and activist Susan Brownmiller first suggested, in her 1975 book *Against Our Will: Men,*

---

[7] Gaca (2010) is a detailed study of the practice of andrapodizing in Greek narratives of warfare. On sexual violence against female war captives, see also Gaca (2011), Gaca (2014), and Gaca (2015); the latter focuses specifically on the representation of this practice as a key element of 'populace-ravaging warfare' in Homeric poetry and Athenian tragedy.

[8] The episode summarized here is related by Thucydides at 3.1–50.

[9] For another example, see below, pp. 174–5, on the Athenians' subjugation of Melos in 416 BCE.

[10] See Card (1996) on the use of rape as a martial weapon in a broad range of historical and contemporary contexts.

Women and Rape, that wartime rape—as distinct from rape perpetrated in other contexts—was a subject meriting serious attention.[11] Sexual violence remains a powerful and terrifying tool of subjugation, and continues to be employed by fighting forces today, in some cases on a vast scale; this is referred to by scholars of conflict-related violence as 'mass martial rape'.[12] Although there is no straightforward equivalence between the English word 'rape' and any single Greek term,[13] the kind of treatment of a subjugated population which we see played out in ancient Trojan War narratives falls into the broad category which international relations researchers Isikozlu and Millard describe in their suggested typology of wartime rape as 'sexual slavery', whereby individuals are considered to be the 'property' of the combatant.[14] Such sexual slavery is still a feature of some modern-day conflicts: Isikozlu and Millard point in particular to the war of the 1990s in Rwanda, where the rape of up to half a million Tutsi women perpetrated by Hutu militia—known as the Interahamwe—was a weapon of genocide, and to the conflict in the same decade in Bosnia-Herzegovina, where the forcible removal of Muslim women and girls from their homes to be used as sex slaves was one element of Serb militia tactics.[15] Imagery and language surrounding both war and sex has evolved in such a way as to create a symbolic link between the two: still today sexual encounters might be described as

---

[11] Brownmiller (1991 [1975], pp. 31–113) takes a detailed transhistorical view of wartime rape, ranging from pre-modern conflicts to those of the twentieth century. Gottschall (2004) provides a brief overview of some of the literature on wartime rape.

[12] On the term 'mass martial rape', see Card (1996). Leatherman (2011, p. 2) notes the astonishing numbers of women estimated to have been raped in post-Cold War conflicts alone; she cites statistics suggesting that, for example, 'as many as 500,000 women were raped in the Rwandan genocide; 60,000 in the wars in Bosnia and Herzegovina and Croatia; and 64,000 internally displaced women were victims of sexual violence in Sierra Leone during the decade of civil war from 1991–2001'.

[13] Rabinowitz (2011, p. 6) and Cantarella (2006, pp. 243–4). The fullest discussion of the (il) legalities, in a classical Athenian context, of actions which would in modern terms be considered as rape remains Omitowoju (2002).

[14] Isikozlu and Millard (2010). The authors of this report set out fully the characteristics, recent geopolitical contexts for, and different types of 'sexual slavery' as it occurs in wartime at pp. 43–9. On wartime sexual slavery in modern-day contexts, see also Ward et al. (2007, pp. 16–19).

[15] On sexual violence in the Rwandan genocide, see Nowrojee (1996). Stiglmayer (1994) provides several examples from Bosnia and Herzegovina. The United Nations produces an annual report, 'Conflict-Related Sexual Violence', which provides a detailed overview of current instances of wartime sexual violence, the regions affected and the scale of the issue. At the time of writing, the most recently available report was that covering 2019, accessible at https://www.un.org/sexualviolenceinconflict/wp-content/uploads/2020/07/report/conflict-related-sexual-violence-report-of-the-united-nations-secretary-general/2019-SG-Report.pdf. Most recently, evidence has begun to emerge about the perpetration of rape by Russian soldiers in the conflict in Ukraine. See Boesten (2022).

'conquests', while descriptions of invasions might refer to the 'rape' of a territory, and the representation of weapons of war as phallic symbols has become a widely used trope.[16]

The notion that female survivors are utterly at the mercy of their captors, with no agency of their own, remains as pervasive in some accounts of recent atrocities as it does in ancient descriptions of the aftermath of war. In particular, the horrific first-person testimonies gathered in Binaifer Nowrojee's 1996 report on the Rwandan genocide for Human Rights Watch read as chilling contemporary echoes of the millennia-old stories of the women of Troy. The women's accounts collected here describe their witnessing the Interahamwe's murder of the men and boys in their family before themselves being taken by force, then raped and mutilated. One survivor, 'Marie-Claire', reported when discussing her rapist: 'He said "we have all the rights over you and we can do whatever we want." They had all the power—our men, our husbands, were all exterminated. We have no mother, no father, no brothers.'[17] Strikingly, the way in which 'Marie-Claire' refers to the deaths of her family calls to mind Andromache's reflection, in the *Iliad*, that she had lost her father, mother, and brothers, and that she would soon also lose her husband (*Iliad* 6.413–30).[18] Elsewhere in Nowrojee's report, 'Clementine' recalls being told by her captors, 'You must accept everything that we do to you now.'[19] This kind of ownership of female survivors by a victorious militia recalls the wholesale capture and violation of women after the killing of their male relatives in ancient Greek conflicts.[20]

First-hand testimonies like those collected in Nowrojee's report are, however, difficult to locate. This results from a combination of the culture of shame surrounding rape, the effects of trauma—which can suppress individuals' ability or willingness to speak of their suffering—and the reluctance or inability of researchers to identify the existence of such atrocities.[21] Journalist Alexandra Stiglmayer writes of her experiences of interviewing survivors of the war in Bosnia-Herzegovina, 'In the refugee camps we visited, how frequently we were told, "Of course we have cases of rape; I can

[16] Porter (1986, p. 233) and Seifert (1994, p. 60). Mechling (2008) discusses in detail the 'symbolic equivalence' of the penis and weapons.
[17] Nowrojee (1996, pp. 27–8).
[18] For a fuller discussion of this scene in the *Iliad*, see above, p. 24.
[19] Nowrojee (1996, p. 28).
[20] Although progress towards gender equality has been made in recent decades, at the time of the conflict Rwandan women were largely dependent on their male relatives for their legal and social status. See Nowrojee (1996, p. 4 and pp. 14–16).
[21] See, for example, Seifert (1994, pp. 66–9) and Heineman (2011, ed., p. 7).

show you the women, but they don't talk about it. They withdraw, they don't say much, they sit in a corner and cry…They won't talk with us, let alone you." [22] In a stark illustration of the impact which trauma has on individuals, one Rwandan survivor, Françoise Kayitesi, told researchers, 'I feel like I can never experience joy, and I do not wish to speak about what I experienced. I can't even write down what happened to me. When I try, I stop after one page and burn the writing.' [23] The challenges of gaining an understanding of this aspect of women's lives are therefore even more pronounced than those which I have observed elsewhere in this book.

While the political, social, and cultural circumstances under which ancient drama was produced differed considerably from the contexts of more recent wars, Athenian tragedy nonetheless delves into aspects of armed conflict which remain pertinent in contemporary societies. As I have noted in earlier chapters, the critical distance afforded by mythical narratives—set in a distant past but with characters who face challenges and dilemmas which might resonate for their audiences—can stimulate reflection on complex and emotive real-world issues. Athenian drama could exercise a profound effect on ancient spectators' emotions, [24] and in particular the performance of tragedies focusing on war and its aftermath could offer a way for audiences to reflect on their own experiences of collective trauma. [25] Shay, for example, views Athenian theatre, which was performed by and for combat veterans, as a form of 'cultural therapy', and Meineck suggests that it offers a form of 'cultural catharsis' for those who have experienced combat. [26] Yet Athenian drama was written and performed by men, for a predominantly—if not exclusively—male audience. [27] Therefore the

[22] Stiglmayer (1994, p. 83).
[23] Quoted in de Brouwer and Ka Hon Chu (2009, eds., p. 135).
[24] Meineck (2019, pp. 71–2) observes that 'Greek drama aimed to provoke the audience to feel for others, often marginalised, powerless and foreign characters, or mythological personages in the depths of despair'. Meineck (2018) considers in depth the emotional power of theatre as a live art form.
[25] Tragedy was performed at a competitive annual civic and religious festival funded by the state, the City Dionysia, which took place over several days in the spring. The festival's ceremonial aspects emphasized the collective responsibility of members of the democratic city as well as the state's responsibility towards those who fought on Athens' behalf. For example, each year there was a pre-performance parade of orphans whose fathers had died in battle, raised at the city's expense and gifted with a full set of costly hoplite armour. On the format and significance of the City Dionysia, and its function as a performance of Athenian civic ideology, see Goldhill (1986, pp. 75–7). Meineck (2012, pp. 10–11) outlines the links between ancient combat and the theatre.
[26] Shay (2002, p. 153); Meineck (2012).
[27] See Goldhill (1994) on the gender of Athenian theatre audiences.

traumas of women which were played out on the ancient tragic stage differed significantly from the experiences of spectators who, as combatants, may well have been responsible themselves for inflicting such atrocities on subjugated populations.[28] With this in mind, the presence of captive women on stage invited ancient audiences not so much to see their own experiences reflected back to them but instead to bear witness to the particular suffering of female survivors.[29] Today Athenian tragedy still has the capacity to move modern audiences deeply. I suggest that observing the painful experiences of Euripides' Andromache and Sophocles' Tecmessa onstage prompts us to reflect more closely on conflict-related trauma and its impact on those who live through it, even—or perhaps especially—if this is far beyond the realm of our own personal experience.[30]

War's immediate aftermath: Euripides' *Trojan Women*

As noted earlier, Homeric poetry, which focuses predominantly on the actions of male combatants, rarely dwells at length on the suffering of women in the aftermath of conflict.[31] In light of this, and given that even in contemporary society it can be difficult to gain an insight into women's experiences of wartime trauma, it might seem all the more remarkable to a modern reader that one ancient tragedian not only highlights the brutality endured by the women of Troy, but also on several occasions places the survivors' trauma at the very centre of his works. As discussed in Chapter 2, in the late fifth century BCE the Athenian playwright Euripides adapted elements of the Trojan War story as the basis for several of his dramatic works. As well as his Iphigenia plays examining the story of Agamemnon's sacrifice of his daughter at the start of the war, Euripides also wrote a series of tragedies which focused on the female Trojan survivors after the Greek army's

[28] I discuss a specific example of this, the Athenians' treatment of Melos, below at pp. 174–5.
[29] For a reading of another ancient tragedy, Sophocles' *Trachiniae*, as an exercise in bearing witness to female trauma, see Weiberg (2020).
[30] Modern adaptations of ancient plays often draw on their potential for encouraging reflection on current events. One recent example of this is *Queens of Syria*, an adaptation of Euripides' *Trojan Women*, which was first performed in Jordan in 2013 and later taken on tour around the UK. The performers were a group of Syrian women whose own experiences of war were woven into a contemporary version of the ancient play. For full details of the production, see the project report by Developing Artists (2016). Clapp (2016) offers a sense of the content and delivery of the performance.
[31] On the lack of attention to the wartime brutalization of women in the Homeric poems, see above, pp. 25–6.

sacking of their city. Three of Euripides' extant plays foreground Trojan women's experiences after the defeat of their homeland: his *Andromache* and *Hecuba*, which have at their centre the two most prominent royal women of Troy, and his *Trojan Women*, which is named after the play's chorus of female survivors. These re-imaginings of the aftermath of the war dwell in vivid and often shocking detail on the effects of war on women whose husbands, sons, fathers, and brothers have been murdered at the hands of an invading army. *Andromache* is set several years after the war and finds Andromache living in the home of her captor, Neoptolemus, Achilles' son.[32] I will return to consider that play in a later section. First, however, I turn to Euripides' exploration of the experiences of soldiers' wives in the immediate aftermath of conflict. My main focus in this section is on *Trojan Women*, where Andromache occupies a prominent role, although first I will touch briefly on *Hecuba*, whose central focus is on the figure of Hecuba as queen and mother of warriors, but whose chorus of female survivors also invites the audience to imagine the final moments together of these women and their soldier husbands. In particular, *Trojan Women* highlights the blurring of the distinction between legitimate marriages and the forced subjugation perpetrated by the victors, as well as highlighting Andromache's lack of agency within a patriarchal system. Any sense that she may have control over her own fate is illusory: it becomes clear that the only choice which she and her co-survivors have is between complying with their captors' demands or taking their own lives.

Hecuba—which was probably produced in the 420s BCE[33]—is set immediately after Troy's fall, and takes its audience into the camp of the Greeks where the captive women await their fate. This play frames Hecuba's reversal of fortune, from queen of Troy and mother of great warriors to enslaved captive, as symbolizing the utter devastation of the city itself. Euripides foregrounds Hecuba's grief at the fall of the city, as well as at the deaths of her husband Priam and their sons. This grief is compounded by the Greeks' sacrifice of Hecuba's daughter Polyxena at the tomb of Achilles, and the discovery that her youngest son Polydorus has been murdered by Polymestor, who had been entrusted with keeping the child safe during the war. Towards the end of the play Hecuba and the other captive women take revenge for

---

[32] Neoptolemus is named as Pyrrhus in some versions of the tradition (this is the name used for him in Barker's version of the story with which I opened this chapter).

[33] The scholarly consensus favours a date for *Hecuba* in the mid to late 420s BCE. See Collard (1991, pp. 34–5).

Polydorus' death by blinding Polymestor and killing his sons. The focus throughout remains on Hecuba, both as a former queen and as a bereaved mother. Although there is no role here for Hector's widow Andromache, the chorus of this play do nonetheless remind the audience of the plight of warriors' widows. In their first ode they sing of being taken at spearpoint by the Greeks (*Hecuba* 100–3), and later they contemplate at length their enslavement and uncertain future, anticipating their journey from Troy to Europe and a life with unknown masters (444–83).[34] In their final ode (905–51), the women of the chorus also reflect specifically on the loss of their husbands, evoking an image of a husband and wife in their bedroom as they share their final moments together on the night of Troy's fall. The intimacy and apparent ordinariness of the scene they recall—as the wife arranges her hair in the mirror while her husband retires to bed (914–26)—contrasts starkly with the horrors of war and its aftermath which have been the focus of the play so far. The time between that last moment together and the one in which the women now exist is elided in the ode, as the chorus reflect upon how, 'after seeing my husband killed [θανόντ' ἰδοῦσ' ἀκοίταν], I am led away to the ocean's sea, looking back at the city' (936–9); they sing of being overcome by grief (τάλαιν' ἀπεῖπον ἄλγει, 942). The horrors to which they have been subjected in the intervening time are here left to the audience's imagination, although Hecuba's descriptions elsewhere in the play of the brutality of the Greeks fill in some of these gaps; she refers, for example, to the dragging of women away from the altars where they sought refuge (289–90).

Euripides' *Trojan Women* is, like *Hecuba*, set immediately after the fall of the city and highlights the plight of the women bereaved, raped, displaced, and enslaved as a result of war. Produced in 415 BCE, the play is set in the camp of the Greeks, where the women lament the loss of their loved ones and their city as they wait to learn which of the Greek warriors has chosen each of them as his captive. Although the scenario and characters were drawn from myth, the events played out on stage would strike a familiar chord for an Athenian audience. Many spectators would have served on military missions during the ongoing Peloponnesian War, undertaking siege warfare as well as exacting often brutal punishment on enemy states. In the years immediately prior to the play's first performance, the Athenians had laid siege to Melos, a small island which had remained neutral in the war. In 416 BCE, when the Melians refused to support Athens against

---

[34] Mossman (1995, pp. 69–93) discusses in detail the role of the chorus in this play. See also Foley (2015, pp. 61–6).

Sparta, the Athenians massacred all of the island's male citizens and enslaved the women and children.[35] Although the Athenian historian Thucydides does not record what happened to the Melian women and children who were enslaved, it is likely that at least some of them would have been brought back to Athens. The sight onstage of captive women bound for foreign shores after the destruction of their homeland must, therefore, have evoked comparisons with the plight of the Melians. *Trojan Women*, in its detailed study of the suffering which women might endure at the hands of a conquering army, invites its audience to consider the impact of war on non-combatants and reads as an indictment of the Athenians' brutality towards the people they had subjugated.[36] For a twenty-first-century audience, it can also provoke reflection on the violation of women, which is still a feature of conflicts around the globe today.

Our attention in *Trojan Women* is focused largely on the individual fates of Hecuba, Andromache, and Cassandra. Each woman represents the suffering of a different generation of Trojan women as, respectively, the elderly mother of warriors, the wife of a fallen soldier, and the young unmarried woman. Euripides also uses a chorus of captive women to examine the collective experience of the city's female survivors. These women are 'wretched captive(s) of the spear' (τάλαινα δοριάλωτος, 517); here, as in the Homeric texts, the notion of being 'spear-won' alludes to the violence to which war captives could often be subjected.[37] The chorus sing of their harrowing memories as they lament the fall of Troy, conjuring images of trembling children clinging to their mothers as the city was stormed, its men slaughtered, and its women raped (555–67, 1081–99). Each woman will be a 'prize' (στέφανος, 565) for a Greek warrior,[38] and—in a hint at the sexual violence which she will endure—will now be expected to 'bear sons for Greece' (Ἑλλάδι κουροτρόφον, 566). The play's central figure is the Trojan queen Hecuba, who remains onstage throughout, and who embodies the trauma

---

[35] Thucydides 5.84–116 narrates the story of Melos' demise, including the now-famous 'Melian dialogue' in which he relates a version of the conversation which was said to have taken place between the Athenians and the Melians prior to Athens' decision.

[36] The extent to which *Trojan Women* was intended as a comment on the Athenians' behaviour towards the Melians has been much debated. Goff (2012, pp. 27–35) provides a helpful summary of the arguments on both sides of the 'Melos interpretation' of the play. See also Croally (1994, pp. 232–4).

[37] On the notion of being 'spear-won' in Homeric poetry, and the brutal implications of this, see above, pp. 25–6.

[38] The word στέφανος refers to a victory crown or wreath and is usually associated with athletics but here refers to the women as a metaphorical 'crown' for the victorious army.

experienced collectively by the women of Troy.[39] She has witnessed the loss of her sons in battle, the murder of her husband Priam at the hands of the Greeks, and the destruction of her city. Her daughters too will suffer; in the course of the play, she learns of the sacrifice of her child Polyxena at Achilles' tomb, and the presence of Cassandra also focuses our attention on this daughter's doomed future. In keeping with my concern in this book to examine the depiction of warriors' wives, however, it is Andromache, as war-ravaged widow of a fallen warrior, who will be the main focus in my discussion of the play.

Unlike Hecuba, Andromache is present only for around 200 of the play's 1300 lines. Nonetheless, Euripides' depiction of her here draws our attention to the trauma endured by a war widow whose fate will now be determined by the conquering army. Andromache's entrance in *Trojan Women* echoes our first encounter with her in the *Iliad*, as she is accompanied by Astyanax, to whom the chorus refer as 'Hector's child' (571). In contrast with the scene in the *Iliad*, however, mother and son are now treated as spoils of war; they are being transported in a cart belonging to the enemy along with the rest of the loot, including the dead Hector's weapons, which was 'taken by the spear' (δοριθήρατος, 574) from Troy (572–6). Together Andromache and Hecuba lament for the city of Troy and for their loved ones; the two women have in common their grief for Hector as Hecuba mourns him as her child (588–9) and Andromache as her husband (587). Andromache then shares the news that the Greeks have murdered Hecuba's daughter Polyxena (623–4), before delivering a longer speech of her own in which she reflects on her role as Hector's wife and on her own fate now that he is dead (634–83). After Hecuba's response, in which the older woman advises Andromache on how to cope with what life has thrown at her, the herald Talthybius arrives with news that the Greeks intend to kill Andromache's infant son Astyanax.[40] Andromache's final speech in the play (740–79) is a heart-rending lament for the fate of her child before he is taken away. She too leaves the stage at this point. When Talthybius returns shortly afterwards, bringing Astyanax's body on Hector's shield, he reports that Andromache has already been taken away to Greece by Achilles' son Neoptolemus (1123–30) having pleaded for her child to be given to Hecuba for burial.

---

[39] Raudnitz (2018, pp. 124–55) presents a detailed reading of Hecuba's character in *Trojan Women*, with a particular focus on her trauma.

[40] In the play Astyanax's death represents the future which Troy has been denied. See, for example, Hecuba's lament for her dead grandson at 1156–1206, in which she reflects on the life that Astyanax could have had had he been allowed to grow to adulthood.

Like the Andromache of the *Iliad*, Euripides' Andromache retains the role of the ideal wife of Troy's greatest warrior, exemplifying the characteristics that mark women out as desirable partners. She reflects (645-6), 'I worked hard in Hector's house at the things which are considered respectable for women [ἃ γὰρ γυναικὶ σῶφρον']': this included remaining indoors and not allowing herself to be influenced by other women's gossip (650-3). Meanwhile, she recalls, 'I kept for my husband a silent tongue and a peaceful demeanour' (γλώσσης τε σίγην ὄμμα θ' ἥσυχον πόσει / παρεῖχον, 654-5), observing when to yield to him and when to assert herself. This picture of passivity, quietness, and introspection has much in common with the model military spouse whom we have encountered in earlier chapters.[41] Andromache's marriage to Hector is also idealized here, as she goes on to make a comparison with the horror of the situation which she now faces: she reflects (673-8),

> Darling Hector, I was content with you, a husband endowed with intelligence, good birth, wealth and bravery. You took me, pure, from my father's house and first joined in marriage [ἐζεύξω] with me, a virgin. And now you are lost and I shall be carried on a ship to Greece, a prisoner, to wear the yoke of slavery [αἰχμάλωτος ἐς δοῦλον ζυγόν].

The Greek terminology used here emphasizes the ghastly contrast between Andromache's past and her present. The verb relating to marriage, ἐζεύξω (676), derives from a root meaning 'yoking', to refer to the joining of a husband and wife; similarly, the 'yoke of slavery', δοῦλον ζυγόν (678) also relates to the binding action but here recalls the yoking of beasts in order to compel them to serve their owners.

By setting up Andromache's marriage as the ideal, Euripides is also able to create a contrast between her relationship with Hector and the relationship with Neoptolemus into which she will now be forced. She reflects (658-60) that it is the same virtuous qualities which made her a worthy wife for Hector that have now attracted the attention of Neoptolemus: 'For when I was captured, Achilles' son wanted to take me as his wife [με...λαβεῖν δάμαρτα]' (660-1). The Greek term which Andromache uses for 'wife' here, δάμαρ, is usually applied to a legitimate spouse,[42] yet clearly—as Euripides had also explored in his earlier tragedy *Andromache*, which I will discuss

---

[41] See above, p. 9, p. 48, p. 90, and p. 111, with Enloe (2000, pp. 162-3).
[42] Barlow (1986), at line 660.

further in the next section—her relationship with Neoptolemus does not equate to that which she shared with Hector. She is still addressed by Talthybius as 'wife of Hector (Ἕκτορος δάμαρ), once the bravest of the Phrygians' (709), although, with Hector's death, she has now lost all of the protection which that status afforded her. Her lack of agency is also underscored repeatedly by the herald as he delivers the news that her child will be killed. The Greek text here uses three different phrases to emphasize her powerlessness: Talthybius insists (728–30), 'do not consider yourself strong when you have no strength [μήτε σθένουσα μηδὲν ἰσχύειν δόκει]; for you have no power [ἔχεις γὰρ ἀλκὴν οὐδαμῇ]...your city and your husband are destroyed, and you are overcome [κρατῇ δὲ σύ]'. He advises Andromache not to struggle, but to remain silent and bear her misfortunes (σιγῶσα δ᾽ εὖ τε τὰς τύχας κεκτημένη, 737) in the hope that the Greeks will not deny her son burial. The notion that Andromache is dependent on her husband for her identity and status recalls her portrayal in the *Iliad*, and her dependency and subsequent helplessness become all the more apparent here, now that Hector is no longer alive.[43]

Andromache articulates the horror of her situation in a heart-rending lament for her child (740–79) in which she kisses Astyanax goodbye; this is her final speech in the play. In her words to Astyanax, she emphasizes the way in which the norms of marriage and family life have been dismantled by war, as she refers to 'my unhappy marriage bed and the wedding [λέκτρα τἀμὰ δυστυχῆ τε καὶ γάμοι] by which I came once to Hector's home' (744–5). She closes this final speech by saying, 'I've come to a fine wedding [καλὸν...ὑμέναιον] indeed, having lost my own child' (778–9). The reference to Andromache's 'wedding' to Neoptolemus echoes the earlier description of herself as his 'wife'; once again we are reminded of the gulf between her marriage to Hector and her new life as captive and forced sexual partner to an enslaver. It is, however, important to bear in mind that the contrast between forced concubinage and legitimate marriage would be perceived differently by a fifth-century-BCE Athenian spectator than by a modern audience. In ancient Athens, women's agency was already limited by the patriarchal structure of society, in which a marriage was the legal process of transfer of a woman from her father to a husband.[44] While a modern reader might be most concerned with the contrast between mutually consensual

---

[43] See above, pp. 24–7, on Andromache's dependence on Hector in the *Iliad*.

[44] For a summary of the law relating to Athenian marriage, see Cantarella (2006, pp. 245–7).

relationships and those into which women are forced against their will, a key issue at stake here for an ancient Athenian audience would be the use of force to take the property of another man.

Nonetheless, the sense that war disrupts the legitimate marriages which thrive in peacetime, and replaces these with relationships like that which is forced upon Andromache and her co-survivors, is present throughout *Trojan Women*. Towards the end of her opening song, Hecuba sings, 'Oh sorrowful wives of bronze-speared Trojans, and ill-wedded girls, Troy is smouldering; let us lament it' (ὦ τῶν χαλκεγχέων Τρώων / ἄλοχοι μέλεαι / καὶ κόραι δύσνυμφαι, / τύφεται Ἴλιον, αἰάζωμεν, 142–5). Her words allude both to the mourning widows like Andromache who have lost their husbands to war and to the unmarried young women who will be 'ill-wedded' (δύσνυμφαι) as they are subjected, as spear-won women, to a distorted version of marriage.[45] In this play it is Cassandra who represents the latter group; the god Poseidon announces in the play's prologue that Agamemnon will 'forcibly wed'(γαμεῖ βιαίως, 44) her, and it is clear that she will be expected to submit to him sexually. Talthybius refers to the Greek leader's improper relationship with Cassandra as 'shady nuptials' (σκότια νυμφευτήρια, 252),[46] and Hecuba reflects, 'I never thought you would be contracted to marriage by the spear, under Argive (Greek) weapons' (ὡς οὐχ ὑπ' αἰχμῆς <σ'> οὐδ' ὑπ' Ἀργείου δορὸς / γάμους γαμεῖσθαι τούσδ' ἐδόξαζόν ποτε, 346–7).[47] In her delirium, Cassandra also sings a version of a celebratory marriage hymn, addressed to Hymenaeus, god of marriage (308–41); such a song would be appropriate for a proper wedding ritual in peacetime, yet in the context of her enforced capture and sexual enslavement to the victorious Greek commander, it becomes a reflection

---

[45] Improper marriage of various kinds is a recurring theme throughout this play; it is particularly present too in the references to the relationship of Helen and Paris, which was the catalyst for the Trojan War. For example, Andromache says that the Greeks destroyed Troy 'for the sake of a hateful marriage' (λεχέων στυγερῶν χάριν, 598); the chorus later reiterate that Troy's losses have been 'for the sake of one woman and her hateful marriage' (μιᾶς γυναικὸς καὶ λέχους στυγνοῦ χάριν, 781). Elsewhere Hecuba also describes her own suffering as having come about 'because of one marriage of one woman' (διὰ γάμον μιᾶς ἕνα / γυναικός, 498–9). A significant proportion of the play is devoted to the *agōn* in which Hecuba and Helen debate the extent to which Helen and the problems associated with her 'marriage' to Paris, is to blame for the war.

[46] The translation 'shady nuptials' is Gaca's (2015, p. 287), although for γαμεῖ βιαίως she uses 'forcibly copulate'. In the case of the latter I favour 'forcibly wed' since it retains the sense of γαμεῖ as referring to marriage. Croally (1994, pp. 87–8) also discusses the translation of the terms used here, noting that that words with the Greek root γαμ- can refer to other kinds of sexual union as well as marriage.

[47] The Greek phrase translated here as 'contracted to marriage' is γάμους γαμεῖσθαι.

on just how far from normality are the horrors which this community of women will continue to endure.[48]

The euphemistic descriptions of the relationships of captive women to their enslavers as 'marriages', and the representation of wartime rape victims as the 'wives' of their abductors find striking parallels in the stories of survivors of recent wars. First-hand testimony provided by survivors of the Rwandan genocide illustrates the insidious way in which rape under these circumstances can become conflated—by both its perpetrators and its victims—with legitimate marriage. 'Francoise', a Rwandan survivor abducted by Interahamwe militia in 1994, later recalled how she was taken back to their camp to perform, under duress, the duties expected of a wife:

> They told me, You will be our wife. If you die, you will die here... I did all the ordinary things a woman does: cooking, sweeping, washing clothes. I was never given a gun. Sometimes I had to work in the vegetable garden... They forced me to have sex with them every day, whenever they wanted.[49]

Time and again, in the case of the Rwandan genocide, the language used to describe the relationships of women with the rapists who took them away from their homes echoes that of the ancient descriptions of the Trojan survivors' relationship with their captors. Survivor accounts gathered by Nowrojee frequently state that the soldiers would proclaim that the women they captured and raped were being taken as their 'wives'. In some cases even distorted versions of the proper rituals ordinarily associated with marriage in peacetime were carried out; in one case a militia leader officiated over a 'marriage ceremony' in which four young women were 'married' to members of his group.[50]

Nowrojee's account of the experiences of Rwandan women also highlights an aspect of their situation that is present too in ancient tragedy: the need to comply with their captors' demands in order to survive, which can lead to the blurring of the distinction between rape and a legitimate marriage. In her discussion of captive women in ancient tragedy, Scodel refers to this inner conflict over whether to resist or to yield to the men on whom

---

[48] Rabinowitz (2011, pp. 14–15) discusses the blurring of the lines between marriage and sexual slavery in *Trojan Women*.
[49] Ward et al. (2007, pp. 34–5).   [50] Nowrojee (1996, pp. 33–7).

their security now depends as the 'captive's dilemma'.[51] As one survivor of the Rwandan genocide, 'Marie-Claire', acknowledged, 'To survive, you had to let yourself be raped.'[52] Reflecting on the reconfiguring of martial rape as 'marriage', Nowrojee writes,

> Many of the women who were held in these forced 'marriages', show enormous internal conflict when they describe the situation. On the one hand, they had no choice and in most cases despise the man whom they refer to as their 'husband'. On the other hand, they also realize that without the protection of this very man (who in many cases murdered the rest of their family), they would most probably be dead today.[53]

This is illustrated starkly in the account given by 'Ancille', who recounted, 'He would lock me in the house in the day and in the evening he would come home and I would be his wife...I wouldn't say that I was taken by force. I did it to save my life. He was my husband.' 'Ancille' told investigators that, with nowhere else to go, she had no choice but to yield to the demands of the man whom she hated.[54]

The 'captive's dilemma' is conspicuous too in *Trojan Women*. Andromache articulates her own agonizing predicament (661–70):

> And if I push aside my darling Hector and open my heart to my present husband [τὸν παρόντα πόσιν], I will appear treacherous to the dead. But if I hate [Neoptolemus] I shall be hated by my master. And yet they say that just one night diminishes a woman's hostility to a man's bed. I despise the woman who casts out her previous husband [ἄνδρα τὸν πάρος] and loves another in a new bed. Not even a horse when separated from its mate will easily bear the yoke.

Andromache's condemnation of women who are disloyal to their husbands, in a play where Helen's betrayal of Menelaus for the sake of her relationship with Paris is also the focus of debate, might seem more appropriate as a comment on adulterers than on women who betray their dead husbands. Here, however, it highlights the impossible bind in which

---

[51] Scodel (1998).   [52] Nowrojee (1996, p. 27).
[53] Nowrojee (1996, p. 34).   [54] Nowrojee (1996, p. 34).

Andromache and her co-survivors have found themselves.[55] Hecuba also
recognizes the need to comply in order to survive, advising Andromache
to set aside her grief for Hector and to, 'Honour your present master, giving him incentive to love you for your actions' (τίμα δὲ τὸν παρόντα
δεσπότην σέθεν, / φίλον διδοῦσα δέλεαρ ἀνδρὶ σῶν τρόπων, 699–700).[56] The
only alternative to compliance in these circumstances is suicide; Hecuba's
own resolve to survive weakens later in the play as she attempts to rush
into the flames of Troy, suggesting that it would be best for her to die
along with the city itself (1282–3). Andromache also suggests that
Polyxena was fortunate to die, in comparison with what she herself is suffering while still alive (630–1); death, she suggests, is preferable to living a
painful life (637).[57]

The lack of agency which I have highlighted elsewhere in this book
as a recurring element of the experiences of many soldiers' wives—both
in ancient mythical narratives and in reality—becomes even more
pronounced in situations such as that faced by the Trojan women after
the fall of their city. The already considerable traumas of bereavement
and the loss of their homes are compounded by the brutality which they
suffer at the hands of their captors. As a widow, Andromache is vulnerable
to being preyed on by the conquering army, and will be passed to another
man to use as he pleases. She has little choice but to submit to her captor;
the alternative is death. Where *Trojan Women*, like *Hecuba*, focuses on
the implications of this lack of agency in the immediate aftermath of a
military defeat, Euripides' earlier *Andromache* had looked further into
the future, imagining the longer-term consequences for Andromache of
her survival and her submission to Neoptolemus. It is to this play that
I now turn.

[55] Note that Cassandra also yields to her captor; Scodel (1998, p. 147) suggests that she 'goes
beyond necessary acquiescence in her concubinage to Agamemnon: she celebrates it as a marriage'. With this in mind, Cassandra's marriage-song might read not as a sign of madness but as
an extreme manifestation of the survival tactics necessary for women in her situation.

[56] Hecuba also suggests that this will secure a future for Andromache and her son so that
they may return to Troy one day; the women do not yet know that the Greeks plan to murder
Astyanax.

[57] In Euripides' *Hecuba*, Polyxena ultimately goes willingly to her death, asserting that
this is preferable to a life of slavery (*Hecuba* 349–78). Within the Trojan mythic cycle,
the sacrifice of Polyxena at the tomb of Achilles before the Greeks sail home mirrors the
sacrifice of another adolescent girl, Iphigenia, on the Greek side before the expedition to
Troy: see Anderson (1997, pp. 60–1). I discuss the sacrifice of Iphigenia at length above,
in Chapter 2.

Longer-term repercussions: Euripides' *Andromache*

> I have not just one but many things to lament: my native city,
> the death of Hector, and the difficult lot to which I was yoked
> when I fell, undeservedly, on the day of slavery.
>
> (Euripides, *Andromache* 96–9)

Andromache's reflection on her situation at the beginning of the play which is named after her summarizes the multiple traumas which she has endured since the fall of Troy; this play invites its audience to consider the continuing impact of war for female survivors whose lives have been catastrophically upended. Where Euripides' *Trojan Women* portrays her in the immediate aftermath of the city's defeat, his earlier *Andromache*, produced in around 425 BCE,[58] is set in Greece in the years after the Greeks' victory. In this play, we meet Andromache after she has been living for several years in Phthia with her captor Neoptolemus, son of the man who killed her husband; she has also borne him a child. Meanwhile, Neoptolemus has also married Hermione, daughter of Menelaus and Helen. Jealous of Andromache, Hermione has been scheming against her while Neoptolemus is away visiting the oracle at Delphi, and Hermione's father Menelaus is now plotting the deaths of Andromache and her son. The play opens with Andromache taking refuge at the sanctuary of Thetis, having hidden her son. Having found the child, Menelaus lures her away from the protection of the sanctuary with the promise that if she allows herself to be killed, the child will be saved; this is soon revealed to be a trick, however. Mother and child are eventually saved by the intervention of Peleus (father of Achilles and therefore Neoptolemus' grandfather). Hermione too has a change of heart, prompted by fear of Neoptolemus' anger upon his return, and attempts suicide. Subsequently Orestes arrives and takes Hermione away with him to Argos, declaring that she was betrothed to him before she married Neoptolemus. The play closes with the news that Orestes has arranged for Neoptolemus' murder at Delphi; after the arrival of Neoptolemus' corpse onstage we learn from Thetis that Andromache will now go with her child to Molossia, where she will be married to the Trojan survivor Helenus.

[58] The play is difficult to date precisely. See Lloyd (2005, pp. 12–13). A note on the ancient text also suggests that *Andromache* may first have been performed outside Athens, although it is difficult to be certain about the truth of this claim, and it seems likely that, as was the case with other plays, it was performed in multiple locations. See Allan (2000, pp. 149–60).

Andromache reflects the ancient Greek patriarchal norms which we have seen played out elsewhere: even my brief summary of the play reveals that much of its plot revolves around the transfer of ownership of women between men. This is not unique to the enslaved Andromache: the high-status Hermione too is passed to another man at the end of the play after her husband's death. As well as highlighting the lack of female agency which is also evident in *Trojan Women*, this earlier play provides a fuller picture of Andromache's past and continuing trauma, examining the ongoing consequences of war for this warrior's wife. In particular, Euripides' portrayal of the enslaved widow highlights the shame and precarity of her current situation. Yet ultimately the play, despite its apparent focus on Andromache, also reminds us that voices like hers are often rendered silent by the men who dominate the narrative. Nonetheless, this ancient text provides us, through the character of Andromache, with an opportunity to bear witness to the impact of wartime atrocities on female survivors. Not only does tragedy depict on stage the intense emotions induced by suffering, but it also has the power to evoke strong emotions in its audiences, and to encourage us to empathize with its characters. As Euripides' Andromache describes her own suffering and expresses her grief, the play's spectators may also come to empathize with her responses to trauma, even if her experiences might be far removed from their own.

In the early part of the play, Euripides gives Andromache the voice to talk about the traumas she has endured in the past, and those which she continues to endure as Neoptolemus' forced concubine.[59] In introducing herself in the play's opening prologue, Andromache summarizes her experiences, emphasizing the contrast between her past life as Hector's wife and her present situation as Neoptolemus' spear prize (5–15):

I, Andromache, was enviable in times past, but now am the most wretched woman of all... I saw my husband Hector killed by Achilles [ἥτις πόσιν μὲν Ἕκτορ' ἐξ Ἀχιλλέως / θανόντ' ἐσεῖδον], and the son I bore to my husband thrown from the steep towers when the Greeks took the land of Troy. And I, from a household considered the freest, came to Greece as a slave,

---

[59] In modern scholarship on the play, Andromache is frequently referred to as Neoptolemus' 'concubine' (see, for example, Allan (2000, p. 17 and *passim*) and Lloyd (2005, pp. 7–10)), yet this word alone is inadequate to capture the full horror of her situation as a war captive and rape victim. I therefore prefer the term 'forced concubine'. For a discussion of the representation of concubines in tragedy more broadly, see Foley (2001, pp. 87–105).

given to the islander Neoptolemus as a choice spear prize [δορὸς γέρας] from the Trojan spoils.

In contrast to the *Iliad*, where Andromache does not directly witness Hector's death but sees Achilles' later defilement of his corpse, the Greek text here appears to imply that she saw her husband killed; as for many survivors of such disturbing experiences, the horror of those events is still vivid in Andromache's memory years after the events she describes. She later elaborates further on the traumas she has endured, with a sung lament in which her grief is palpable; for an ancient audience Euripides' use of the metre usually associated with elegiac poetry would also heighten the emotional impact of her song.[60] Here the audience views Troy's last days from her perspective, as she recalls the destruction of Troy 'with spear and fire' (δορὶ καὶ πυρί, 105), the death of Hector, and Achilles' defilement of his corpse by dragging him around Troy (106–8), before reflecting on her own enslavement (109–14):

I myself was led from my bedroom to the shore of the sea, putting hateful slavery about my head [δουλοσύναν στυγερὰν ἀφιβαλοῦσα κάραι]. Many tears flowed down my cheeks, when I left behind my city, my bedroom, and my husband in the dust. Unhappy me, why must I still see the light as Hermione's slave?

Her recollection emphasizes the loss of everything she had before—her city, her home, her husband, and her freedom—and, as in *Trojan Women*, she implies here that death would be preferable to life as a slave.[61] The sense that she is enduring a kind of living death recurs later in the play too, as she tells Menelaus, 'The death which you have decided for me is not so terrible; for I was destroyed when the wretched city of the Phrygians [Troy] was ruined, along with my glorious husband' (453–6). Meanwhile, repeated references to the death of Hector and the destruction of Troy suggest that these are the indelible traumatic memories which she frequently revisits in her mind. Elsewhere, for example, she tells Menelaus of the horror of witnessing Achilles' cruel treatment of Hector's corpse and the brutality which she herself subsequently endured (399–403):

---

[60] Allan (2000, pp. 55–6) discusses the way in which the structure and metre of this song would emphasize Andromache's grief for an ancient audience.

[61] See *Trojan Women* 636–40, as noted above at p. 182.

I witnessed the slaughtered Hector dragged behind a chariot, and Troy burning pitifully; I myself went as a slave to the Argive ships, dragged by the hair, and when I arrived at Phthia I was married to Hector's murderers [φονεῦσιν Ἕκτορος νυμφεύομαι].[62]

As in the *Trojan Women*, her relationship with Neoptolemus is equated here to a marriage despite the fact that he is her enslaver and rapist. Andromache also emphasizes that she was innocent of any wrongdoing, asking, 'What city did I betray? Which of your children did I kill? What house have I burned?' (388–9). There is a striking sense here that the consequences of men's actions are most brutal for the women who have played no part themselves in waging war.

For Andromache, the traumas of bereavement—with the loss of her child as well as her husband—and the razing of her home were merely the start of a series of horrors. This play invites us to witness the ongoing ordeal of a survivor who has been enslaved, raped, taken far from home, and forced to serve her captor. Andromache refers to Neoptolemus as her master (δεσπότῃ δ' ἐμῷ, 25) and herself as his slave (δοῦλος, 30; cf. 64, 110), and makes it clear that she slept with him against her will, stating that 'I shared his bed unwillingly' (οὐχ ἑκοῦσα τῷδ' ἐκοινώθην λέχει, 38), and later that 'I was forced to sleep with my master' (ἐκοιμήθην βίᾳ / σὺν δεσπόταισι, 390–1). This is the ownership of one human being by another, and the non-consensual sexual relationship has resulted for Andromache in the birth of another child (24). It is a precarious existence for the child as well as for her, and the temporary absence of their master has made them both even more vulnerable; in her opening speech, Andromache reveals that since Neoptolemus married Hermione, she has been persecuted by her master's wife who, in her jealousy, accuses Andromache of practising witchcraft to make Hermione childless (29–35). The child's life is also at risk as Menelaus plans to kill him (47–8, 68–9). The chorus, who are themselves slaves from Phthia, remind Andromache too of her helplessness. They acknowledge that she is 'distraught from fear' (ἀτυζομέναι, 131) but insist that resistance to Menelaus' plot against her is futile and advise her to leave the shrine and accept her current status: 'recognize that you, a foreign slave from another city, are in a strange land where you can see none of your loved ones,

---

[62] The plural form of 'murderers' (φονεῦσιν) is used here as a way of generalizing, since of course it was not Neoptolemus but his father Achilles who killed Hector.

unhappiest of women, most wretched bride [παντάλαινα νύμφα]' (136–40). Menelaus' later observation that if a woman 'loses her husband she loses her life' (373), although spoken in the context of his defence of Hermione's relationship with Neoptolemus, is borne out by the fragile existence which Andromache endures after her widowhood.[63]

Euripides also provides here a snapshot of the shame and stigma that attach to a forced concubine. There is a focus throughout the play on the impropriety of a household in which a man has two women as his sexual partners,[64] and we are reminded repeatedly of the contrast in status between the two women who share Neoptolemus' bed. Hermione's opening words to Andromache make this contrast clear; she points out that she is wearing the rich clothes that formed part of the dowry she brought with her when she married Neoptolemus (147–53) before declaring, 'You, a slave and spear-won woman [δούλη καὶ δορίκτητος γυνή], plan to throw me out and take this house for yourself' (156–7).[65] The nurse later makes a point of emphasizing the distinction between a legitimate marriage and Andromache's relationship with her captor when she tries to reassure Hermione that Neoptolemus will not reject her on his return: 'Your husband will not reject his marriage with you like that, persuaded by the worthless words of a barbarian woman. In you he does not have a spear-captive from Troy [αἰχμάλωτον ἐκ Τροίας]; you are the daughter of a noble man whom he took with a rich dowry and from a city of considerable prosperity' (869–73). The contrast between the two women is particularly apparent in the play's first *agōn*, a verbal contest between Hermione and Andromache.[66] Here, Hermione's opening tirade reveals her abhorrence for the woman who previously shared her husband's bed, and she casts slurs against Andromache which draw on common stereotypes used to denigrate non-Greeks (170–6):

---

[63] Even the case which Peleus later makes for saving her life initially rests as much on the question of who has ownership of Andromache as his possession, and how he should treat her, as it does on humane principles. When Menelaus argues that it was he who took Andromache prisoner, Peleus retorts that his grandson, Neoptolemus, took her as his prize, and that she should be treated well (585–8).

[64] The choral ode at lines 465–93 focuses on the strife caused when a man shares his bed with two women; Orestes reiterates the point in his later conversation with Hermione (909).

[65] Hermione's anxiety seems to be fuelled primarily by Andromache's fertility and her own inability to conceive: see Vester (2009). Allan (2000, pp. 167–70) suggests that this may relate to anxieties in fifth-century-BCE Athens concerning the legitimacy of children, after the passing of a law which defined citizens only as those born of two citizen parents.

[66] For an analysis of the formal structure and rhetorical features of this *agōn*, see Allan (2000, pp. 128–36).

You've reached such a level of ignorance, wretched woman, that you dare to sleep with the son of the man who killed your husband, and bear the children of murderers. The whole barbarian race is the same: fathers sleep with daughters, sons with mothers, and sisters with brothers, loved ones murder each other, and there is no law to stop it.

Her accusation takes no account of the fact that, as Neoptolemus' slave, Andromache had no choice but to sleep with him; Hermione's words further stigmatize her and conflate enforced enslavement with the incest and kin-killing which she claims are characteristic of all non-Greeks.[67]

Andromache's response to Hermione in her own defence (183–231) reflects further on her own powerlessness, as well as revisiting the image of the ideal wife, which is an essential aspect of her character. Touching on the contrast between her relationship with Neoptolemus and Hermione's 'legitimate marriage' (γνησίων νυμφευμάτων, 193), she ridicules the suggestion that she wants to usurp Hermione; not only is she helpless in light of Troy's destruction (194–8), but she has no motive to do so. She makes the point that as a slave, she would not want to bear further children who would only themselves be 'slaves, and a wretched burden for me' (δούλους ἐμαυτῇ τ' ἀθλίαν ἐφολκίδα, 200); in a reminder of the servitude of any offspring she might produce, she also points out that her own children would never be viewed as kings in Phthia even if Hermione were unable to give birth (201–2). In what follows, she explains why Hermione is hated by Neoptolemus: this is not, Andromache says, because of any witchcraft but because she is unpleasant to live with, particularly because she boasts of the superiority of her own wealth, family, and homeland over those of Neoptolemus (205–12). Hermione therefore fails to meet the submissive ideal that Andromache upholds: 'Even if a woman is given to a bad husband, she must show him affection and not compete with him in pride' (213–14). By contrast, Andromache positions herself as having been a virtuous wife to Hector, even going so far as to indulge his affairs and to breastfeed his illegitimate children (222–5). 'In doing this,' she says, 'I drew my husband to me through my virtue [τῇ ἀρετῇ]' (226–7).[68]

---

[67] There is also a logical absurdity in Hermione's accusation; she implies that Andromache is entirely to blame for what she represents as Neoptolemus' indecent polygamy (177–80), yet this overlooks the fact that his relationship with Andromache began *before* his marriage to Hermione.

[68] The mention of Hector's infidelities here might seem jarring in comparison with the portrayal of his relationship with Andromache in the *Iliad*. Allan (2000, p. 135) suggests that the

The audience's sympathies are directed towards Andromache throughout the play, partly by way of the contrast that Euripides draws between her dignity, despite her suffering, and the cruel and unpleasant behaviour of Hermione. Andromache's self-sacrifice in offering to die for her son reinforces the impression of her virtue, and the moving lament between mother and child as they await their death (501–36)—to which Menelaus is cruelly impervious—stirs the audience's pity. Here Andromache once again longs for Hector's protection, reminding the audience of her vulnerability in widowhood, even long after she has been integrated into her captor's household: 'Husband, husband, if only I could have your hand and spear as allies, son of Priam!' (523–4). The chorus too sympathize with Andromache rather than Hermione: after her description of the indignities she has suffered they declare, 'I pity [ὤκτιρ'] her for what I have heard. For misfortunes, even those of a stranger, are pitiable [οἰκτρά] to all mortals' (421–2; cf. 498–500, where they express their sympathy for both mother and child). Earlier in the play they had commented too that Andromache was 'most pitiable' (οἰκτροτάτα, 141) when she first came to the house of their masters, but that they kept silent in fear of reprisal from Hermione (141–6). In bearing witness to Andromache's ongoing suffering the play's external audience, like the chorus who form its internal audience, is also invited to feel their own pity for her situation. The emotions provoked may have been all the more intense for ancient spectators with their own direct experience of war and its aftermath than for some modern audiences, many of whom have not lived through conflict in the same way. By placing Andromache's pain under the spotlight, Euripides invites us—here, as in his *Trojan Women*—to reflect on, and empathize with, the ongoing consequences of wartime trauma for its survivors.

Even despite the focus on Andromache's trauma in the early part of this tragedy, however, for much of Euripides' play, its title character is rendered silent. Soon after Peleus' arrival at line 547, our attention moves away from Andromache altogether. After begging Peleus for help (569–76), she remains onstage, unspeaking, as her fate is argued over by Menelaus and Peleus. She speaks only once more (750–6), to thank Peleus for saving her life, and to express her concern that she and her son may still be recaptured

addition of this detail is intended to illustrate 'Andromache's generosity and her less destructive method of coping with sexual rivalry'.

on their journey back to Phthia; this is the last we hear from her.[69] The remainder of the play's 1288 lines are given over to the plot's subsequent focus on Hermione, the arrival of Orestes, and the news that he has arranged the death of Neoptolemus. What little mention is made of Andromache here re-emphasizes her lack of agency and the stigma surrounding her position in the household. Hermione reports to Orestes, for example, that her actions against Andromache were influenced by other women who taunted her by asking, 'Will you put up with that wretched captive slave-woman [τὴν κακίστην αἰχμάλωτον...δούλην] in your bed?' (932–3). The last we hear of Andromache is Thetis' report that she will now marry Helenus, brother of Hector, and live with him in Molossia, along with her son, whose descendants will become kings (1243–7). Scodel reflects that within the terms of the play 'Andromache, for all her suffering, is an exceptionally successful character', largely as the marriage to Helenus represents a return to her first marital family, and her son (in some versions of the tradition named as Molossus) will found a new royal line.[70] Yet this eventual outcome does not diminish the trauma that she has undergone, and the indignity she has suffered as a captive, and we might well reflect on how little control she has over her own future.

Andromache's story here, then, is one of a warrior's wife whose first marriage is cut short by the death of her husband at the hands of the enemy. Her new 'marriage' as the spear-bride of Neoptolemus, warrior son of her dead husband's killer, supplants her previous relationship with Hector in the most brutal way imaginable. Euripides gives her the voice to describe elements of her horrific experience in the first half of the play, and invites his audience to reflect on the horrors of conflict-induced trauma for non-combatants. Yet even here, where the central character is a female survivor of wartime violence, displacement, and sexual slavery, Andromache's silence in the second half of the play is telling. In some respects, it anticipates the silence (or silencing) of wartime rape survivors in the millennia which have passed since *Andromache* was first produced. This silencing is a feature too of Sophocles' representation of another conflict survivor, Tecmessa, as I shall consider in the next and final section of this chapter.

---

[69] While some scholars assert that Andromache leaves the stage at line 765, after speaking these words, others argue that she remains onstage, but unspeaking, for the rest of the play. For a discussion of the possible staging of this final portion of the play, with Andromache present, see Golder (1983).

[70] Scodel (1998, p. 150).

Living with a wounded warrior: Sophocles' Tecmessa

While Euripides' plays are the most detailed surviving ancient tragic representations of female survivors of the Trojan War, one earlier Athenian tragedy
from the fifth century BCE also dramatizes the impact of this conflict on a
captive woman. Sophocles' *Ajax*—most likely dating from the 440s BCE[71]—
focuses on one of the foremost Greek fighters at Troy, but also features Ajax's
forced concubine Tecmessa, who was captured after he murdered her family
when the Greeks sacked her homeland in Phrygia. She subsequently bore
Ajax a son. Deeply troubled by an insult to his honour committed by the
Greek leaders, Ajax commits appalling acts of violence—witnessed by
Tecmessa—and ultimately dies by suicide in Sophocles' play. Where the plays
of Euripides discussed earlier in this chapter examine closely the experiences
of captive women, however, Sophocles' *Ajax* is concerned mainly with the
male hero at its centre. Sophocles uses Tecmessa primarily as a vehicle for
shedding light on the figure of Ajax, and seems largely unconcerned with
exploring her trauma in any depth. Nonetheless, I suggest that we can use
this text as a prompt to think about the experiences of the spouses of soldiers
who are scarred by war; Tecmessa, although not a warrior's wife in the same
sense as Andromache, endures at close quarters the consequences of her
intimate partner's conflict-induced breakdown. In this respect elements of
her story might be familiar to the modern-day spouses of traumatized
soldiers who return from the front line psychologically damaged by what
they have undergone there.[72] In this section, I offer a reading of Sophocles'
Tecmessa which acknowledges her own trauma as a survivor of conflict-
related violence as well as a witness to Ajax's mental anguish.

   In brief, the plot of Sophocles' *Ajax* is as follows. The play is opened by
the goddess Athena, who informs Odysseus that Ajax is resentful that the
Greek leaders have awarded Achilles' armour (the prize of honour for the
foremost fighter) to Odysseus instead of to him. As a result, Ajax set out to
kill Agamemnon and Menelaus, the commanders who made the decision.

---

[71] It is difficult to date the play securely. See Finglass (2011, pp. 1–11), for a full discussion of
the evidence.
[72] Elsewhere in the surviving corpus of Athenian tragedy the figure of Heracles offers
another insight into the effects of war trauma on a veteran and his family. Euripides' *Heracles
Mainomenos* (usually translated as 'The Madness of Heracles') and Sophocles' *Trachiniae* focus
on the return home of the hero Heracles and the impact of this on his family. As these stories
are not part of the Trojan War cycle, however, they fall outside the scope of my work in this
book. See further Rabinowitz (2014, pp. 191–6), Rowland (2017, pp. 1–32), and Weiberg
(forthcoming, Chapters 3 and 4).

Athena herself has intervened to prevent him from doing so, having inflicted a kind of madness on Ajax, who has unwittingly slaughtered the animals that the Greeks have taken as spoils, along with their herdsmen. We briefly see Ajax here in an exchange with Athena where, delusional, he tells her that he has killed the sons of Atreus (Agamemnon and Menelaus) and plans to torture Odysseus, whom he believes he is holding captive; he has become convinced that the animals he killed are the other Greek warriors. Tecmessa, having witnessed the aftermath of the bloodbath the previous evening, relates a graphic account of what she saw to the chorus, who are the crew of Ajax's ship and the soldiers under his command. On discovering that he has been duped into killing livestock rather than his intended targets, Ajax, despite appeals from Tecmessa and the chorus, is driven by shame to take his own life. His death takes place less than two thirds of the way into the play and, in a departure from Athenian tragic convention, happens on stage in full view of the audience. The rest of the play focuses first on the discovery of his body by Tecmessa and the chorus and then on a quarrel between the Greek warriors over whether his body should be buried. His brother Teucer argues for the performance of the funerary rituals, and Agamemnon and Menelaus oppose this on the grounds that Ajax has betrayed the army. The situation is resolved by the intervention of Odysseus, who persuades Agamemnon and Menelaus to allow Ajax a proper funeral.

While my focus here is on Tecmessa's role within *Ajax*, and the ways in which aspects of her experience might seem relatable to some contemporary military spouses, a brief overview of possible interpretations of Ajax's character and actions is crucial to understanding the play. In recent decades, since Jonathan Shay's work comparing the mental states of Homeric heroes and Vietnam veterans,[73] scholars have debated the extent to which modern diagnoses might be used to describe the mental states of characters found in ancient texts. Some interpretations suggest, for example, that particular mythical figures, including Ajax, might be described retrospectively as exhibiting symptoms of what would now be diagnosed as post-traumatic stress disorder (PTSD).[74] First described by medical professionals in the wake of the Vietnam War, PTSD refers to a collection of often debilitating symptoms which can result from an individual's exposure to an abnormal amount of trauma-induced stress. Among other things, these symptoms

---

[73] Shay (1994) and (2002). See further my Introduction, p. 2.

[74] See in particular Doerries (2015, pp. 57–152). On the ways in which contemporary reworkings of Ajax's story have interpreted it through the lens of PTSD, see Cole (2019).

might include: intrusive memories, dreams or flashbacks; a persistent nega-tive emotional state (for example, fear, anger, or guilt); irritable or reckless behaviour; and hypervigilance.[75] Scholarship on the psychological effects of ancient combat has produced a range of interpretations, from those who, like Tritle, argue for the existence of PTSD in the ancient world to others such as Crowley who see the diagnosis as a culturally specific phenomenon which cannot be retrospectively applied to either real or fictional ancient people.[76] As I have made clear elsewhere in this book, my own approach resists universalizing tendencies; rather than drawing straightforward equivalences between ancient and modern circumstances I believe that it is possible to highlight points of similarity while also acknowledging the often vast differences between past and present historical, social, and cultural contexts. Crucially in the case of Ajax, his violent outburst and suicide is not the direct result of having witnessed or participated in disturbing events in combat. Instead, his fury stems initially from a sense of injustice that the prize which he felt should rightly have been his has gone to an unworthy rival.[77] The transgression against him represents an extreme affront to his honour and a contravention of the moral values governing heroic conduct within the society of which he is a part. The harm he has suffered is there-fore a kind of 'moral injury' and it is this which leads to his extreme psycho-logical distress.[78] Aspects of his resulting behaviour—delusions, erratic

[75] The diagnostic criteria for PTSD were first set out in the third edition of the American Psychiatric Association's *Diagnostic and Statistical Manual of Medical Disorders* (*DSM*), pub-lished in 1980. The *DSM* is now in its fifth edition (*DSM-5*) and the criteria have been amended with each new edition. See American Psychiatric Association (2013, pp. 271–2).

[76] Tritle (2000, p. 96) sees Ajax as 'an ancient Greek equivalent to the traumatized veteran from Vietnam'. Crowley (2012) argues against such universalizing tendencies. The papers col-lected by Meineck and Konstan (2014, eds.), which also include contributions by Tritle and Crowley, provide a broad sample of the range of views held by ancient world scholars on the topic. Gardner (2019, pp. 8–28) provides a comprehensive overview of the scholarship on trauma and the ancient world, and herself argues for a culturally and historically specific read-ing of the Trojan War heroes' responses to overwhelming events.

[77] At the start of the play, Athena explains to Odysseus that Ajax is 'weighed down by anger because of Achilles' armour' (χόλῳ βαρυνθεὶς τῶν Ἀχιλλείων ὅπλων, 41). For a reading of the play that sees it as an exploration of the Homeric 'heroic code' relating to honour and shame through the character of Ajax, see Knox (1961). On the ways in which Ajax's behaviour relates to the Greek heroic principle of 'helping friends and harming enemies', see also Blundell (1991, pp. 60–105).

[78] Sherman (2015, pp. 23–56) demonstrates that 'moral injury'—where individuals have witnessed or been involved in behaviours that contradict their own moral values—is a feature of the experience of many combat veterans and can lead to a sense of resentment or betrayal. For some, it might also coexist with combat trauma; see Shay (2014). Weiberg (forthcoming, Chapter 2) provides a reading of Aeschylus' *Agamemnon* that frames Clytemnestra as having been wounded by moral injury.

outbursts, and extreme violence—are indeed very similar to those witnessed in soldiers suffering from combat trauma or PTSD, yet it is the sense of betrayal which drives him.[79] His anguish on becoming aware of the actions he has committed in his frenzy comes not from a sense of shame that he has tried to murder the Greek leaders, but instead from the humiliation that he has been thwarted in his attempt to take revenge against them.

Tecmessa occupies a specific role as witness to, and narrator of, Ajax's actions in Sophocles' play, and, as will later become clear, elements of her experience may resonate with the partners of military veterans in the aftermath of combat. Yet the differences between her status and identity and those of contemporary military spouses are vast. Hers is not a mutually consensual marriage; like Andromache and the women of Troy portrayed in Euripides' plays, Tecmessa is a forced concubine and a survivor of wartime rape. The chorus describe her as Ajax's 'spear-won bedmate' (λέχος δουριάλωτον, 211), and 'ill-fated bride, captive of his spear' (τὴν δουρίληπτον δύσμορον νύμφην, 894). She points out that she is now a slave, although she was born to a free father (487–9); Ajax destroyed her homeland with his spear, and both of her parents are dead (515–17). Some interpretations of the text claim that there are hints of affection between Ajax and Tecmessa; several translators and editors suggest that the chorus say that Ajax 'maintains affection' (στέρξας ἀνέχει, 212)[80] for Tecmessa, and note that she reflects that, despite his recent outburst, he has been kinder to her in the past (808). Yet it is difficult to read either of these points as evidence of a genuinely warm relationship between captor and captive. The vocabulary used by the chorus at 212 is open to an alternative interpretation; Finglass points out that it is possible that the text should actually read στέρξασαν ἔχει and therefore translate as '[Ajax] possesses you, as you acquiesce.'[81] Elsewhere, it may be tempting to read Tecmessa's grief primarily as a sign of her care for Ajax; for example, when he prays for death, she asks, 'What should I live for when you are dead?' (τί γὰρ δεῖ ζῆν με σοῦ τεθνηκότος, 393) For a woman who—like the Andromache of Euripides' plays discussed earlier—is wholly dependent on her captor this is, however, not so much an expression of her concern for him but rather one of extreme anxiety about her own future safety.

---

[79] See Meineck (2012, p. 16).

[80] Garvie (1998), for example, translates these words as 'shows constant affection'. Foley (2001, p. 91) compares Tecmessa to Briseis in the *Iliad*, suggesting that she has 'come to care for the captor who destroyed her city and family'.

[81] Finglass (2009, pp. 85–9), and Finglass (2011, commenting on lines 211–13).

Later, as she tries to dissuade him from suicide, Tecmessa's lengthy plea to Ajax not to abandon her, and their son, to be the slaves of other men (492–513), and her assertions that 'I have nothing left to look to except you' (514–15) and, 'My safety depends wholly on you' (519) underscore the fact that she and her son are completely reliant on him.[82] Like Andromache and the Trojan women discussed earlier, Tecmessa has had to comply—and even perhaps to show Ajax some affection—in order to protect herself and her child. When, then, she says to him 'Since I came to your bed I have been well-disposed towards you' (ἐπεὶ / τὸ σὸν λέχος ξυνῆλθον, εὖ φρονῶ τὰ σά, 490–1), this seems less a declaration of affection than a reminder that she has done what is necessary to stay alive.[83] When she implores Ajax not to take his own life, she is pleading too for her own future.

For Sophocles, Tecmessa is of far less interest as a character in her own right than as a device for illuminating Ajax, the play's central figure.[84] As witness to Ajax's initial outburst, Tecmessa performs the role conventionally occupied by a messenger in tragedy, narrating what has taken place for the chorus and the audience; later her conversations with Ajax help to reveal further his state of mind. In the early part of the play, Tecmessa gives two accounts of the events of the previous evening, the first (201–56) a brief general summary of what she saw, with disturbing descriptions of Ajax's delusional state and the brutal slaughter of the livestock. Her second, more detailed account (284–330) is prompted by the chorus' desire for further details as they attempt to comprehend what has happened. Here Tecmessa relates events from the point at which Ajax left the hut with the intention of hunting down and killing the Greek chieftains. Her reports incorporate vivid and gruesome details of the ordeal, including graphic descriptions of the specific kinds of torture Ajax inflicted upon his victims (235–44, 298–300), as well providing an insight into Ajax's emotional state. For example, she recalls his delusional behaviour as he imagined that the beasts

---

[82] This speech is particularly striking for its similarities to that of Andromache to Hector in *Iliad* 6 (discussed above, pp. 21–32). Here Tecmessa's words echo those of Andromache and simultaneously draw attention to comparison between Andromache as royal wife of a fighter who will die on the battlefield and Tecmessa as Ajax's enslaved spear-bride. See Ormand (1996, pp. 49–52), Hesk (2003, pp. 63–9), and Barker (2009, pp. 293–5). On the relationship between *Ajax* and the *Iliad* more broadly, see also Burian (2012, pp. 70–1).

[83] On the 'captive's dilemma' and the need for women captured in war to acquiesce to their captors in order to survive, see above, pp. 180–1.

[84] This lack of focus on Tecmessa is true too of much of the scholarship on *Ajax*. One exception in providing a close reading of the interactions between Tecmessa and Ajax is Hesk (2003, pp. 52–73). For discussions of Tecmessa's character, see also Burian (2012, pp. 75–7), Roisman (2019), and Esposito (2019).

he was torturing were the Greek leaders (301–4). This, she says, then gave way to despair and lamentation once he returned to his senses and realized that he had been duped (306–22). He now lies among the slaughtered herd in silence, not eating or drinking (323–5) and it is clear to Tecmessa that he means to do some harm (326).[85]

Later in the play, Tecmessa moves from the position of witness and narrator to become Ajax's interlocutor. After he has offered his own perspective on the betrayal and humiliation he has suffered (430–80) she attempts to persuade him not to end his life, first with the speech in which she envisages the future which she and their child will face in the event of Ajax's death (485–524) and then in dialogue with him. Here she appeals to Ajax's sense of shame (Greek αἰδώς), a powerful motivating factor for the heroes of the Trojan epics;[86] she reminds him that, in the event of his death, others will pour scorn on her, and that their 'words will be shameful for you and your family' (σοὶ δ' αἰσχρὰ τἄπη ταῦτα καὶ τῷ σῷ γένει, 505). She goes on to appeal to this same sense of shame where his elderly parents are concerned, telling him to 'feel shame' (the Greek has the instruction αἴδεσαι twice in quick succession, at lines 506 and 507) at the thought of abandoning his mother and father, before pleading with him to pity the son who will be deprived of his guardianship in future (510). That Ajax is ultimately unmoved by any of these appeals reflects the extent to which the shame of the betrayal which he has endured outweighs, for him, the thought of his reputation being tarnished further in future.

With the focus of the audience's attention so overwhelmingly on Ajax himself throughout the play, there is—in contrast with Euripides' examinations of the experiences of Trojan survivors—little space left for exploring Tecmessa's own trauma here. Although her eyewitness accounts, with all their macabre detail, convey a sense of the terror of the onlooker who has witnessed such horrors, and although her pleas to Ajax outline the precarity of her situation as a war captive, her words give little sense of the emotional

---

[85] Ajax's behaviour is referred to at various points in the play as 'sickness' or 'madness'. For example, at line 207, Tecmessa says that Ajax has 'been sick/unwell' (νοσήσας); shortly afterwards she says he has been 'seized by madness' (μανίᾳ γὰρ ἁλούς, 216). At lines 609–11, the chorus describe him as δυσθεράπευτος, 'hard to heal', and as θεία μανίᾳ ξύναυλος, 'living with divine madness'; in the same ode they say that he is 'sick', νοσοῦντα (625, cf. 635). That the Greek text uses terms relating to both madness and sickness interchangeably prefigures some of the ways in which mental illness (including PTSD) is still misunderstood and stigmatized today: see Mittal et al. (2013). For a detailed study of the representation of madness in tragedy, see Padel (1995), with a particular focus on *Ajax* at pp. 65–77.

[86] Roisman (2019, p. 105).

impact which witnessing Ajax's recent outburst has had on her.[87] The one emotion of her own that she names is fear, and she mentions this only briefly. She specifically reports having been afraid when Ajax returned to his senses and began demanding for her to tell him what had happened (311–16):

> He sat there for a long time, not speaking; then, with terrible words, he threatened me if I did not reveal everything about the disaster. And he asked me about the situation he was in. And I, friends, in fear [δείσασα], told him everything that had been done as far as I knew.

Tecmessa also later refers to her fear for their child Eurysaces in the face of Ajax's violence. When Ajax asks to see his son she tells him (531), 'I let him go away in my fear [φόβοισί]'; she clarifies that she did so 'in case the poor boy should encounter you and die' (533). She mentions her own fear just once more, in dialogue with Ajax where, when he tells her she is talking too much, she replies 'Yes, because I'm frightened' (ταρβῶ γάρ, 593). Of course in performance the actor playing Tecmessa would also be able to convey a great deal of unspoken emotion through, for example, body language and tone of voice, yet the words of the text themselves convey little about her own state of mind.

We might shed more light on the nature of what Tecmessa endures when exposed to Ajax's violent outburst if we consider the lived experience of women who have been in relationships with wounded warriors. Indeed, Bryan Doerries' work with the *Theater of War* project, which presented adapted readings of *Ajax*, along with other Greek tragedies, to communities of veterans and their families in the US, revealed that the figure of Tecmessa often resonated with wives and widows who had been confronted by the psychological effects of war on their partners.[88] One of these women, Sheri Hall, reflected, on hearing Tecmessa's pleas that Ajax consider the impact on his family, 'That's me. I hid our kids away. I begged and pleaded for him to get

---

[87] Settle (2020) explores the way in which the recollections of Ajax's violence in the play constitute a 'core trauma pattern' whereby the audience, through Tecmessa's accounts, is invited to bear witness to the trauma which has taken place offstage.

[88] On *Theater of War*'s readings of *Ajax*, and audience responses to these, see Doerries (2015, pp. 111–52). In a similar vein, Meineck (2012, p. 16), when referring to readings of Tecmessa's account of Ajax's behaviour as part of his *Ancient Greeks/Modern Lives* project, notes that 'Tecmessa's situation resonates with the spouses of combat veterans who have frequently related how their husbands or wives return home with a plethora of psychological problems that are then visited on the family'.

help. And the only difference between her and me was I didn't go to his soldiers…'[89] Meanwhile the playwright Timberlake Wertenbaker set her 2013 retelling of the story of Ajax, *Our Ajax*, on a British army base in Afghanistan, with Ajax as a British general, traumatized by his experiences in the conflict. The play features a contemporary version of Tecmessa, envisaged here as a Middle Eastern woman whose family has been killed in the war and who has ended up marrying Ajax, largely for her own protection. Wertenbaker's play, in its exploration of Tecmessa's own challenges alongside those of Ajax, offers an example of the way in which the ancient story might be used illuminate the emotional experiences of modern-day spouses of combat veterans.[90]

Women who have themselves endured the challenges of living with a traumatized veteran often relate experiences which call to mind some of the things which Tecmessa describes in Sophocles' play. One work which vividly documents the impact of war on the lives of women at home is *Vietnam Wives*, written by Aphrodite Matsakis, a counselling psychologist experienced in working with veterans, who had observed that the main focus of public attention and published work in the aftermath of Vietnam War had tended to be the veterans themselves. First published in 1988, with a revised second edition produced in 1996, *Vietnam Wives* collates testimony from the wives of returning soldiers. As noted above, the particular circumstances and value system driving Ajax's behaviour differ from those which prevail in modern contexts, yet his actions and emotional state in many ways resemble those of combatants who have been mentally scared in modern-day conflicts; so too the impact of his behaviour on those closest to him finds parallels in the experiences of contemporary military spouses. There are countless such examples woven into Matsakis' work, which illustrates in depth the scale of the impact of their partners' suffering on these women's lives.[91] Matsakis' work captures a sense of the unpredictability, the fear, and the exhaustion which can become a core part of life with a traumatized veteran. Laura, for example, recalled,

[89] Doerries (2015, p. 143).

[90] The play was initially titled *The Suicide of Colonel A. Ajax*, then performed as *Ajax in Afghanistan* before being renamed *Our Ajax*. For a discussion of the play and its representation of female trauma, see Shannon (2014, pp. 165–75).

[91] For an insight into the experiences of couples dealing with combat trauma in the wake of a different modern conflict, the war in Iraq, see Finkel's 2013 *Thank You For Your Service*. This work of non-fiction journalism charts the stories of a battalion of returning combatants and, although the focus is predominantly on service personnel themselves, it highlights some of the challenges faced by their partners as they deal with the consequences of PTSD. Elsewhere, Dekel et al. (2005) presents the findings of a study of nine women whose husbands were Israeli veterans formally diagnosed with PTSD; the women reflect on the impact of dealing with their husband's violence, delusional episodes, and suicidal ideation.

I was eight months pregnant and sick with the flu when my husband shot the phones, barricaded the house, and threatened to kill the first person in uniform who tried to enter the door. When the postman ran screaming down the block about the 'weirdo' acting up again, my eight-year-old hid under the bed crying. That 'weirdo' was his Daddy...[92]

Another woman, Lorraine, told Matsakis a similar tale of her own fear of her husband's violence, and the steps she took, like Tecmessa, to protect her children: 'When Len was angry, nothing was safe... If I felt a beating coming on, I'd lock the children in their bedroom or, if there was time, drive them to my mother's. Eventually, however, Len would wear out and everything would be peaceful.'[93] The swings from chaos to calm and back again which Lorraine describes call to mind Tecmessa's comparison of the end of Ajax's violent episode to the passing of a raging storm, when the lightning and the wind ceases (257–9). Lorraine, whose husband eventually died by suicide, described to Matsakis her own emotional state while he was alive, saying that she was 'psychologically defeated' and 'in a state of constant confusion' as a result of Len's mood swings:

I was tired of walking on eggshells and having one anxiety attack after another. My thinking had become distorted, too, as I was always trying to find answers to problems over which I had no control. I was always irritable and depressed and when he'd been gone for hours, wandering aimlessly in the streets, I didn't know who was closer to suicide, him or me.[94]

As Lorraine's testimony suggests, one of the recurring themes that characterizes the accounts of partners of traumatized veterans is a fear that their spouse will take their own life. As we have seen, this is a key element of Tecmessa's experience in Sophocles' play too, although, as noted earlier, her fear for her own future security as a war captive—rather than any love for him as her partner—is the driving factor of her attempts to dissuade Ajax from suicide. Yet the interaction of Ajax and Tecmessa regarding his intention to end his life also bears a resemblance to one of the difficulties which contemporary soldiers' spouses face when trying to connect emotionally with a partner who is mentally wounded. The refusal or inability of some

---

[92] Matsakis (1996, p. 9).
[93] Matsakis (1996, p. 14). Matsakis discusses in further detail at pp. 228–77 the impact on children of living with a traumatized veteran parent.
[94] Matsakis (1996, pp. 14–15).

veterans to engage with those closest to them, resisting attempts at communication or offers of help, is a common feature of such accounts: Matsakis refers to this disengagement and impenetrability of Vietnam veterans as being like 'living with the ice man'.[95] Lisa, one of the women whose story Matsakis tells, described her husband as being 'so numb that sometimes he's like a statue', and as putting up a 'wall'; meanwhile another wife of a Vietnam veteran referred to living with her emotionally inert husband as 'like being on a starvation diet'.[96]

Tecmessa hints at a similar kind of impenetrability when she reports that Ajax silenced her as she tried to intervene when he set out on his mission (292–3); he later refuses to answer her directly when she challenges him as to what he intends to do next, replying, 'Don't question, don't examine me' (586). In the exchange between the couple which follows, he blocks every one of Tecmessa's attempts to engage with him. He repeatedly demands her silence, telling her to 'Speak to those who are listening' (591) and insisting that she is saying too much (592) before ordering her to close the door as quickly as possible (593); thus he quite literally shuts her out. His final words to Tecmessa underline the futility of her attempted intervention, as he tells her (594–6) that she is foolish if she thinks she can 'educate' him (this is the sense of the Greek verb παιδεύω which is used here, with the implication that she cannot change his mind). His masking of his emotions is, however, at its height in the speech that he makes immediately before his suicide. In what is often referred to by scholars as his 'deception speech', Ajax seems to suggest that, softened by pity for Tecmessa and Eurysaces (650–3), he has had a change of heart, and that he no longer wishes for death. His speech here is ambiguous, and the chorus' joyful response in the ode which immediately follows suggests that they have interpreted his declared intentions to go to a secluded place and hide his sword (654–60) as indicative of a decision to carry on living. In fact, as soon becomes clear, he will instead use this weapon against himself.[97]

In Sophocles' play the prophecy that Ajax will not live until the end of the day is relayed to the chorus by a messenger (748–83); in the moments after this news arrives we witness Tecmessa's response to the unfolding situation. When the chorus call her to relay the messenger's news, her exhaustion in

[95] See Matsakis (1996, pp. 54–81), for many examples of this turning off of emotions and refusal, or inability, to engage with others.

[96] Matsakis (1996, p. 61).

[97] There is a long-running discussion among scholars as to Ajax's intentions in this speech. Segal (1999, pp. 432–3 n. 9) gives a helpful summary of some of these differing points of view.

the wake of Ajax's outburst is palpable: she asks wearily why they have disturbed her, when she has 'only just gained respite from relentless troubles'
(ἀρτίως πεπαυμένην / κακῶν ἀτρύτων, 787–8). As the significance of the
messenger's report dawns, she expresses her psychological anguish in a way
which connects this to physical pain, declaring, μ' ὠδίνειν τί φῇς, 'I am in
agony at what you are saying' (794); the Greek verb used here can also refer
to the physical pain of childbirth.[98] In what follows, the chorus are unable to
locate Ajax; Tecmessa is the first to discover his body and responds with
cries of grief (ἰώ μοί μοι, 'Alas!' at 891; ἰώ τλήμων, 'Alas, wretched me!' at 893),
then lamenting, 'I am lost, destroyed, utterly ruined, friends' (οἴχωκ', ὄλωλα,
διαπεπόρθημαι, φίλοι, 896). She then attends to Ajax's body, covering him
with a cloak to hide his wounds (915–19), before joining with the chorus in
a short lament in which she once again refers to the threat of fresh enslavement which hangs over her and Eurysaces (944–5).[99] Her final speech in the
play (961–73) is a searing criticism of those under whose command Ajax
was fighting in which she suggests that although the Greek leaders failed to
appreciate him when he was alive they will miss him in battle now that he is
dead. She reflects that 'his death is as bitter [πικρός] to me as it is sweet to
them, and was a delight to him' (966–7). Her final words in the play (972–3)
are a brief summary of her grief, contrasting what she assumes will be the
Greek commanders' indifference to his death with the devastating impact
it will have on her personally: 'For them, Ajax exists no more, but in his
death he has left me with sorrows and lamentation [λιπὼν ἀνίας καὶ γόους
διοίχεται]'.

With more than 400 lines remaining after Tecmessa speaks her final
words, Ajax's brother Teucer arrives on stage. But where is Tecmessa for the
remainder of the play? Teucer sends her to fetch Eurysaces (985–99), and
she reappears with the child at around line 1170, but she does not speak
again. It is telling that, now that she has served the dramatic functions given
to her by Sophocles—in illuminating Ajax's character, and then in being the
first to find his body—she is apparently no longer of interest. From this
point, the dead hero's corpse dominates both the stage and the dialogue, as
the male characters argue over whether or not to give him a proper burial
after the betrayal which he has committed. Ajax's son is paid some attention

---

[98] The Greek language often uses words that link physical and emotional pain: for example,
ἄλγος can be used to refer both to grief and to pain felt in the body.
[99] For an analysis of the poetic and dramatic impact of Tecmessa's display of her grief here,
see Esposito (2019).

here—Teucer instructs the boy to sit by his father's corpse (1171–5)—but, as the only woman in the drama, Tecmessa is overlooked in the dialogue from now on.[100] She is overshadowed here by the presence of Ajax's body, his brother and son, and the commanders whose actions led to his death; it is the men who take up space and whose voices we hear. We might compare here the silence of Andromache in the second half of Euripides' *Andromache*, as discussed earlier in this chapter; even there, however, we are given a sense of what will happen next for Andromache. In Sophocles' play, the audience is left to wonder about Tecmessa's future fate and to imagine her private anguish after the play has ended. Like her counterparts elsewhere in the mythical tales of the Trojan War, as well as many real-life spouses of soldiers across the centuries, she is primarily defined by her relationship to the warrior whose story takes centre stage.

At a time when it can still be difficult to locate women's own accounts of their lived experience of conflict-related trauma, witnessing the suffering of a Tecmessa or an Andromache might prompt reflection—for modern audiences just as for those who first saw these plays on the ancient stage—on the harsh realities of war, and on its impact on non-combatants. Euripides' Trojan War plays offer a closer examination of the experiences of the female survivors of violence and displacement than Sophocles' *Ajax*; yet even the latter can yield insights into the survivor's experience if we actively choose to focus on Tecmessa's struggles, both as a survivor of wartime violence and as the partner of a troubled warrior. These ancient narratives offer us the opportunity to understand more deeply the ongoing emotional impact of wartime bereavement, violation, and displacement, as well as—for Tecmessa—the challenges of living alongside a soldier who has himself been mentally wounded. In societies and settings where male voices, and the voices of those who participate directly in combat, tend to speak the loudest, Athenian tragedy offers one way in to thinking about the stories which, even today, often remain untold. These dramatizations of the female survivors of Troy are not merely the invention of mythmakers; they are powerful reflections on the brutality of conflict, both for women who lived at the time when Sophocles and Euripides were producing their plays, and for those women who have endured similar horrors ever since.

---

[100] It is not clear from the text where Tecmessa is positioned in relation to the corpse, and much is left open to the decision of a director. Finglass (2011, p. 469) suggests that she might crouch down with Eurysaces to protect Ajax's body. By contrast, for example, Seale (1982, p. 173) assumes that she remains some distance away.

Epilogue

This book opened with the final words of Hector to Andromache in the sixth book of the *Iliad*, in which the Trojan hero declares to his wife that 'the war shall be the men's concern', before he heads out onto the battlefield for the final time. When narratives of armed conflict and its aftermath place at their centre male protagonists, their triumphs and their challenges, the sentiment Hector expresses might seem inescapable. Just as the presence of Ajax, both in life and in death, dominates the stage in the Sophoclean play which bears his name as its title, so too Odysseus' story is the central focus of the epic poem named after him. Even in versions of the Trojan War myths that centre female experiences—notably the tragedies of Euripides—we have seen that women like Andromache and the other female survivors of the sack of Troy have limited agency and are, as quite literally the property of the victors, largely at the mercy of the male fighters who ultimately control their destiny.

This may all seem largely unsurprising to readers of this book who were already familiar with ancient Greek epic and tragedy; both genres are cultural products of patriarchal societies within which gender roles were starkly divided, and the stories they tell reflect that divide. Put simply, in these ancient works, men participate in the fighting while women are largely confined to the domestic sphere. Today too, in societies where, even despite progression towards greater gender parity in many areas, military personnel are still predominantly male, the stories of combatants remain far more visible, and have been the subject of greater public attention, than those of the women with whom they share their lives. When the spotlight does fall on the spouses of serving soldiers, the picture which results is often as much a myth as the figures whom we meet in the ancient tales of the Trojan War; these women frequently represent an idealized image of femininity, largely confined to domestic roles and serving patiently and without complaint alongside husbands who have been called to do their duty in the military sphere.[1]

---

[1] Shotbolt (2011) provides a neat summary of the way in which this mythologizing of contemporary military wives operates in practice.

Warriors' Wives: Ancient Greek Myth and Modern Experience. Emma Bridges, Oxford University Press.
© Emma Bridges 2023. DOI: 10.1093/oso/9780198843528.003.0008

A recurrent theme of the preceding chapters has been the ways in which the voices of the women closest to military personnel—both those whom we encounter in surviving ancient texts and those for whom this is present-day lived experience—have traditionally been given less space to tell their stories than those of the heroes with whom they share their lives. Silencing can take many forms, not all of them as blunt as the Iliadic Hector's outright dismissal of Andromache's concerns. It may consist of, for example, simply reproducing narratives which centre one type of perspective—in this case that of the male 'heroes'—or ignoring the voices whose presence represents an alternative perspective upon that narrative; it might involve perpetuating the shame or stigma associated with speaking out about difficult experiences such as rape or trauma; or it may take the form of trivializing the experiences of women in order to privilege male perspectives. It can result in the creation of one-dimensional stereotypes such as that of the faithful Penelope-figure and her opposite, the adulterous Clytemnestra; viewed uncritically, such stereotypes encourage the oversimplification of complex and personal responses to particular situations. Happily many modern reinterpretations of ancient myth—several of which I have drawn on for my chapter openings—provide versions of the ancient narratives which do place the female characters at the centre, and which imagine the responses of those women to the situations in which the ancient narratives locate them. As the ancient Greeks themselves knew, myth is inherently malleable, and is always open to being rewritten in new contexts; the production of new creative receptions of classical stories is one way of reclaiming those stories and centring the voices of those who are marginalized in the ancient texts.

If, then, we take the approach of actively seeking out and listening to the voices of the wives of warriors in contexts where military action is the focus of attention, it soon becomes apparent that war has never been exclusively 'men's concern'. Even the ancient versions of episodes from the Trojan War illustrate that conflict inevitably has a profound impact on the lives of the women for whom the battlefield itself is out of bounds. As Homeric poetry and Athenian tragic drama illustrate, it is the wives of warriors who must live with the repercussions of wars waged by their husbands, as they endure the pain of separation, the anguish of bereavement, and the horrors associated with trauma and rape. The voices of the women who live through these challenges may occupy less space in some of the ancient narratives, yet if we actively set out to listen to those voices it is still possible to unearth the alternative perspectives which they offer on the consequences of military action; in many cases, the stories in which they participate reflect situations which were of pressing concern to audiences in whose societies armed conflict was an ever-present aspect of life.

We might, of course, lament that the surviving tales of the battles which raged around Troy were produced by male authors and for predominantly male audiences; yet, while remaining alert to the interpretative challenges which this presents, I hope that my discussions of the female characters whom we encounter in epic poetry and tragedy have provided my readers with some fresh insights into the psychological, emotional, and social impacts of life with a warrior. Just as, in the ancient texts, we often need to look a little harder to find the stories of the mythical heroes' wives, so too in our own world it is not always easy to unearth the perspectives of the women who live side-by-side with serving military personnel and veterans. Alongside the mythical spouses of the Trojan War heroes, in the course of this book we have encountered just a few of the women who have lived through the experience of being 'married to the military' in more recent times. We have heard their voices in interviews with journalists or scholars, and we have read some of their autobiographical reflections on life with a member of the armed forces, whether in the form of memoirs, blogposts, or poetry. These are the women who have endured separation and bereavement, who have lived through the challenges of being in a relationship with a serving soldier—often sacrificing parts of their own identity in the process—or who have survived the most brutal treatment at the hands of enemy fighters. Even now, they are rarely the focus of attention for the public, the media, or policy makers; like the Homeric Penelope, they are more used to occupying the margins of the stories of the men on whom the spotlight falls.

Still today too, then, war is very much the concern of the women who share their lives with military personnel: the Penelopes who still wait and wonder whether their absent warriors will return home alive while they keep the home fires burning; the Clytemnestras, resentful of the sacrifices the military has demanded of them; the Andromaches, bereaved, violated, or displaced from war-ravaged territories; and the Tecmessas, coping with the fear and grief which are ubiquitous elements of life with a wounded warrior. If at times these women seem less vocal, and demand less of our attention, than the men who still today occupy centre stage in narratives of war, that should merely make us more determined to seek out their stories, and to listen more carefully to what they have to tell us.

References

Adams, Abigail E. (1997), 'The "military academy": metaphors of family for pedagogy and public life', in Weinstein and White (eds.), pp. 63–77.

Aducci, C. J., Joyce A. Baptist, Jayashree George, Patricia M. Barros, and Briana S. Nelson Goff (2011), 'The recipe for being a good military wife: how military wives managed OIF/OEF deployment', *Journal of Feminist Family Therapy* 23.3–4, 231–49.

Allan, William (2000), *The Andromache and Euripidean Tragedy*. Oxford: Oxford University Press.

Allen-Hornblower, Emily (2016), *From Agent to Spectator: Witnessing the Aftermath in Ancient Greek Epic and Tragedy*. Berlin and Boston: de Gruyter.

American Psychiatric Association (2013), *Diagnostic and Statistical Manual of Mental Disorders*. 5th edition (*DSM-5*). Washington and London: American Psychiatric Publishing.

Amory, Anne (1963), 'The reunion of Odysseus and Penelope', in Charles H. Taylor (ed.) *Essays on the Odyssey: Selected Modern Criticism*. Bloomington: Indiana University Press, pp. 100–36.

Anderson, Michael J. (1997), *The Fall of Troy in Early Greek Poetry and Art*. Oxford: Oxford University Press.

Andres, Manon, Karin De Angelis, and David McCone (2015), 'Reintegration, reconciliation and relationship quality', in Moelker et al. (eds.), pp. 145–60.

Anonymous (2014), 'I'm a woman who cheated on her deployed husband, this is why I did it', Thoughtcatalog.com blogpost (18 November 2014) (https://thoughtcatalog.com/anonymous/2014/11/im-a-woman-who-cheated-on-her-deployed-husband-this-is-why-i-did-it, accessed 4 August 2022.)

Armitage, Simon (2014), *The Last Days of Troy*. London: Faber and Faber.

Atwood, Margaret (2005), *The Penelopiad*. Edinburgh: Canongate.

Austin, Norman (1975), *Archery at the Dark of the Moon: Poetic Problems in Homer's Odyssey*. Berkeley and Los Angeles: University of California Press.

Bacalexi, Dina (2016), 'Personal, paternal, patriotic: the threefold sacrifice of Iphigenia in Euripides' *Iphigenia in Aulis*', *Humanitas* 68, 51–76.

Baker, Catherine (2018), 'Unsung heroism? Showbusiness and social action in Britain's military wives choir(s)', in Veronica Kitchen and Jennifer G. Mathers (eds.), *Heroism and Global Politics*. New York: Routledge.

Baptist, Joyce A., Yvonne Amanor-Boadu, Kevin Garrett, Briana S. Nelson Goff, Jonathan Collum, Paulicia Gamble, Holly Gurss, Erin Sanders-Hahs, Lizette Strader, and Stephanie Wick (2011), 'Military marriages: the aftermath of Operation Iraqi Freedom (OIF) and Operation Enduring Freedom (OEF) deployments', *Contemporary Family Therapy* 33, 199–214.

Barker, Elton and Joel Christensen (2013), *Homer: A Beginner's Guide*. London: Oneworld.

Barker, Elton T. E. (2009), *Entering the Agon: Dissent and Authority in Homer, Historiography and Tragedy*. Oxford: Oxford University Press.

Barker, Pat (2019 [2018]), *The Silence of the Girls*. London: Penguin.

Barker, Pat (2022 [2021]), *The Women of Troy*. London: Penguin.

Barlow, Shirley A. (1986), *Euripides: Trojan Woman*. Warminster: Aris and Phillips.

Bedell, Geraldine (2009), 'The knock at the door: three Afghan war widows talk about the day they lost their hero', *The Guardian*, 18 October 2009. (https://www.theguardian.com/world/2009/oct/18/afghanistan-war-widows-love-loss, accessed 4 August 2022)

Bergren, Ann L. T. (1983), 'Language and the female in early Greek thought', *Arethusa* 16, 69–95.

Betensky, Aya (1978), 'Aeschylus' *Oresteia*: the power of Clytemnestra', *Ramus* 7, 11–25.

Biank, Tanya (2006), *Under the Sabers: The Unwritten Code of Army Wives*. New York: St. Martin's Press.

Black, William G. (1993), 'Military-induced family separation: a stress reduction intervention', *Social Work* 38, 273–80.

Blondell, Ruby (2013), *Helen of Troy: Beauty, Myth, Devastation*. Oxford: Oxford University Press.

Blundell, Mary Whitlock (1991), *Helping Friends and Harming Enemies: A Study in Sophocles and Greek Ethics*. Cambridge: Cambridge University Press.

Boesten, Jelke (2022), 'Sexual violence as a weapon of war in Ukraine', *British Medical Journal* 2022, 377.

Boorstein, Michelle (2012), 'Military wives stay mum on the subject of infidelity', *Washington Post*, 21 November 2012. (Online edition: https://www.independent.co.uk/news/world/americas/military-wives-stay-mum-on-the-subject-of-infidelity-8339507.html, accessed 4 August 2022.)

Booth, Bradford and Suzanne Lederer (2012), 'Military families in an era of persistent conflict', in Janice H. Laurence and Michael D. Matthews (eds.), *The Oxford Handbook of Military Psychology*. Oxford: Oxford University Press, pp. 365–80.

Boss, Pauline (1999), *Ambiguous Loss: Learning to Live with Unresolved Grief*. Cambridge, Mass: Harvard University Press.

Boss, Pauline (2006), *Loss, trauma and resilience: therapeutic work with ambiguous loss*. New York: Norton.

Boss, Pauline (2007), 'Ambiguous loss theory: challenges for scholars and practitioners', *Family Relations* 56, 105–10.

Boston, Anne (1988, ed.), *Wave Me Goodbye: Stories of the Second World War*. London: Virago.

Bourke, Joanna (2007), *Rape: A History from 1860 to the Present Day*. London: Virago.

Bowling, Ursula B. and Michelle D. Sherman (2008), 'Welcoming them home: supporting service members and their families in navigating tasks of reintegration', *Professional Psychology: Research and Practice* 39.4, 451–8.

Bradley, Keith and Paul Cartledge (2011, eds.), *The Cambridge World History of Slavery Volume I*. Cambridge: Cambridge University Press.

Braybon, Gail and Penny Summerfield (1987), *Out of the Cage: Women's Experiences in Two World Wars*. London: Pandora Press.

Bremmer, Jan N. (2010), 'Greek normative animal sacrifice', in Daniel Ogden (ed.), *A Companion to Greek Religion*. Oxford: Wiley-Blackwell, pp. 132–44.

Bridges, Emma (2015a), Interview with Caroline Horton, *Practitioners' Voices in Classical Reception Studies*. https://www.open.ac.uk/arts/research/pvcrs/2015/horton.

Bridges, Emma (2015b), Interview with Robert Icke, *Practitioners' Voices in Classical Reception Studies*. http://www.open.ac.uk/arts/research/pvcrs/2015/icke.

Bridges, Emma (2015c), '"The greatest runway show in history": Paul Violi's "House of Xerxes" and the Herodotean spectacle of war', in Anastasia Bakogianni and Valerie M. Hope (eds.), *War as Spectacle: Ancient and Modern Displays of Armed Conflict*. London: Bloomsbury, pp. 111–27.

Brittain, Vera (1978 [1933]), *Testament of Youth: An Autobiographical Study of the Years 1900–1925*. London: Virago.

Brown, David (2011), 'Bereaved relatives berate Blair at Iraq war hearing: the Chilcot inquiry', *The Times*, 22 January 2011, p. 24.

Brownmiller, Susan (1991 [1975]), *Against Our Will: Men, Women and Rape*. London: Penguin.

Budin, Stephanie Lynn (2016), *Artemis*. London and New York: Routledge.

Buitron-Oliver, Diana and Beth Cohen (1995), 'Between Skylla and Penelope: female characters of the *Odyssey* in archaic and classical Greek art', in Cohen (1995, ed.), pp. 29–58.

Burian, Peter (2012), 'Polyphonic *Ajax*', in Kirk Ormand (ed.), *A Companion to Sophocles*. Oxford: Blackwell, pp. 69–83.

Burke, Carol (1989), 'Marching to Vietnam', *The Journal of American Folklore* 102, 424–41.

Burns, Richard Allen (2012), 'Where is Jody now? Reconsidering military marching chants', in Eric A. Eliason and Tad Tuleja, *Warrior Ways: Explorations in Modern Military Folklore*. Logan: Utah State University Press, pp. 79–98.

Campbell, Brian and Lawrence A. Tritle (2013, eds.), *The Oxford Handbook of Warfare in the Classical World*. Oxford: Oxford University Press.

Cantarella, Eva (2006), 'Gender, sexuality, and law', in Michael Gagarin and David Cohen (eds.), *The Cambridge Companion to Ancient Greek Law*. Cambridge: Cambridge University Press, pp. 236–53.

Card, Claudia (1996), 'Rape as a weapon of war', *Hypatia* 11.4, 5–18.

Carey, Christopher (1995), 'Rape and adultery in Athenian law', *Classical Quarterly* 45, 405–17.

Caruth, Cathy (1995, ed.), *Trauma: Explorations in Memory*. Baltimore and London: Johns Hopkins University Press.

Centre for Social Justice (2016), 'Military families and transition' (https://www.centreforsocialjustice.org.uk/library/military-families-and-transition, accessed 4 August 2022).

Cesur, Resul and Joseph J. Sabia (2016), 'When war comes home: the effect of combat service on domestic violence', *The Review of Economics and Statistics* 48.2, 209–25.

Christensen, Joel (2020), *The Many-Minded Man: The Odyssey, Psychology, and the Therapy of Epic*. Ithaca and London: Cornell University Press.

Clapp, Susannah (2016), '*Queens of Syria* review—the most urgent work on the London stage', *The Observer*, 10 July 2016. (https://www.theguardian.com/stage/2016/jul/10/queens-of-syria-review-young-vic-euripides-trojan-women, accessed 4 August 2022).

Clark, Raymond J. (1990), 'The returning husband and waiting wife: folktale adaptations in Homer, Tennyson and Pratt', *Folklore* 91.1, 46–62.

Clayton, Barbara (2004), *A Penelopean Poetics: Reweaving the Feminine in Homer's Odyssey*. Lanham, Maryland and Oxford: Lexington Books.

Cohen, Beth (1995, ed.), *The Distaff Side: Representing the Female in Homer's Odyssey*. New York and Oxford: Oxford University Press.

Cohler, Deborah (2017), 'Consuming *Army Wives*: military domesticity and nationalist neoliberalism on TV', *Critical Military Studies* 3:3, 235–51.

Cole, Emma (2019), 'Post-traumatic stress disorder and the performance reception of Sophocles' *Ajax*', in Stuttard (ed.), pp. 151–60.

Collard, Christopher (1991), *Euripides: Hecuba*. Warminster: Aris and Phillips.

Collard, Christopher and James Morwood (2017, eds.), *Euripides: Iphigenia at Aulis* (2 vols.) Liverpool: Liverpool University Press.

Colloff, Pamela (2004), 'Life during wartime', *Texas Monthly* February 2014 (Online edition: https://www.texasmonthly.com/articles/life-during-wartime/, accessed 4 August 2022).

Coser, Lewis A. (1974), *Greedy Institutions: Patterns of Undivided Commitment*. New York: Free Press.

Cox, Fiona and Elena Theodorakopoulos (2019, eds.), *Homer's Daughters: Women's Responses to Homer in the Twentieth Century and Beyond*. Oxford: Oxford University Press.

Cree, Alice (2018), 'The hero, the monster, the wife: geographies of remaking and reclaiming the contemporary military hero' (unpublished doctoral thesis, University of Durham).

Cree, Alice (2019), 'People want to see tears: military heroes and the "Constant Penelope" of the UK's Military Wives Choir', *Gender, Place and Culture* 26, 1–21.

Creech, Suzannah K., W. Hadley, and B. Borsari (2014), 'The impact of military deployment and reintegration on children and parenting: a systematic review', *Professional Psychology: Research and Practice* 45(6), 452–64.

Croally, N. T. (1994), *Euripidean Polemic: The Trojan Women and the Function of Tragedy*. Cambridge: Cambridge University Press.

Crowley, Jason (2012), *The Psychology of the Athenian Hoplite*. Cambridge: Cambridge University Press.

Crowley, Jason (2014), 'Beyond the universal soldier: combat trauma in classical antiquity', in Meineck and Konstan (eds.), pp. 105–30.

Cuchet, Violaine Sebillotte (2015), 'The warrior queens of Caria (fifth to fourth centuries BCE): archeology, history, and historiography', in Fabre-Serris and Keith (eds.), pp. 229–46.

Cyrino, Monica S. (2010), *Aphrodite*. London and New York: Routledge.

Davis, Jennifer, David B. Ward and Cheryl Storm (2011), 'The unsilencing of military wives: wartime deployment experiences and citizen responsibility', *Journal of Marital and Family Therapy* 37.1, 51–63.

Deacy, Susan and Fiona McHardy (2015), 'Ajax, Cassandra and Athena: retaliatory warfare and gender violence at the Sack of Troy', in Geoff Lee, Helene Whittaker, and Graham Wrightson (eds.), *Ancient Warfare: Introducing Current Research, Volume I*. Cambridge: Cambridge Scholars Publishing, pp. 252–72.

De Angelis, Karin and Mady Wechsler Segal (2015), 'Transitions in military and family as greedy institutions: original concept and current applicability', in Moelker et al. (eds.), pp. 22–42.

Debnar, Paula (2010), 'The sexual status of Aeschylus' Cassandra', *Classical Philology* 105, 129–45.

de Brouwer, Anne-Marie and Sandra Ka Hon Chu (2009, eds.), *The Men who Killed Me: Rwandan Survivors of Sexual Violence*. Vancouver: Douglas &McIntyre.

de Burgh, H. Thomas, Claire J. White, Nicola T. Fear and Amy C. Iversen (2011), 'The impact of deployment to Iraq or Afghanistan on partners and wives of military personnel', *International Review of Psychiatry* 23, 192–200.

Dekel, Rachel, Hadass Goldblatt, Michal Keidar, Zahava Solomon, and Michael Polliack (2005), 'Being a wife of a veteran with posttraumatic stress disorder', *Family Relations* 54, 24–36.

Dekel, Rachel, Yoav Levinstein, Alana Siegel, Shimon Fridkin, and Vlad Svetlitsky (2016), 'Secondary traumatization of partners of war veterans: the role of boundary ambiguity', *Journal of Family Psychology* 30.1, 63–71.

Department of Defense (2020), '2020 Demographics: Profile of the Military Community'. (https://download.militaryonesource.mil/12038/MOS/Reports/2020-demographics-report.pdf, accessed 7 November 2022).

de Souza, Philip (2013), 'War at sea', in Campbell and Tritle (eds.), pp. 369–94.

Developing Artists (2016), '*Queens of Syria* UK theatre tour 2016: project report'. (Available to download at https://www.developingartists.org.uk/queens-of-syria, accessed 4 August 2022.)

Dimiceli, Erin E., Mary A. Steinhardt, and Shanna E. Smith (2009), 'Stressful experiences, coping strategies, and predictors of health-related outcomes among wives of deployed military servicemen', *Armed Forces and Society* 36, 351–73.

Doerries, Bryan (2015), *The Theatre of War: What Ancient Greek Tragedies Can Teach Us Today*. Melbourne and London: Scribe.

Doherty, Lillian E. (1995), *Siren Songs: Gender, Audiences, and Narrators in the Odyssey*. Ann Arbor: University of Michigan Press.

Dowson, Jane (1996, ed.), *Frances Cornford: Selected Poems*. London: Enitharmon Press.

Doyle, Andrea (2008), 'Cassandra—feminine corrective in Aeschylus's *Agamemnon*', *Acta Classica* 50, 57–75.

Dubrow, Jehanne (2010), *Stateside: Poems*. Evanston, Illinois: Northwestern University Press.

Ducrey, Pierre (2015), 'War in the feminine in ancient Greece', in Fabre-Serris and Keith (eds.), pp. 181–99.

Easterling, Beth, and David Knox (2010), 'Left behind: how military wives experience the deployment of their husbands', *Journal of Family Life*, 1–22.

Easterling, Pat E. (1997, ed.), *The Cambridge Companion to Greek Tragedy*. Cambridge: Cambridge University Press.

Egan, Rory B. (2007), 'The prophecies of Calchas in the Aulis narrative of Aeschylus' *Agamemnon*', *Mouseion Series III* Vol. 7, 179–212.

Elshtain, Jean Bethke (1991), 'Sovereignty, identity, sacrifice', *Social Research* 58, 545–64.

Elshtain, Jean Bethke (1995 [1987]), *Women and War*. Chicago and London: University of Chicago Press.

Emlyn-Jones, Chris (1984), 'The reunion of Penelope and Odysseus', *Greece and Rome* second series 31.1, 1–18.

Ender, Morten G., Kathleen M. Campbell, Toya J. Davis, and Patrick R. Michaelis (2007), 'Greedy media: army families, embedded reporting, and war in Iraq', *Sociological Focus* 40.1, 48–71.

Enloe, Cynthia (2000), *Maneuvers: The International Politics of Militarizing Women's Lives*. Berkeley, Los Angeles, and London: University of California Press.

Enloe, Cynthia (2014, 2nd edn), *Bananas, Beaches and Bases: Making Feminist Sense of International Politics*. Berkeley and Los Angeles: University of California Press.

Erikson, Kai (1995), 'Notes on trauma and community', in Caruth (ed.), pp. 183–99.

Esposito, Stephen (2019), 'A grief observed: Tecmessa and her sadness-work in Sophocles' *Ajax*', in Stuttard (ed.), pp. 117–30.

Fabre-Serris, Jacqueline and Alison Keith (2015, eds.), *Women and War in Antiquity*. Baltimore: Johns Hopkins University Press.

Fallon, Siobhan (2011), *You Know When the Men Are Gone*. New York and London: Penguin.

Felson, Nancy (1994), *Regarding Penelope: From Character to Poetics*. Princeton: Princeton University Press.

Felson, Nancy and Laura Slatkin (2004), 'Gender and Homeric epic', in Robert Fowler (ed.) *The Cambridge Companion to Homer*. Cambridge: Cambridge University Press, pp. 91–114.

Felson-Rubin, Nancy (1996), 'Penelope's perspective: character from plot', in Schein, pp. 163–83.

Figley, Charles R. (1993), 'Coping with stressors on the home front', *Journal of Social Issues* 49(4), 51–71.

Finglass, Patrick (2007), *Pindar: Pythian Eleven*. Cambridge: Cambridge University Press.

Finglass, Patrick (2009), 'Sophocles' Tecmessa: characterisation and textual criticism', *Eikasmos* 20, 85–96.

Finglass, Patrick (2011), *Sophocles: Ajax*. Cambridge: Cambridge University Press.

Finkel, David (2013), *Thank You For Your Service*. Melbourne and London: Scribe.

Fisher, Ian (1997), 'Army's adultery rule is don't get caught', *New York Times*, 17 May 1997. (Online edition: https://www.nytimes.com/1997/05/17/us/army-s-adultery-rule-is-don-t-get-caught.html, accessed 4 August 2022).

Foley, Helene P. (1978), '"Reverse similes" and sex roles in the *Odyssey*', in John Peradotto and J. P. Sullivan (eds.), *Arethusa* 11, 7–25.

Foley, Helene P. (1982), 'Marriage and sacrifice in Euripides' *Iphigeneia in Aulis*', *Arethusa* 15, 159–80.

Foley, Helene P. (1985), *Ritual Irony: Poetry and Sacrifice in Euripides*. Ithaca and London: Cornell University Press.

Foley, Helene P. (1995), 'Penelope as moral agent', in Cohen, pp. 93–115.

Foley, Helene P. (2001), *Female Acts in Greek Tragedy*. Princeton: Princeton University Press.

Foley, Helene P. (2015), *Euripides: Hecuba*. London and New York: Bloomsbury.

Fuhrer, Therese (2015), 'Teichoskopia: female figures looking on battles', in Fabre-Serris and Keith (eds.), pp. 52–70.

Gaca, Kathy L. (2010), 'The andrapodizing of war captives in Greek historical memory', *Transactions of the American Philological Association* 140, 117–61.

Gaca, Kathy L. (2011), 'Girls, women, and the significance of sexual violence in ancient warfare', in Heineman (ed.) pp. 73–88.

Gaca, Kathy L. (2014), 'Martial rape, pulsating fear, and the sexual maltreatment of girls (παῖδες), virgins (παρθένοι), and women (γυναῖκες) in antiquity', *American Journal of Philology* 135, 303–57.

Gaca, Kathy L. (2015), 'Ancient warfare and the ravaging martial rape of girls and women: evidence from Homeric epic and Greek drama', in Mark Masterson, Nancy Sorkin Rabinowitz, and James Robson (eds.), *Sex in Antiquity: Exploring Gender and Sexuality in the Ancient World*. Abingdon and New York: Routledge, pp. 278–97.

Gainsford, Peter (2003), 'Formal analysis of recognition scenes in the *Odyssey*', *Journal of Hellenic Studies* 123, 41–59.

Gantz, Timothy (1982), 'Inherited Guilt in Aischylos', *Classical Journal* 78, 1–23.

Gantz, Timothy (1993), *Early Greek Myth: A Guide to Literary and Artistic Sources. Volume Two*. Baltimore and London: Johns Hopkins University Press.

Gardner, Lyn (2014), 'Simon Armitage on rewriting Homer: Lily Cole's Helen is "an Iraqi supergun"', *The Guardian*, 8 May 2014 (https://www.theguardian.com/stage/2014/may/08/simon-armitage-the-last-days-of-troy-lily-cole-homer, accessed 4 August 2022).

Gardner, Melissa J. (2019), 'Odyssean perspectives on trauma' (unpublished doctoral thesis, University of Durham).

Garvie, A. F. (1986), *Aeschylus: Choephori*. Oxford: Oxford University Press.

Garvie, A. F. (1998), *Sophocles: Ajax*. Warminster: Aris and Phillips.

George, Lisa Rengo (2001), 'The conjecture of a sleeping mind: dreams and the power of Clytemnestra in the *Oresteia*', *Eranos* 99, 75–86.

Georgoudi, Stella (2015), 'To act, not submit: women's attitudes in situations of war in ancient Greece', in Fabre-Serris and Keith (eds.), pp. 200–13.

Gerardi, Steven M. (1999), 'Part I. Work hardening for warriors: occupational therapy for combat stress casualties', *Work* 13.3, 185–95.

German, Lindsay (2013), *How a Century of War Changed the Lives of Women*. London: Pluto Press.

Gibert, John (1995), *Change of Mind in Greek Tragedy*, Hypomnemata 108. Göttingen: Vandenhoeck and Ruprecht.

Gibert, John (2005), 'Clytemnestra's first marriage: Euripides' *Iphigenia in Aulis*', in Victoria Pedrick and Steven M. Oberhelman (eds.), *The Soul of Tragedy: Essays on Athenian Drama*. Chicago and London: University of Chicago Press, pp. 227–48.

Gideons, Valli (2018), 'Transition. What really happens after military deployment homecoming', 'My Battle Call' blogpost, 3 June 2018. (https://mybattlecall.com/2018/06/03/transition-how-post-deployment-feels/, accessed 27 January 2022.)

Gilchrist, Katie E. (1997), 'Penelope: A Study in the Manipulation of Myth' (unpublished doctoral thesis, University of Oxford).

Gober, Sharon J. (2005), 'The reintegration of military families following long term separation'. Dissertation submitted in partial requirement for the degree Doctor of Philosophy, Arizona State University.

Goff, Barbara (2012), *Euripides: Trojan Women*. London: Bloomsbury.

Golder, Herbert (1983), 'The mute Andromache', *Transactions of the American Philological Association* 113, 123–33.

Goldhill, Simon (1986), *Reading Greek Tragedy*. Cambridge: Cambridge University Press.

Goldhill, Simon (1992), *Aeschylus: The Oresteia*. Cambridge: Cambridge University Press.

Goldhill, Simon (1994), 'Representing democracy: women at the Great Dionysia', in Robin Osborne and Simon Hornblower (eds.), *Ritual, Finance, Politics: Athenian Democratic Accounts Presented to David Lewis*. Oxford: Oxford University Press, pp. 347–69.

Goldhill, Simon (2022), *What is a Jewish Classicist? Essays on the Personal Voice and Disciplinary Politics*. London, New York, and Dublin: Bloomsbury.

Gottschall (2004), 'Explaining wartime rape', *Journal of Sex Research* 41, 129–36.

Gray, Harriet (2016), 'Domestic abuse and the public/private divide in the British military', *Gender, Place and Culture* 23, 912–25.

Graziosi, Barbara (2016), *Homer*. Oxford: Oxford University Press.

Graziosi, Barbara and Johannes Haubold (2010), *Homer, Iliad Book VI*. Cambridge: Cambridge University Press.

Grethlein, Jonas (2007), 'The poetics of the bath in the *Iliad*', *Harvard Studies in Classical Philology* 103, 25–49.

Griffin, Jasper (1980), *Homer on Life and Death*. Oxford: Clarendon Press.

Hall, Edith (1997), 'The sociology of Athenian tragedy', in Easterling (1997), pp. 93–126.

Hall, Edith (2008), *The Return of Ulysses: A Cultural History of Homer's Odyssey*. London and New York: I. B. Tauris.

Hall, Edith (forthcoming), *Aeschylus: Agamemnon*. Warminster: Aris and Phillips.

Hallett, Judith P. and Thomas Van Nortwick (1997, eds.), *Compromising Traditions: The Personal Voice in Classical Scholarship*. London and New York: Routledge.

Harrell, Margaret C. (2000), *Invisible Women: Junior Enlisted Army Wives*. Santa Monica, CA and Arlington, VA: RAND.

Harrell, Margaret C. (2001), 'Army officers' spouses: have the white gloves been mothballed?', *Armed Forces and Society* 28, 55–75.

Harsh, Philip W. (1950), 'Penelope and Odysseus in *Odyssey* XIX', *American Journal of Philology* 71, 1–21.

Hart, Peter. J. (2010), 'The White Feather Campaign: A Struggle with Masculinity During World War I', *Inquiries Journal 2.02* (http://www.inquiriesjournal.com/a?id=151, accessed 4 August 2022).

Haynes, Natalie (2019), *A Thousand Ships*. London: Pan Macmillan.

Hedayat, Samira (2019), 'What is a Gold Star Family?', United Services Organization, 24 September 2019 (https://www.uso.org/stories/2471-what-is-a-gold-star-family, accessed 4 August 2022).

Heilbrun, Carolyn G. (1991), 'What was Penelope unweaving?', in Heilbrun, *Hamlet's Mother and Other Women: Feminist Essays on Literature*. London: The Women's Press, pp. 103–11.

Heineman, Elizabeth D. (2011, ed.), *Sexual Violence in Conflict Zones: From the Ancient World to the Era of Human Rights*. Philadelphia, PA: University of Pennsylvania Press.

Heiselberg, Maj Hedegaard (2017), 'Fighting for the family: overcoming distances in time and space', *Critical Military Studies* 3.1, 69–86.

Heitman, Richard (2005), *Taking Her Seriously: Penelope and the Plot of Homer's Odyssey*. Ann Arbor: University of Michigan Press.

Herman, Judith (1992), *Trauma and Recovery*. New York: Basic Books.

Hesk, Jon (2003), *Sophocles: Ajax*. London: Duckworth.

Holm, Seth (2012), 'Dyeing bronze: new evidence for an old reading of *Agamemnon* 612', *Classical Quarterly* 62, 486–95.

Hölscher, Uvo (1996, tr. Simon Richter), 'Penelope and the suitors', in Schein (ed.), pp. 133–40.

Hopkins, C. Quince (1999), 'Rank matters but should marriage? Adultery, fraternization, and honor in the military', *UCLA Women's Law Journal* 9, 177–262.

Horn, Denise M. (2010), 'Boots and bedsheets: constructing the military support system in a time of war', in Laura Sjoberg and Sandra Via (eds.), *Gender, War, and Militarism: Feminist Perspectives*. Oxford: Praeger, pp. 57–68.

Houppert, Karen (2005), *Home Fires Burning: Married to the Military for Better or Worse*. New York: Random House.

Huebner, Angela J., Jay A. Mancini, Ryan M. Wilcox, Saralyn R. Grass and Gabriel A. Grass (2007), 'Parental deployment and youth in military families: exploring uncertainty and ambiguous loss', *Family Relations* 56.2, 112–22.

Huffman, Amanda (2018), 'The stressful lead up to say goodbye'. 'Airman to Mom' blogpost, 6 February 2018 (https://www.airmantomom.com/2018/02/say-goodbye/, accessed 4 August 2022).

Hunt, Peter (2018), *Ancient Greek and Roman Slavery*. Malden: Wiley Blackwell.

Hyde, Alexandra (2015), 'Inhabiting no-man's land: the military mobilities of army wives' (unpublished doctoral thesis, London School of Economics and Political Science).

Icke, Robert (2015), *Aeschylus, Oresteia: A New Adaptation*. London: Oberon.

Instone, S. J. (1986), '*Pythian* 11: did Pindar err?', *Classical Quarterly* 36, 86–94.

Isikozlu, Elvan and Ananda S. Millard (2010), 'Brief 43: Towards a typology of wartime rape', Bonn International Center for Conversion. (https://www.bicc.de/uploads/tx_bicctools/brief43.pdf, accessed 4 August 2022.)

Jaffe, Greg (2010), 'When the messages home stop', *Washington Post* Friday 5 November 2010. (Online edition: http://www.washingtonpost.com/wp-dyn/content/article/2010/11/04/AR2010110407432.html, accessed 4 August 2022.)

Jervis, Sue (2007), 'Moving experiences: responses to relocation among British military wives', in Anne Coles and Anne-Meike Fechter (eds.), *Gender and Family Among Transnational Professionals*. New York and London: Routledge, pp. 103–23.

Jervis, Sue (2011), *Relocation, Gender, and Emotion: A Psycho-Social Perspective on the Experiences of Military Wives*. London: Karmac.

Kachadourian, Lorig K., Brian N. Smith, Casey T. Taft, and Dawne Vogt (2015), 'The impact of infidelity on combat-exposed service members', *Journal of Traumatic Stress* 28, 418–25.

Karakurt, Gunnur, Abigail Tolhurst Christiansen, Shelley M. MacDermid Wadsworth, and Howard M. Weiss (2012), 'Romantic relationships following wartime deployment', *Journal of Family Issues* 34, 1427–51.

Karanika, Andromache and Vassiliki Panoussi (2020, eds.), *Emotional Trauma in Greece and Rome: Representations and Reactions*. London and New York: Routledge.

Katz, Marylin Arthur (1981), 'The divided world of *Iliad* VI', in Helene Foley (ed.), *Reflections of Women in Antiquity*. London and New York: Routledge, pp. 19–44.

Katz, Marylin Arthur (1991), *Penelope's Renown: Meaning and Indeterminacy in the Odyssey*. Princeton: Princeton University Press.

Kermode, Mark (2020), '*Military Wives* review—on song with chalk-and-cheese Kristin Scott Thomas and Sharon Horgan', *The Guardian* 8 March 2020 (https://www.theguardian.com/film/2020/mar/08/military-wives-review-kristin-scott-thomas-sharon-horgan-peter-cattaneo, accessed 4 August 2022).

Klay, Phil (2014), *Redeployment*. Edinburgh: Canongate.

Knobloch, Leanne K. and Jennifer A. Theiss (2014), 'Relational turbulence within military couples during reintegration following deployment', in Shelley MacDermid Wadsworth and David S. Riggs (eds.), *Military Deployment and its Consequences for Families*. New York: Springer, pp. 37–60.

Knox, Bernard M. W. (1961), 'The *Ajax* of Sophocles', *Harvard Studies in Classical Philology* 65, 1–37.

Komar, Kathleen L. (2003), *Reclaiming Klytemnestra: Revenge or Reconciliation*. Urbana and Chicago: University of Illinois Press.

Konishi, Haruo (1989), 'Agamemnon's reasons for yielding', *American Journal of Philology* 110, 210–22.

Lattimore, Richmond (1967), *The Odyssey of Homer*. New York: Harper.

Leatherman, Janie L. (2011), *Sexual Violence and Armed Conflict*. Cambridge: Polity Press.

Lester, Nicola (2015), 'When a soldier dies', *Critical Military Studies* 1.3, 249–53.

Leyva, Meredith (2003), *Married to the Military: A Survival Guide for Military Wives, Girlfriends, and Women In Uniform*. New York: Simon and Schuster.

Lissarrague, François (2015), 'Women arming men: armor and jewelry', in Fabre-Serris and Keith (eds.), pp. 71–81.

Lloyd, Michael (2005, 2nd edn.), *Euripides: Andromache*. Warminster: Aris and Phillips.

London, Andrew S., Elizabeth Allen, and Janet M. Wilmoth (2012), 'Veteran status, extramarital sex, and divorce: findings from the 1992 national health and social life survey', *Journal of Family Issues* 34.11, 1452–73.

Luschnig, C. A. E. (1988), *Tragic Aporia: A Study of Euripides' Iphigenia at Aulis*. Berwick, Victoria, Australia: Aureal Publications.

Lutz, Catherine and Jon Elliston (2002), 'Domestic terror', *The Nation* (14 October, 2002), 18–20.

MacEwen, Sally (1990, ed.), *Views of Clytemnestra, Ancient and Modern*. Lewiston: Edwin Mellen Press.

Macintosh, Fiona, Pantelis Michelakis, Edith Hall, and Oliver Taplin (2006, eds.), *Agamemnon in Performance 458 BC to AD 2004*. Oxford: Oxford University Press.

Macleod, C. W. (1982), 'The politics of the *Oresteia*', *Journal of Hellenic Studies* 102, 124–44.

Maguire, Laurie (2009), *Helen of Troy: From Homer to Hollywood*. Oxford: Wiley-Blackwell.

Marcotte, Amanda (2017), 'Meet the "Dependa": an ugly meme—and sexist stereotype—used to slur military spouses', *Salon*, 15 May 2017 (https://www.salon.com/2017/05/15/meet-the-dependa-an-ugly-meme-and-sexist-stereotype-used-to-slur-military-spouses/, accessed 4 August 2022).

Marquardt, Patricia A. (1985), 'Penelope "*ΠΟΛΥΤΡΟΠΟΣ*"', *American Journal of Philology* 106, 32–48.

Mason, Patience H. C. (1990), *Recovering From the War: A Guide for All Veterans, Family Members, Friends and Therapists*. Florida: Patience Press.

Mateczun, John M. and Elizabeth K. Holmes (1996), 'Return, readjustment and reintegration: the three R's of family reunion', in Ursano and Norwood (eds.), pp. 369–92.

Matheson, Susan B. (2005), 'A farewell with arms: departing warriors on Athenian vases', in Judith M. Barringer and Jeffrey M. Hurwitt (eds.), *Periklean Athens and its Legacy: Problems and Perspectives*. Austin: University of Texas Press, pp. 23–35.

Matsakis, Aphrodite (1996, 2nd edn.), *Vietnam Wives*. Baltimore: Sidran Press.

McClure, Laura (1997), 'Clytemnestra's binding spell (*Ag.* 958–974)', *Classical Journal* 92, 123–40.

McClure, Laura (1999), *Spoken Like a Woman: Speech and Gender in Athenian Drama*. Princeton: Princeton University Press.

McConnell, Justine (2016), 'Review: Radical re-envisionings: the Almeida Theatre's *Oresteia* and *Medea*', *Arion* 23, 151–66.

McCoskey, Denise Eileen (1998), ' "I, whom she detested so bitterly": Slavery and the violent division of women in Aeschylus' *Oresteia*', in Sandra R. Joshel and Sheila Murnaghan (eds.), *Women and Slaves in Greco-Roman Culture: Differential Equations*. London and New York: Routledge, 35–55.

McCray, Myriam Levesque (2015), 'Infidelity, trust, commitment, and marital satisfaction among military wives during husbands' deployment' (unpublished doctoral thesis, Walden University).

McCubbin, Hamilton I., Edna J. Hunter and Barbara B. Dahl (1975), 'Residuals of war: families of prisoners of war and servicemen missing in action', *Journal of Social Issues* 31.4, 95–109.

McNeil, Lynda (2005), 'Bridal cloths, cover-ups, and *kharis*: the "carpet scene" in Aeschylus' *Agamemnon*', *Greece and Rome* 52, 1–17.

Meade, Marion (1989), *Dorothy Parker: What Fresh Hell Is This?* New York: Penguin.

Mechling, Jay (2008), 'Gun play', *American Journal of Play* 1, 192–209.

Medina, Beate (2013), 'Afterword: A surviving spouse speaks', in Raymond Monsour Scourfield and Katherine Theresa Platoni (eds.), *War Trauma and Its Wake: Expanding the Circle of Healing*. New York: Routledge, pp. 317–30.

Meineck, Peter (2012), 'Combat trauma and the tragic stage: "Restoration" by cultural catharsis', *Intertexts* 16.1, 7–24.

Meineck, Peter (2018), *Theatrocracy: Greek Drama, Cognition, and the Imperative for Theatre*. London and New York: Routledge.

Meineck, Peter (2019), 'The remains of ancient action: understanding affect and empathy in Greek drama', in Rick Kemp and Bruce McConachie (eds.), *The Routledge Companion to Theatre, Performance, and Cognitive Science*. Abingdon and New York: Routledge, pp. 66–74.

Meineck, Peter and David Konstan (2014, eds.), *Combat Trauma and the Ancient Greeks*. New York: Palgrave Macmillan.

Meridor, Racanana (1987), 'Aeschylus *Agamemnon* 944–57: Why does Agamemnon give in?', *Classical Philology* 82, 38–43.

Michelakis, Pantelis (2006), *Euripides: Iphigenia at Aulis*. London: Duckworth.

Michelini, Ann N. (1999–2000), 'The expansion of myth in late Euripides: *Iphigeneia at Aulis*', in Martin Cropp, Kevin Lee, and David Sansone (eds.), *Euripides and Tragic Theatre in the Late Fifth Century* (*Illinois Classical Studies* 24–25). Champaign: University of Illinois Press, pp. 41–57.

Millay, Edna St Vincent (1954), *Mine the Harvest*. New York: Harper & Brothers.

Ministry of Defence (2022), 'UK Armed Forces biannual diversity statistics 1 April 2022, https://www.gov.uk/government/statistics/uk-armed-forces-biannual-diversity-statistics-april-2022/uk-armed-forces-biannual-diversity-statistics-1-april-2022, accessed 7 November 2022).

Mitchell-Boyask, Robin (2006), 'The marriage of Cassandra and the *Oresteia*: text, image, performance', *Transactions of the American Philological Association* 136, 269–97.

Mittal, Dinesh, Karen L. Drummond, Dean Blevins, Geoffrey Curran, Patrick Corrigan, and Greer Sullivan (2013), 'Stigma associated with PTSD: perceptions of treatment seeking combat veterans', *Psychiatric Rehabilitation Journal* 36.2, 86–92.

Moelker, René, Manon Andres, Gary Bowen, and Philippe Manigart (2015, eds.), *Military Families and War in the 21st Century: Comparative Perspectives*. New York: Routledge.

Moore, Bret A. (2012, ed.), *Handbook of Counseling Military Couples*. New York: Routledge.

Moreau, Donna (2005), *Waiting Wives: The Story of Schilling Manor, Home Front to the Vietnam War*. New York: Atria Books.

Morrell, Kenneth Scott (1997), 'The fabric of persuasion: Clytemnaestra, Agamemnon, and the sea of garments', *Classical Philology 92*, 141–65.

Moskos, Charles C. and Frank R. Wood (1988, eds.), *The Military: More Than Just a Job?* Washington, DC and London: Pergamon Brassey's.

Mossman, Judith (1995), *Wild Justice: A Study of Euripides' Hecuba*. Oxford: Oxford University Press.

Murnaghan, Sheila (2011, 2nd edn), *Disguise and Recognition in the Odyssey*. Lanham, Maryland: Lexington Books.

Murnaghan, Sheila (2015), 'Tragic realities: fictional women and the writing of ancient history', *EuGeStA 5*, 178–96.

Murray, Abby E. (2018), *How to Be Married After Iraq*. Georgetown, Kentucky: Finishing Line Press.

Murray, Kimberly (2011), 'Emotion work on the home front: the special case of military wives' (unpublished MA thesis, University of Arkansas).

Myrsiades, Kostas (2011), 'Introduction: is there early recognition in the *Odyssey*?', *College Literature 38.2*, ix–xi.

Naiden, Fred (2015), 'Sacrifice', in Esther Eidinow and Julia Kindt (eds.), *The Oxford Handbook of Ancient Greek Religion*. Oxford: Oxford University Press, pp. 463–75.

Nappi, Marella (2015), 'Women and war in the *Iliad*: rhetorical and ethical implications', in Fabre-Serris and Keith (eds.), pp. 34–51.

NATO (2019), 'Summary of the national reports of NATO member and partner nations to the NATO Committee on Gender Perspectives' (https://www.nato.int/nato_static_fl2014/assets/pdf/2021/9/pdf/NCGP_Full_Report_2019.pdf, accessed 7 November 2022).

Norwood, Ann E., Carol S. Fullerton, and Karen P. Hagen (1996), 'Those left behind: military families', in Ursano and Norwood (eds.), pp. 163–96.

Novak, Marian Faye (1991), *Lonely Girls with Burning Eyes: A Wife Recalls Her Husband's Journey Home from Vietnam*. Boston, Toronto and London: Little, Brown and Company.

Nowrojee, Binaifer (1996), 'Shattered lives: sexual violence during the Rwandan genocide and its aftermath', *Human Rights Watch* (https://www.hrw.org/reports/pdfs/r/rwanda/rwanda969.pdf, accessed 4 August 2022).

Nussbaum, Martha C. (2001, revised edn.), *The Fragility of Goodness: Luck and Ethics in Greek Tragedy and Philosophy*. Cambridge: Cambridge University Press.

Olson, S. Douglas (1990), 'The stories of Agamemnon in Homer's *Odyssey*', *Transactions of the American Philological Association 120*, 57–71.

Olson, S. Douglas (1995), *Blood and Iron: Stories and Storytelling in Homer's Odyssey*. Leiden, New York, and Köln: Brill.

Omitowoju, Rosanna (2002), *Rape and the Politics of Consent in Classical Athens*. Cambridge: Cambridge University Press.

Ormand, Kirk (1996), 'Silent by convention? Sophocles' Tekmessa', *American Journal of Philology 117*, 37–64.

Padel, Ruth (1995), *Whom Gods Destroy: Elements of Greek and Tragic Madness*. Princeton: Princeton University Press.

Pantelia, Maria (1993), 'Spinning and weaving: ideas of domestic order in Homer', *American Journal of Philology 114*, 493–501.

Parker, Dorothy (1928), *Sunset Gun*. New York: Sun Dial Press.

Payen, Pascal (2015), 'Women's wars, censored wars? A few Greek hypotheses (eighth to fourth centuries BCE)', in Fabre-Serris and Keith (eds.), pp. 214–27.

Petropoulos, J. C. B. (2011), *Kleos in a Minor Key: The Homeric Education of a Little Prince*. Cambridge, Mass. and London: Harvard University Press.

Porter, Roy (1986), 'Rape—does it have a historical meaning?', in Tomaselli and Porter (eds.), pp. 216–36.

Price, Siân (2011), *If You're Reading This: Last Letters from the Front Line*. Barnsley: Pen and Sword.

Provost, Julie (2019), 'The night before they deploy'. 'Soldier's Wife, Crazy Life' blog-post, 12 September 2019 (https://soldierswifecrazylife.com/night-before-they-deploy/, accessed 4 August 2022).

Rabinowitz, Nancy (1993), *Anxiety Veiled: Euripides and the Traffic in Women*. Ithaca and London: Cornell University Press.

Rabinowitz, Nancy (2014), 'Women and war in tragedy', in Meineck and Konstan (eds.), pp. 185–206.

Rabinowitz, Nancy Sorkin (2001), 'Personal voice/feminist voice', *Arethusa* 34, 191–210.

Rabinowitz, Nancy Sorkin (2011), 'Greek tragedy: a rape culture?', *EuGeStA* 1, 1–21.

Raeburn, David and Oliver Thomas (2011), *The Agamemnon of Aeschylus: A Commentary for Students*. Oxford: Oxford University Press.

Raudnitz, Sophie (2018), 'Tracing the establishment of political society: remembering and forgetting in ancient Greek literature' (unpublished doctoral thesis, The Open University).

Rawlings, Louis (2013), 'War and warfare in ancient Greece', in Campbell and Tritle (eds.), pp. 3–28.

Rees, Owen (2019), 'We need to talk about Epizelus: PTSD and the ancient world', *Medical Humanities* 46, 46–54.

Reilly, Catherine (1984, ed.), *Chaos of the Night: Women's Poetry and Verse of the Second World War*. London: Virago.

Rhodes, P. J. (2007), 'The impact of the Persian Wars on classical Greece', in Emma Bridges, Edith Hall, and P. J. Rhodes (eds.), *Cultural Responses to the Persian Wars: Antiquity to the Third Millennium*. Oxford: Oxford University Press, pp. 31–45.

Rieu, E. V. (1946), *Homer: The Odyssey*. London: Penguin.

Roisman, Hanna M. (2019), 'Tecmessa', in Stuttard (ed.), pp. 97–115.

Rosenbloom, David (1995), 'Myth, history, and hegemony in Aeschylus', in Barbara Goff (ed.), *History, Tragedy, Theory: Dialogues on Athenian Drama*. Austin: University of Texas Press, pp. 91–30.

Roth, Paul (1993), 'The theme of corrupted *xenia* in Aeschylus' *Oresteia*', *Mnemosyne* 46, 1–17.

Rousseau, Philippe (2015), 'War, speech, and the bow are not women's business', in Fabre-Serris and Keith (eds.), pp. 15–33.

Rowland, Richard (2017), *Killing Hercules: Deianira and the Politics of Domestic Violence from Sophocles to the War on Terror*. Oxford and New York: Routledge.

Russo, Joseph, Manuel Fernández-Galiano, and Alfred Heubeck (1992), *A Commentary on Homer's Odyssey Volume III: Books XVII–XXIV*. Oxford: Oxford University Press.

Rutherford, R. B. (1992, ed.), *Homer: Odyssey Books XIX and XX*. Cambridge: Cambridge University Press.

Sahlstein, Erin, Katheryn C. Maguire and Lindsay Timmerman (2009), 'Contradictions and praxis contextualised by wartime deployment: wives' perspectives revealed through relational dialectics', *Communication Monographs* 76, 421–42.

Sammons, Benjamin (2010), *The Art and Rhetoric of the Homeric Catalogue*. Oxford: Oxford University Press.

Schein, Seth L. (1996, ed.), *Reading the Odyssey: Selected Interpretive Essays*. Princeton, New Jersey: Princeton University Press.

Scodel, Ruth (1996), 'Δόμων ἄγαλμα: virgin sacrifice and aesthetic object', *Transactions of the American Philological Association* 126, 111–28.

Scodel, Ruth (1998), 'The captive's dilemma: sexual acquiescence in Euripides *Hecuba* and *Troades*', *Harvard Studies in Classical Philology* 98, 137–54.

Scodel, Ruth (2001), 'The suitors' games', *American Journal of Philology* 122, 307–27.

Seaford, Richard (1984), 'The last bath of Agamemnon', *Classical Quarterly* 34, 247–54.

Seaford, Richard (2017), 'Laughter and tears in early Greek literature', in Margaret Alexiou and Douglas Cairns (eds.), *Greek Laughter and Tears: Antiquity and After*. Edinburgh: Edinburgh University Press, pp. 27–35.

Seale, David (1982), *Vision and Stagecraft in Sophocles*. London and Canberra: Croom Helm.

Segal, Charles (1999), *Tragedy and Civilization: An Interpretation of Sophocles*. Norman: Oklahoma University Press.

Segal, Mady Wechsler (1988), 'The military and the family as greedy institutions', in Moskos and Wood (eds.), pp. 79–97.

Seifert, Ruth (1994), 'War and rape: a preliminary analysis', in Stiglmayer (ed.), pp. 54–72.

Settle, Trigg (2020), 'Aspects of violence, trauma, and theater in Sophocles' *Ajax*', in Karanika and Panoussi (eds.), pp. 11–29.

Shannon, Peggy (2014), 'Catharsis, trauma and war in Greek tr agedy: an inquiry into the therapeutic potential of Greek tragedy with special reference to the female experience' (unpublished doctoral thesis, Royal Holloway University of London).

Shay, Jonathan (1994), *Achilles in Vietnam: Combat Trauma and the Undoing of Character*. New York: Scribner.

Shay, Jonathan (2002), *Odysseus in America: Combat Trauma and the Trials of Homecoming*. New York: Scribner.

Shay, Jonathan (2014), 'Moral injury', *Psychoanalytic Psychology* 31, 182–91.

Sherman, Nancy (2007), *Stoic Warriors: The Ancient Philosophy Behind the Military Mind*. Oxford: Oxford University Press.

Sherman, Nancy (2010), *The Untold War: Inside the Hearts, Minds, and Souls of Our Soldiers*. New York and London: Norton.

Sherman, Nancy (2015), *Afterwar: Healing the Moral Wounds of Our Soldiers*. Oxford: Oxford University Press.

Sherratt, Susan and John Bennet (2017, eds.), *Archaeology and Homeric Epic*. Oxford and Philadelphia: Oxbow Books.

Shotbolt, Vicky (2011), 'I know the real military wives', *The Guardian*, 21 December 2011 (https://www.theguardian.com/commentisfree/2011/dec/21/the-real-military-wives, accessed 4 August 2022).

Siegel, Herbert (1981), 'Agamemnon in Euripides' *Iphigenia at Aulis*', *Hermes* 109, 257–65.

Silva, Maria de Fátima (2010), 'Euripides' *Orestes*: the chronicle of a trial', in Edward M. Harris, Delfim F. Leão, and P. J. Rhodes (eds.), *Law and Drama in Ancient Greece*. London: Duckworth, pp. 77–93.

Snyder, Douglas K., Christina Balderrama-Durbin, Caitlin Fissette, David M. Scheider, J. Kelly Barnett, and Samuel Fiala (2012), 'Infidelity', in Moore (2012, ed.), pp. 219–35.

Sokoloff, Sally (1999), ' "How are they at home?" Community, state, and servicemen's wives in England, 1939–45', *Women's History Review* 8, 27–52.

Solomon, Denise Haunani (2015), 'Relational turbulence model', in C. R. Berger, M. E. Roloff, S. R. Wilson, J. P. Dillard, J. Caughlin, and D. Solomon (eds.), *The International Encyclopedia of Interpersonal Communication* (10.1002/9781118540190.wbeic174, accessed 4 August 2022).

Sommerstein, Alan H. (2012), *Aeschylean Tragedy*. London: Bloomsbury.

Steiner, Deborah (2010, ed.), *Homer: Odyssey Books XVII and XVIII*. Cambridge: Cambridge University Press.

Steinman, Ron (2002), *Inside Television's First War: A Saigon Journal*. Columbia, Missouri: University of Missouri Press.

Stiglmayer, Alexandra (1994, ed.), *Mass Rape: The War Against Women in Bosnia-Herzegovina*. Lincoln and London: University of Nebraska Press.

Stiglmayer, Alexandra (1994), 'The rapes in Bosnia-Herzegovina', in Stiglmayer (ed.), pp. 82–169.

Stuttard, David (2019, ed.), *Looking at Ajax*. London: Bloomsbury.

Suzuki, Mihoko (1989), *Metamorphoses of Helen: Authority, Difference, and the Epic*. Ithaca and London: Cornell University Press.

Synodinou, Katerina (2013), 'Agamemnon's change of mind in Euripides' *Iphigeneia at Aulis*', *Logeion* 3, 51–65.

Taplin, Oliver (1977), *The Stagecraft of Aeschylus: The Dramatic Use of Exits and Entrances in Greek Tragedy*. Oxford: Oxford University Press.

Taplin, Oliver (1978), *Greek Tragedy in Action*. Berkeley and Los Angeles: University of California Press.

Taylor, Paul (2011, ed.), 'War and sacrifice in the post-9/11 era: the military-civilian gap', *Pew Social and Demographic Trends* (https://www.pewresearch.org/fact-tank/2011/10/06/war-and-sacrifice-in-the-post-911-era-the-military-civilian-gap/, accessed 4 August 2022).

Tomaselli, Sylvana and Roy Porter (1986, eds.), *Rape*. Oxford: Blackwell.

Tritle, Lawrence A. (2000), *From Melos to My Lai: War and Survival*. London: Routledge.

Tritle, Lawrence A. (2014), ' "Ravished minds" in the ancient world', in Meineck and Konstan (eds.), pp. 87–103.

Tsagalis, Christos (2004), *Epic Grief: Personal Laments in Homer's Iliad*. Berlin and New York: de Gruyter.

Turkeltaub, Daniel (2015), 'Penelope's lion, θυμολέων husband, and θυμός-destroying pain', *The Classical Journal* 110, 279–302.

Turner, Sarah Victoria (2015), 'The poetics of permanence? Inscriptions, memory and memorials of the First World War in Britain', *Sculpture Journal* 24, 73–96.

Ursano, Robert J. and Ann E. Norwood (1996, eds.), *Emotional Aftermath of the Persian Gulf War: Veterans, Families, Communities, and Nations*. Washington and London: American Psychiatric Press.

Vavrus, Mary Douglas (2013), 'Lifetime's *Army Wives*, or I married the media-military-industrial complex', *Women's Studies in Communication* 36:1, 92–112.

Verity, Anthony (2016), *The Odyssey*. Oxford: Oxford University Press.

Vester, Christina (2009), 'Bigamy and bastardy, wives and concubines: civic identity in *Andromache*', in J. R. C. Cousland and James R. Hume (eds.), *The Play of Texts and Fragments: Essays in Honour of Martin Cropp*, Leiden and Boston: Brill, pp. 293–305.

Villanueva, Tino (2013), *So Spoke Penelope*. Cambridge, Mass.: Grolier Poetry Press.

von Bothmer, Dietrich (1949), 'The arming of Achilles', *Bulletin of the Museum of Fine Arts* 47, 84–90.

Ward, Jeanne, Christopher Horwood, Claire McEvoy, Pamela Shipman, and Lauren Rumble (2007), *The Shame of War: Sexual Violence Against Women and Girls in Conflict*, United Nations Office for the Coordination of Humanitarian Affairs/Integrated Regional Information Networks.

Ware, Vron (2010), 'Lives on the line', *Soundings* 45, 147–58.

Weiberg, Erika L. (2020), 'Learning to bear witness: tragic bystanders in Sophocles' *Trachiniae*', in Karanika and Panoussi (eds.), pp. 177–91.

Weiberg, Erika L. (forthcoming), *Performing Gender and Trauma in Greek Tragedy*.

Weinstein, Laurie and Helen Mederer (1997), 'Blue Navy blues: submarine officers and the two-person career', in Weinstein and White (eds.), pp. 7–18.

Weinstein, Laurie and Christie C. White (1997, eds.), *Wives and Warriors: Women and the Military in the United States and Canada*. Westport, Connecticut and London: Bergin and Garvey.

Welwei, Karl-Wilhelm (2006), 'The Peloponnesian War and its aftermath', in Konrad H. Kinzl (ed.), *A Companion to the Classical Greek World*. Oxford: Blackwell, pp. 526–43.

Wertenbaker, Timberlake (2013), *Our Ajax*. London: Faber and Faber.

Wilson, Emily (2017), *The Odyssey*. New York: W. W. Norton and Company.

Wilson, Hannah M. N. and Craig D. Murray (2016), 'The experience of deployment for partners of military personnel: a qualitative meta-synthesis', *Journal of Couple and Relationship Therapy* 15.2, 102–20.

Wohl, Victoria (1998), *Intimate Commerce: Exchange, Gender, and Subjectivity in Greek Tragedy*. Austin: University of Texas Press.

Wolfe, Rachel M. E. (2009), 'Woman, tyrant, mother, murderess: an exploration of the mythic character of Clytemnestra in all her forms', *Women's Studies* 38, 692–719.

Woodford, Susan (1993), *The Trojan War in Ancient Art*. Ithaca: Cornell University Press.

Worman, Nancy (2001), 'The voice which is not one: Helen's verbal guises in Homeric epic', in André Lardinois and Laura McLure (eds.), *Making Silence Speak: Women's Voices in Greek Literature and Society*. Princeton: Princeton University Press, pp. 19–37.

Yerkes, S. A. and H. C. Holloway (1996), 'War and homecomings: the stressors of war and returning from war', in Ursano and Norwood (eds.), pp. 25–42.

Zeitlin, Froma (1965), 'The motif of the corrupted sacrifice in Aeschylus' *Oresteia*, *Transactions and Proceedings of the American Philological Association* 96, 463–508.

Zeitlin, Froma (1996), *Playing the Other: Gender and Society in Classical Greek Literature*. Chicago: University of Chicago Press.

Zeitlin, Froma (2004), 'The artful eye: vision, ecphrasis and spectacle in the Euripidean theatre', in Simon Goldhill and Robin Osborne (eds.), *Art and Text in Ancient Greek Culture*. Cambridge: Cambridge University Press, pp. 138–96.

Index of passages discussed

For the benefit of digital users, indexed terms that span two pages (e.g., 52–53) may, on occasion, appear on only one of those pages.

General Index

For the benefit of digital users, indexed terms that span two pages (e.g., 52–53) may, on occasion, appear on only one of those pages.